The Bias That Divides Us

The Bias That Divides Us

The Science and Politics of Myside Thinking

Keith E. Stanovich

The MIT Press
Cambridge, Massachusetts
London, England

The MIT Press would like to thank the anonymous peer reviewers who provided comments on drafts of this book. The generous work of academic experts is essential for establishing the authority and quality of our publications. We acknowledge with gratitude the contributions of these otherwise uncredited readers.

This book was set in Stone Serif and Stone Sans by Westchester Publishing Services. Printed and bound in the United States of America.

Library of Congress Cataloging-in-Publication Data

Names: Stanovich, Keith E., 1950– author.
Title: The bias that divides us : the science and politics of myside thinking / Keith E. Stanovich.
Description: Cambridge, Massachusetts : The MIT Press, [2021] | Includes bibliographical references and index.
Identifiers: LCCN 2020029640 | ISBN 9780262045759 (hardcover)
Subjects: LCSH: Prejudices. | Discrimination. | Thought and thinking.
Classification: LCC BF575.P9 .S73 2021 | DDC 153.4/2--dc23
LC record available at https://lccn.loc.gov/2020029640

10 9 8 7 6 5 4 3 2 1

For Paula,
you were with me, my love,
every step of the way

Contents

Preface

In the wake of the 2016 presidential election, there was widespread concern about the accuracy of information available to voters about the issues and the candidates. There were debates about how much "fake news" had affected the election, and there was widespread concern about biased news reporting and censoring by the arbiters of social media. People from both ends of the ideological spectrum thought that the media had failed to present information in an unbiased manner. A polarized electorate seemed to be looking at the world from diametrically opposed perspectives. The cover of *Time* magazine on April 3, 2017, carried the title "Is Truth Dead?" There were many essays and op-eds lamenting that we had become a "post-truth" society, a term that the editors of the Oxford dictionaries had named as the word of the year for 2016.

Despite its popularity, I will not be employing the term post-truth in this volume because it is too often taken to imply that our current society fails to *value* the truth. The crux of our current societal dilemma, however, is not that we have come to disregard the truth or become cavalier toward it, but that we are *selective* in displaying our post-truth tendencies. Neither side in the political debate thinks that everything in society is post-truth. What we do believe is that our political *enemies* are post-truth. We don't think that all the news we see in the media is fake news—only the news that emanates from our political opponents. We believe in *our* truth, in *our* news. We do value truth and facts—but only when they support our views.

What our society is really suffering from is *myside bias*: we evaluate evidence, generate evidence, and test hypotheses in a manner biased toward our own prior beliefs, opinions, and attitudes. We are not living in a post-truth society—we are living in a myside society. Our political peril stems from our inability to *converge* on commonly accepted facts and truth, not from our inability to value or respect facts and truth. In scientific practice, there are mechanisms for converging on the truth—things like publicly agreed upon operational definitions. In real life, however, we tend to define concepts with a myside bias, and this tendency ensures that evidence will not lead to convergence, as it does in science.

That we are facing a myside bias problem and not a calamitous abandonment of the concept of truth is good news in at least one sense: the phenomenon of myside bias has been extensively studied in cognitive science. Understanding it may help to alleviate our present scourge of political divisiveness.

Introducing readers to some of the paradigms used to study myside bias, chapter 1 will demonstrate how behavioral scientists from various disciplines have studied this bias in the lab. We will see that myside bias is ubiquitous—indeed, one of the most universal biases that has been studied. Chapter 2 will deal with the vexing question of whether myside bias, for all the negative effects it seems to have, should really be considered a reasoning error or whether it has some rational justification.

Although psychologists have studied a considerable number of thinking biases, myside bias stands out as unusual in several respects. Chapter 3 will discuss how most biases that have been studied can be predicted from various cognitive abilities (intelligence and executive function measures, for example) and from thinking dispositions related to rationality. In contrast, however, myside bias is *not* predictable from standard measures of cognitive and behavioral functioning. Furthermore, it has very little domain generality: myside bias in one domain is not a very good predictor of myside bias in another. As one of the most unpredictable of the biases in an individual difference sense, myside bias is thus an outlier bias—and that has important social, political, and psychological consequences.

For one, to study it, we need a different type of model—one that does not connect this bias to the traditional types of cognitive abilities and personality traits that psychologists study. Chapter 4 will argue that models focusing on the properties of acquired beliefs rather than cognitive processes provide better frameworks for the study of myside bias.

And because myside bias is not predictable from traditional psychological measures, chapter 5 will explain how it creates a true blind spot among cognitive elites. Cognitive elites (those high in intelligence, executive functioning, or other valued psychological dispositions) often predict that they them-selves are less biased than other people when queried about other well-known psychological biases (overconfidence bias, omission bias, hindsight bias, anchoring bias). They are often correct in their predictions because cognitive sophistication is moderately correlated with the ability to avoid most of the biases that have been studied. But because myside bias is an exception, an outlier, it is the bias where the cognitive elites most often think they are unbiased when in fact they are just as biased as everyone else.

In chapter 6, I explore how this bias blind spot contributes to the ideological polarization of our current politics and to a troubling new trend: the decline of trust in university research as a disinterested arbiter of pressing social issues. I will discuss what can be done to stem the effects of the kinds of myside biases that have led to our poisonous politics and that interfere with our ability to unify as a nation.

Acknowledgments

Throughout the first decade of this century, my research group published a series of papers on myside bias (Macpherson and Stanovich 2007; Stanovich and West 2007, 2008a; Toplak and Stanovich 2003) that each contained a surprising finding: myside bias was not attenuated by cognitive ability. In "Myside Bias, Rational Thinking, and Intelligence" (Stanovich, West, and Toplak 2013), we summarized these converging results, highlighting the unusual individual difference findings. In many heuristics and biases tasks, including ones seemingly similar to myside reasoning paradigms such as belief bias tasks, subjects of higher ability are better able to avoid the bias. In our 2013 paper, we provided a preliminary theoretical context for understanding our curious findings regarding myside bias. *The Bias That Divides Us* fleshes out in considerable detail our theoretical understanding of why myside bias may act differently than other biases reported in the heuristics and biases literature—particularly as regards individual differences.

In our 2013 paper, the social implications of a bias operating independently of cognitive sophistication went unexplored. As described in greater detail in chapter 5 of this volume, the political implications of our blindness to our own myside bias became apparent to me only after the publication of *The Rationality Quotient* (Stanovich, West, and Toplak 2016). Those sociopolitical implications are now explicitly discussed in the chapters to follow.

Although *The Bias That Divides Us* was written without grant support, my laboratory's earlier empirical work on myside bias received welcome support from grants given by the John Templeton Foundation to Keith E. Stanovich and Richard F. West; by the Social Sciences and Humanities Research Council of Canada and by the Canada Research Chairs program to Keith E. Stanovich; and by the Social Sciences and Humanities Research Council of Canada to Maggie E. Toplak.

My thanks to Phil Laughlin, my editor at the MIT Press, whose help with this and previous books has made him a key participant in my laboratory's scientific achievements, for his enthusiastic support of the present project from the very beginning; to Alex Hoopes and Elizabeth Agresta for guidance during the book's production process; to Jeffrey Lockridge for extremely thorough, conscientious, and insightful copyediting; to the three anonymous reviewers secured by Phil who provided extensive and incisive reactions to an outline and proposed structure for the book; to Maggie Toplak and Jonathan Evans for their erudite feedback on the entire manuscript; and to Richard West and Anne Cunningham who spent considerable time with an earlier draft.

But my true Maxwell Perkins for this book was my wife, Paula, who was there at its inception and who edited every chapter and verse. More than halfway into the drafting of the book, in early fall of 2019, Paula was diagnosed with multiple serious heart conditions. The stress of the resulting extensive open-heart surgery she endured was greatly mitigated by the Stanovich support team of Tom Hagen and Wanda Auger on the days surrounding the surgery and Anne Cunningham on Paula's first days home from the hospital. Invaluable members of the Stanovich support team also included Marilyn Kertoy (as always) and Terry Needham; Sue Bert and Jack Buddeke; and Di Rosenblum and Mark Mitshkun. Thanks also to Gary and Mike Carson for their support. After the surgery, Paula and I healed together and continued to write and edit together. Paula had just begun her cardiac rehabilitation program at the hospital when we heard news of a very bad virus coming out of China. Within a few weeks, we were isolated at home. Under lockdown, I worked on the book with Paula's able assistance until it was finally finished, and it, as is my life, is dedicated to her.

1 The Many Faces of Myside Bias

Myside bias occurs across a wide variety of judgment domains. It is displayed by people in all demographic groups, and it is exhibited even by expert reasoners, the highly educated, and the highly intelligent. It has been demonstrated in research studies across a variety of disciplines, including: cognitive psychology (Edwards and Smith 1996; Toplak and Stanovich 2003), social psychology (Ditto et al. 2019a), political science (Taber and Lodge 2006), behavioral economics (Babcock et al. 1995), legal studies (Kahan, Hoffman, et al. 2012), cognitive neuroscience (Westen et al. 2006), and in the informal reasoning literature (Kuhn and Modrek 2018). Myside bias has been found to occur in every stage of information processing. That is, studies have shown a tendency toward biased search for evidence, biased evaluation of evidence, biased assimilation of evidence, biased memory of outcomes, and biased evidence generation (Bolsen and Palm 2020; Clark et al. 2019; Ditto et al. 2019a; Epley and Gilovich 2016; Hart et al. 2009; Mercier and Sperber 2017; Taber and Lodge 2006).

Table 1.1 presents a sampling of myside studies using different paradigms, along with representative citations. Taken collectively, the studies in the table show that myside bias has been displayed in a wide variety of paradigms. This opening chapter will begin by illustrating some of the most easily understandable paradigms—ones that are more like demonstrations—and will then introduce studies that are more technically sophisticated.

One of the most cited demonstrations of myside bias is also one of the oldest. In a classic study, Albert Hastorf and Hadley Cantril (1954) used as a stimulus the film of a notorious football game played by Princeton and Dartmouth in 1951. It was the last game of the year. Princeton was undefeated and featured on its team an All-American player who had been on

Table 1.1

Different Myside Bias Paradigms and Representative Studies of Each Type

Myside bias paradigms	Example studies
Evaluating acts more favorably when they support one's group	Claassen and Ensley 2016; Kahan, Hoffman, et al. 2012; Kopko et al. 2011
Evaluating quality of hypothetical experiments	Lord, Ross, and Lepper 1979; Munro and Ditto 1997; Drummond and Fischhoff 2019
Evaluating quality of informal arguments	Baron 1995; Edwards and Smith 1996; Stanovich and West 1997, 2008a; Taber and Lodge 2006
Applying logical rules better when logical conclusion supports one's strongly held beliefs	Feather 1964; Gampa et al. 2019
Searching or selecting information sources that are likely to support one's position	Hart et al. 2009; Taber and Lodge 2006
Generating arguments	Macpherson and Stanovich 2007; Perkins 1985; Toplak and Stanovich 2003
Covariation detection	Kahan et al. 2017; Stanovich and West 1998b; Washburn and Skitka 2018
Contradiction detection	Westen et al. 2006
De-emphasizing costs of one's moral commitments	Liu and Ditto 2013
Distorting perception of risk and reward in direction of one's preferences	Finucane et al. 2000; Stanovich and West 2008b
Selective use of moral principles	Uhlmann et al. 2009; Voelkel and Brandt 2019
Essay evaluation	Miller, et al. 1993
Written argumentation	Wolfe and Britt 2008
Political approval ratings	Lebo and Cassino 2007
Selectively learning facts favorable to one's political party	Jerit and Barabas 2012
Conditional probability evaluation	Van Boven et al. 2019
Fairness judgments	Babcock et al. 1995; Messick and Sentis 1979
Resisting evidence when it will lead to unwanted societal changes	Campbell and Kay 2014
Interpreting facts in a way favorable to one's group	Stanovich and West 2007, 2008a
Selectively questioning scientific status of evidence	Munro 2010
Four-card selection task	Dawson, Gilovich, and Regan 2002
Inconsistent political judgments	Crawford, Kay, and Duke 2015
Biased perceptions of media reports	Vallone, Ross, and Lepper 1985

the cover of *Time* magazine. The game turned out to be a brutal one, with a large number of penalties and several broken bones. The star player from Princeton left the game before halftime with a broken nose. The game was the subject of controversy, and the student newspapers of each school lamented the poor sportsmanship of the other team.

Hastorf and Cantril (1954) showed the same film of the game to a group of Dartmouth students and to a group of Princeton students and asked them to mark on a piece of paper each time they saw an infraction of the rules. The Dartmouth students reported that an equal number of infractions were committed by both teams (in fact, in the actual game, Dartmouth had committed a greater number), whereas the Princeton students estimated that the Dartmouth team had committed 70 percent of the infractions overall. Of course, in a study this old, the types of carefully controlled conditions that we now take for granted in psychological research were not present. Nevertheless, the study is a classic in showing how people can see the same stimulus and yet interpret it in different ways based on their relationship to the situation (i.e., what "side" they are on). Hastorf and Cantril (1954) themselves made this point by using an ironic title for their study: "They Saw a Game"—drawing attention to the fact that, actually, the subjects had "seen" *different* games based on their relationship to the two opposing teams.

Although the Hastorf and Cantril 1954 study lacked the methodological rigor now expected of such studies, half a century later, Dan Kahan, David Hoffman, and colleagues (2012) were able to replicate the earlier finding with thoroughly modern controls by showing their subjects a film of a protest that had taken place in Cambridge, Massachusetts, in 2009. From the film, it is impossible to tell who the protesters are or what the protest was about—it occurs outside an unidentified building. All that is really discernible is that there is a clash between the protesters and the police in front of the building. The subjects were told that the protesters had been ordered to disperse by the police and were suing the police for doing so. Unlike the Hastorf and Cantril 1954 study, the Kahan, Hoffman, and colleagues 2012 study contained an experimental manipulation: half of the subjects were told that the demonstrators were protesting against the availability of abortion in a reproductive health care center and the other half were told that the protesters were demonstrating outside a military recruiting center against the military's then-existing ban on service by openly gay soldiers.

Kahan, Hoffman, and colleagues (2012) also used assessments of a variety of multidimensional political attitudes, making it possible to assess whether subjects with conservative social attitudes and those with liberal social attitudes[1] assessed the very same protest differently depending on the target of the protest. In fact, the labeling of the protest made an enormous difference in how the two groups of subjects interpreted the clash between the police and the protesters. In the abortion clinic condition, 70 percent of the socially conservative subjects thought that the police had violated the demonstrators' rights, but only 28 percent of the socially liberal subjects thought that they had. The pattern of responses was completely reversed in the condition that was described to the subjects as a protest against restrictions on gay members serving in the military; only 16 percent of the socially conservative subjects thought that the protesters' rights were being violated, whereas 76 percent of the socially liberal subjects thought that they were. The results show why the title to the Kahan, Hoffman, and colleagues 2012 study echoed that of the Hastorf and Cantril 1954 study. "'They Saw a Protest'" refers to the fact that the very same protest—just like the very same football game decades before—was "seen" differently depending upon what side the observers were on.

The Terminology Confusion: "Confirmation Bias," "Belief Bias," and "Myside Bias"

Before we move on to consider some additional myside paradigms and studies, it is important to clarify the terminology used in this domain because it is quite confusing. The three terms "confirmation bias," "belief bias," and "myside bias" are used in a highly inconsistent manner in the scientific literature. The term "confirmation bias" is the most popular term used in the general media; indeed, Google Trends confirms that "confirmation bias" is a vastly more common term than "belief bias" or "myside bias." However, because it is the most confused of all the terms, I will restrict my use of "confirmation bias" in this book to one carefully defined sense. Indeed, as long ago as 1983, two distinguished psychologists, Baruch Fischhoff and Ruth Beyth-Marom (1983), investigating hypothesis testing recommended that the term "confirmation bias" be retired because even then it had already become a catchall phrase incorporating too many different effects. Unfortunately, their recommendation was not adopted, and so a decade later another theorist, Joshua Klayman (1995), expressed his exasperation with the term—saying that there seemed to be as many definitions of confirmation bias as there were studies of it.

The basic problem is that too many different processing tendencies have been swept up into the term confirmation bias, and many of them are not indicators of the type of motivated cognition that underlies true myside bias (Evans 1989; Fischhoff and Beyth-Marom 1983; Hahn and Harris 2014; Klayman and Ha 1987; Nickerson 1998). In his nuanced 1995 paper, Klayman discusses two different definitions of confirmation bias; he calls his first definition the positive test strategy, and this definition is the one I am reserving for the term confirmation bias. A positive test strategy looks for evidence that is expected, given the focal hypothesis in a reasoner's mind. As long as the reasoner deals appropriately with disconfirming evidence, there is nothing nonnormative about a positive test strategy (see Baron 1985; Klayman and Ha 1987; McKenzie 2004; Mercier 2017; Oaksford and Chater 1994, 2003). Klayman's second definition focuses on the psychological disinclination to abandon a currently favored hypothesis and views this type of confirmation bias as a form of motivated cognition (Bolsen and Palm 2020; Kunda 1990). Because I want to emphasize Klayman's (1995) motivated processing category in *The Bias That Divides Us*, I am reserving a separate term—"myside bias"—for this second type of confirmation bias.

To reiterate, I will use the term confirmation bias to refer to the cognitive process of centering the evaluation and testing of evidence on the focal hypothesis.[2] It is not necessarily irrational or nonnormative[3] for a reasoner to display a confirmation bias as long as the reasoner is willing to correctly process the implications of disconfirming evidence when the reasoner encounters it—a point that has been known for quite some time (Baron 1985; Klayman 1995; Klayman and Ha 1987). That is, as long as a reasoner shows appropriate Bayesian updating when encountering disconfirming evidence,[4] seeking tests of the focal hypothesis that the reasoner has in mind is not inappropriate (McKenzie 2004).

That confirmation bias, defined in this manner, does not mean a reasoning error in this case highlights two different senses of the term "bias" in the reasoning literature. The first, evaluatively neutral sense of "bias" simply connotes a processing tendency—"I have a bias to shop at Costco when I'm trying to save money," for example. My use of the term confirmation bias is of this, evaluatively neutral, type.[5] Klayman (1995) distinguishes this first sense of "bias" from a second, very different one, where "bias" refers to a fundamentally flawed reasoning process that often leads to a thinking error. Whether myside bias, as I identify it here, is a bias in the sense of a reasoning error that results from fundamentally flawed thinking will be the subject of chapter 2.

Unlike confirmation bias as I have narrowly defined it, the term "belief bias," used primarily in the syllogistic reasoning literature, is a term that *does* tend to connote a reasoning error. Belief bias occurs when we have difficulty evaluating conclusions that conflict with what we know about the world (Evans 2017). It is most often assessed with syllogistic reasoning tasks in which the believability of the conclusion conflicts with logical validity. Consider the following syllogism and ask yourself if it is valid—whether the conclusion follows logically from the two premises:

Premise 1: All living things need water,

Premise 2: Roses need water,

Therefore roses are living things.

Judge the conclusion as either logically valid or invalid before reading on.

If you are like the approximately 70 percent of university students who have been given this syllogism to evaluate, you will judge the conclusion valid. And if you did think that it was valid, like those 70 percent who did, you would be wrong. Premise 1 says that all living things need water, not that all things that need water are living things. So just because roses need water, it does not follow from premise 1 that roses are living things. If that is still not clear, it will probably become clear after you consider the next syllogism with exactly the same structure:

Premise 1: All insects need oxygen,

Premise 2: Mice need oxygen,

Therefore mice are insects.

Now it seems pretty clear that the conclusion does not follow from the premises. The same thing that made the rose syllogism so hard to evaluate makes the mice syllogism easy.

In both of these syllogisms, prior knowledge about the nature of the world (that roses are living things and that mice are not insects) becomes implicated in a type of judgment that is supposed to be independent of content: a judgment of logical validity. In the rose syllogism, prior knowledge was interfering with your arriving at the correct answer. Even if you answered it correctly, you no doubt felt the conflict. In the mice syllogism, prior knowledge helped you answer correctly. Although belief bias has been most extensively studied in the syllogistic reasoning and conditional reasoning literatures (Evans 2017), it is observed in other paradigms as well (Levin, Wasserman, and Kao 1993; Stanovich and West 1997, 1998b; Thompson and Evans 2012).

Belief bias is not the same as myside bias: belief bias occurs when our real-world knowledge interferes with our reasoning performance, whereas myside bias occurs when we search for and interpret evidence in a manner that tends to favor the hypothesis we *want* to be true (Mercier 2017; Stanovich, West, and Toplak 2013). What turns a belief bias into a myside bias? Myside bias refers to processing in favor of existing opinions that are currently *highly valued*. To use a distinction discussed years ago by Robert Abelson (1988), myside bias concerns the beliefs that we hold with high *conviction*. And, unlike more typical beliefs, convictions are accompanied by emotional commitment and ego preoccupation and tend to have undergone more cognitive elaboration (Abelson 1988; see Fazio 2007; Howe and Krosnick 2017 for more contemporary discussions). Linda Skitka, Christopher Bauman, and Edward Sargis (2005) found that attitudes rooted in moral mandates tended to become convictions that were especially potent predictors of outcome variables (social distance, goodwill, and so on).

To illustrate the difference between a simple belief and a conviction, imagine you were on another planet, called "Zircan" but otherwise almost exactly like Earth, and you heard from someone there that roses were never red but were always brown. You would have no trouble acquiring that belief. You would feel no urge to argue with anyone that roses could be red. On planet Zircan, they simply weren't red, and you would have no trouble giving up the belief that roses could be red. On the other hand, if you were to hear that, on planet Zircan, it was believed that left-handed people were morally inferior to right-handed people, you would not accept that belief and in fact would try to argue against it. You would defend your belief that the moral worth of human beings did not depend on whether they were left-handed or right-handed. That belief would be a conviction for you in a way that the belief that roses could be red would not be.

Convictions often derive from worldviews that spawn "protected values"—those which resist trade-offs with other values (Baron and Spranca 1997). Protected values (sometimes termed "sacred values"; see Ditto, Liu, and Wojcik 2012; Tetlock 2003) are viewed as moral obligations that arise from rules that govern which actions are morally required, forbidden, or permitted, and the thought of violating them often provokes anger. Experiments have shown that subjects are reluctant to engage in monetary trade-offs when protected values are at stake (Baron and Leshner 2000; Bartels and Medin 2007) A belief that is a protected value will not be easily altered by evidence.

In further writings on the idea that some beliefs can become convictions, Robert Abelson (1986; see also Abelson and Prentice 1989) makes the distinction between what he calls "testable beliefs" and "distal beliefs." *Testable* beliefs are closely tied to the real world and the words we use to describe that world (e.g., Roses are red). They can be verified by observations—sometimes easily made personal observations, but other times observations that rely on the expertise of others and the more sophisticated methods of science. In contrast, *distal* beliefs cannot be directly verified by experience, nor can they be easily confirmed by turning to experts or scientific consensus. For example, you may think that pharmaceutical companies make excessive profits, or that your state should spend more on mental health and less on green initiatives. Certainly, economic statistics and public policy facts might *condition* distal beliefs such as these (either strengthening or weakening your attachment to them), but they cannot *verify* your distal beliefs in the same manner that they can verify your testable ones. Many distal beliefs embody our values. When they do, they are apt to become convictions because they will lead to emotional commitment and ego preoccupation, as argued by Abelson (1988). Distal beliefs often derive from our general worldviews or, in politics, from our ideologies.

Myside bias centers on distal beliefs, not testable ones. Belief bias, in contrast, centers on testable beliefs. This is why belief bias is more remediable by education and more correlated with cognitive ability than myside bias is (as will be discussed in subsequent chapters). The belief that health care spending is the second largest item in the US federal budget is a testable belief, whereas the belief that Americans spend too much on health care is a distal belief. Certainly, economic facts might alter our attitude toward the latter belief, but they cannot *verify* this distal belief in the same way they can verify our testable beliefs. The myside bias studies discussed in this book will be almost exclusively about distal beliefs—those which arise from beliefs held with conviction.[6]

To summarize the terminological distinctions as they will be made in *The Bias That Divides Us*: I am calling "confirmation bias" the bias toward looking for positive tests of the hypotheses that are focal in our minds, and "belief bias," the bias that occurs when we have difficulty evaluating conclusions that conflict with what we know about the world. The conclusions that interfere with reasoning in the case of belief bias are testable beliefs. And I am calling "myside bias" the bias that occurs when we evaluate evidence, generate evidence, and test hypotheses in a manner favorable toward our prior opinions and attitudes—where the attitudes in question are convictions (that is, distal beliefs and worldviews to which we show emotional commitment and ego preoccupation). Finally, in this book, I will separate the literature on myside bias from the literature on wishful thinking (Bar-Hillel, Budescu, and Amor 2008; Ditto and Lopez 1992; Lench and Ditto 2008; Weinstein 1980) by dealing only with the former.[7]

Demonstrations of Myside Bias across Paradigms and Types of Thinking

The classic Hastorf and Cantril 1954 study and the follow-up 2012 study by Kahan, Hoffman, and colleagues give a flavor of one type of myside bias, where people evaluate ambiguous acts more favorably when they support their own groups. As you can see in table 1.1, however, myside bias has been demonstrated in a variety of ways using different paradigms that assess many different stages of information processing.

One of the more easily explained demonstrations comes from my lab's work. Several years ago, my colleague Richard West and I presented one group of subjects (university students in the United States) with the following thought problem (see Stanovich and West 2008b for details): First, they were told that, according to a comprehensive study by the US Department of Transportation, a particular German car was eight times more likely than a typical family car was to kill occupants of another car in a crash, and the department was considering a ban on the sale of this German car in the United States. Then they were asked whether they thought that any action should be taken regarding this German car. We found that 78.4 percent of the subjects thought the German car should be banned.

The trick behind the study was that the statistics on the dangerousness of the car in the example were real at the time of the study, but that car was actually *not* a German car but the Ford Explorer, a vehicle manufactured in the United States. In the scenario just presented, subjects were evaluating whether to ban a dangerous German vehicle on American streets. This allowed us to employ a second group of subjects (also US university students) to evaluate the reverse scenario—whether to ban a dangerous American vehicle on German streets. The subjects in this group were told that, according to a comprehensive study by the US Department of Transportation, Ford Explorers were eight times more likely than a typical family car to kill occupants of another car in a crash and that the German Department of Transportation was considering a ban on the sale of the Ford Explorer in Germany.

This second group of subjects answered the same set of questions as the first, but now from the standpoint of the *German* Department of Transportation. We found that, in this case, only 51.4 percent of the subjects thought the Ford Explorer should be banned in Germany. Our study illustrates, clearly and simply, how people judge the same harm more harshly if it is done to their own side. In this case, they saw the dangerous vehicle as much more deserving of being banned if it were a German vehicle in America than if it were an American vehicle in Germany.

Myside bias has been studied much more systematically in other research. For example, assessments of the logical validity of informal arguments have been shown to be infected by myside bias. In one of the oldest studies, Norman Feather (1964) had subjects evaluate syllogisms presented as informal arguments. In a typical trial of his experiment, subjects would be told to accept as fact that a charitable and tolerant attitude toward mankind helps to bring people together in love and harmony; and that Christianity always helps to bring people together in love and harmony. They were then told to evaluate the soundness of the conclusion "Therefore a consequence of Christianity is a charitable and tolerant attitude toward mankind." Although this conclusion is actually not logically valid, those of Feather's (1964) subjects who were ranked high in religiosity found that the invalidity was much harder to detect than subjects who were not highly religious did.

Anup Gampa and colleagues (2019) observed that, when evaluating informal logical arguments, political ideology acted much like religiosity did in the 1964 Feather experiment. Syllogisms with the conclusion "Therefore marijuana should be legal" were easier for liberals and harder for conservatives to judge correctly when the conclusion was valid, whereas syllogisms with the conclusion "Therefore no one has the right to end the life of a fetus" were harder for liberals and easier for conservatives to judge correctly when the conclusion was valid. Performance on the four-card selection task (Wason 1966),[8] another paradigm involving logical reasoning, is also affected by myside bias. Erica Dawson, Thomas Gilovich, and Dennis Regan (2002) found that it was much easier for a subject to find the cards that falsified the rule if the rule stated a negative stereotype with respect to the subject (a female subject testing the rule "All women are poor drivers") than it was to find the cards that falsified the rule if the rule stated a positive stereotype with respect to the subject (an Asian subject testing the rule "All Asian Americans are smart").

Note that the studies by Feather (1964), Gampa and colleagues (2019), and Dawson and colleagues (2002) all demonstrate what transforms a belief bias experiment into a myside bias experiment. In a belief bias syllogistic reasoning experiment, for example, the believability of the conclusion will be manipulated—comparing, say, the believable "Roses are red" conclusion with the unbelievable "Mice are insects" conclusion. The conclusions in this and other belief bias experiments will be testable beliefs—again, using Robert Abelson's (1986) term, whereas, in the myside bias experiments just discussed, the key beliefs are distal beliefs—whether marijuana should be legal or whether Christians are charitable. When we review the individual difference correlates of these biases in chapter 3, we will see that using distal beliefs versus testable beliefs in these paradigms leads to vast differences in our ability to predict who will reason correctly and who will not.

As these myside bias studies show, ideology and politics, which represent distal beliefs that are not easy to empirically verify, are rich sources of myside bias (Ditto et al. 2019a). For example, Jarret Crawford, Sophie Kay, and Kristen Duke (2015) found that when liberal subjects were told that a military general had criticized the president of the United States, they were more likely to excuse the behavior of the general when the president was George W. Bush than when the president was Barack Obama. Conservative subjects, on the other hand, were more likely to excuse the behavior of the general when the president was Obama than when the president was Bush.

Myside bias infects many different kinds of political judgments, and it fuels self-serving decisions in negotiations and in work environments as well. Thus Kyle Kopko and colleagues (2011) found that rulings on the adequacy of challenged ballots in elections were infected by a partisan bias. Thus, too, in examining what subjects thought about the appropriate payment for working on a common task with someone else, David Messick and Keith Sentis (1979) found that subjects who believed they had worked more on the task than the other person tended to think they should be paid more. In contrast, however, subjects who believed they had worked *less* on the common task tended to think both workers should be paid the same.

Such mysided thinking certainly plays out in real life. Max Bazerman and Don Moore (2008) report on a survey where, for subjects in one group, 44 percent thought that if they sued someone and lost their suit, they should pay the legal costs of the person they sued. In contrast, for subjects in a second group, 85 percent thought that if someone sued them and they won the case, the other party should pay their legal costs. Thus subjects' judgments of fairness depended to a great extent on which side of the outcome they were on.

Linda Babcock and colleagues (1995) had dyads of subjects simulate being plaintiff or defendant in an automobile accident case adjudicating damages (an actual case in Texas, where the plaintiff was suing the defendant for $100,000). After being assigned their roles, plaintiffs and defendants both read twenty-seven pages of testimony and then attempted to settle on an amount without going before a judge. They were told that failure to settle would result in a penalty for both parties. Under this condition, 72 percent of the subject dyads reached a settlement. But when the subject dyads in a second group read the twenty-seven pages of testimony *before* they were assigned their roles, 94 percent reached a settlement. The significantly lower settlement rate in the former condition was a result of the subjects' feeling too confident of their respective sides in the case due to their myside orientation while reading the case testimony.

In argument evaluation experiments (Stanovich and West 2008a), we had subjects rate the quality of arguments about abortion (and another issue—lowering the drinking age—that yielded similar results). The pro-choice and pro-life arguments were judged by experts to be similar in quality and strength. Consistent with some previous research (Baron 1995), a strong myside bias was observed. That is, subjects rated the arguments that were consistent with their own position as better than the arguments that were not.

Charles Taber and Milton Lodge (2006) had subjects evaluate pro and con arguments on the issues of affirmative action and gun control. They found that subjects preferred arguments that matched their prior opinions on those two issues over arguments that contradicted their prior opinions, even when the arguments were similar in quality. Taber and Lodge also found that subjects took much more time reading and thinking about arguments when these contradicted their prior opinions because they were selectively generating refutations of them (see Edwards and Smith 1996).

Myside processing undermines our ability to evaluate the evidence produced by scientific studies. Charles Lord, Lee Ross, and Mark Lepper (1979) presented subjects with the design and results of two studies on the effects of capital punishment. One study reported data supporting the deterrent effect of the death penalty, and the second presented data disconfirming it. One group of subjects supported the death penalty and another opposed it (both groups were selected based on their responses to the same questionnaire). Subjects rated the study that confirmed their prior opinion more favorably than the one that disconfirmed it, even though the two studies were designed to be similar in their methodological rigor.

The most cited result from the Lord, Ross, and Lepper 1979 study, however, was the subjects' response to it at the end of the experiment. At first glance,[9] from a Bayesian perspective, it would seem that the two groups would converge in their opinions after reading the two studies, which, taken together, produced mixed evidence. Instead, both groups had processed the studies in a myside manner—accepting the evidence that was favorable to their own view and exaggerating the defects of the evidence that was not. As a result, the groups were even more polarized after reading the two contradictory studies.

Taber and Lodge (2006) observed a similar polarization, but only among those who were ranked high in political knowledge. In fact, the attitude polarization found by Lord, Ross, and Lepper (1979) is not always observed in myside experiments, and when it is observed, it does not always characterize performance on every issue (Gerber and Green 1998; Hahn and Harris 2014; Kuhn and Lao 1996; MacCoun 1998; Munro and Ditto 1997). But whether or not the polarization occurs in experiments, one result is consistently found. The evidence is almost always evaluated with a myside bias.

That subjects critique unfavorable studies and arguments more harshly has been demonstrated many times in the literature. For example, in several experiments, Paul Klaczynski and colleagues (Klaczynski 1997; Klaczynski and Lavallee 2005) presented subjects with flawed experiments and arguments that led to conclusions either consistent or inconsistent with their prior opinions and beliefs. Subjects were then asked to critique the flaws in the experiments. Robust myside bias effects were observed—subjects found many more flaws when the experiment's conclusions were inconsistent than when they were consistent with their prior opinions and beliefs.

People not only *evaluate* arguments in a myside biased manner; they *generate* arguments in a biased manner as well (Perkins 1985). In several experiments, my research group (Toplak and Stanovich 2003; Macpherson and Stanovich, 2007) had subjects explore arguments both for and against various public policy propositions (e.g., "People should be allowed to sell their internal organs"; "Tuition should be raised to cover the full cost of a university education"). When subjects had a strong opinion on the issue, they generated many more arguments for their side than for the opposite one. This was true even when they were given explicit instructions to be unbiased in their reasoning (Macpherson and Stanovich 2007).

Myside bias shows up in more subtle ways as well—both in real life and in the laboratory. In the real world, risk and reward are positively correlated. High-risk activities tend to have greater benefits than low-risk activities do.[10] Contrary to this real-life relationship, studies have found that people's ratings of the risk and reward of various activities are *negatively* correlated (Finucane et al. 2000; Slovic and Peters 2006) both across activities within subjects and across subjects within activities. When something is rated as having high benefits, it tends to be seen as having low risk; and when something is rated as having high risk, it is seen as having low benefits. Paul Slovic and Ellen Peters (2006) suggest that risk perception shows this kind of myside bias because it is driven by affect—if we like the benefits of something, we tend to think it is low risk. Our research group confirmed this finding in a within-subject design (Stanovich and West 2008b). Subjects who saw a benefit in drinking alcohol rated the risks of drinking alcohol as lower than those who saw no such benefit. And subjects who saw substantial benefits in using pesticides rated the risks in using them as lower than subjects who saw no such benefits.

Brittany Liu and Peter Ditto (2013) observed a similar self-serving trade-off when judging the morality of various actions, and they found it on both sides of the political spectrum. Subjects were asked about the moral acceptability of four different actions: the forceful interrogation of terrorist suspects, capital punishment, condom promotion in sex education, and embryonic stem cell research (the first two actions being more often seen as morally acceptable by politically conservative subjects than by politically liberal subjects and the second two being more often seen as morally acceptable by politically liberal subjects than by politically conservative ones). They were asked about the morality of each action in itself, whether it was immoral *even if* effective in fulfilling its intended purpose. The subjects were also asked about the perceived likelihood of beneficial consequences of the action (e.g., whether forceful interrogation produces valid intelligence; whether promoting condom use helps reduce teen pregnancy and sexually transmitted diseases).

For each of the four actions, the more strongly subjects believed that the action was immoral even if it had beneficial consequences, the less strongly they believed it would actually have beneficial consequences. Thus the more strongly subjects endorsed the belief that promoting the use of condoms was morally wrong even if it helped prevent pregnancy and sexually transmitted diseases, the less likely they were to believe that condoms actually were effective at preventing these problems. Thus, too, the more strongly subjects endorsed the belief that the forceful interrogation of terrorist suspects was morally wrong even if it yielded valid intelligence, the less likely they were to believe that it actually did yield valid intelligence. In short, the subjects tended to de-emphasize the costs of their moral commitments, just as the subjects in the Finucane and colleagues 2000 study tended to minimize the risks of activities they approved of.

Michael Huemer (2015) discusses how we use facts to fit our beliefs in mysided ways. He notes that, in the 2×2 matrix of beliefs about capital punishment (whether or not capital punishment deters crime by whether or not many innocent people are convicted of crimes), two of the four cells are overpopulated and two are underpopulated. Thus, although many people believe that capital punishment deters crime and that not many innocent people are convicted of crimes, on the one hand, and many people believe that capital punishment fails to deter crime and that many innocent people are convicted of crimes, on the other, almost no one holds either of the two other conjunctions of beliefs, both of which are quite plausible: that capital punishment deters crime but that many innocent people are convicted of crimes or that capital punishment fails to deter crime but that very few innocent people are convicted of crimes. This suggests that people's evaluations of beliefs about capital punishment are linked not to assessing, independently, the evidence on each belief but, instead, through myside bias, to their convictions about capital punishment.

The myside examples considered so far have largely involved the interpretation of written descriptions of arguments or experiments, but other research shows that myside bias can even affect the interpretation of the *numerical* outcome of an experiment. Subjects' interpretation of covariation data relevant to an experimental outcome can be distorted by their prior hypotheses about the nature of the relationship (Stanovich and West 1998b). In a typical, purely numeric covariation detection experiment not assessing myside bias, subjects are shown data from an experiment examining the relation between a treatment and patient response. They might be told, for instance, that

200 people were given the treatment and improved

75 people were given the treatment and did not improve

50 people were not given the treatment and improved

15 people were not given the treatment and did not improve

In covariation detection experiments, subjects are asked to indicate whether the treatment was effective. The example presented here represents a difficult problem that many people get wrong, believing that the treatment in this example is effective. Subjects focus, first, on the large number of cases (200) in which improvement followed the treatment and, second, on the fact that, of the people who received treatment, many more showed improvement (200) than showed no improvement (75). Because this probability ($200/275 = .727$) seems high, subjects are enticed into thinking that the treatment works. This is an error of rational thinking. Such an approach ignores the probability of improvement where treatment was *not* given. Since this probability is even higher ($50/65 = .769$), the particular treatment tested in this experiment can be judged to be completely ineffective. The tendency to ignore the outcomes in the no-treatment condition and focus on the large number of people in the treatment-improvement group entices many people into viewing the treatment as effective.

Dan Kahan and colleagues (2017) presented difficult problems like this to subjects who were randomly assigned to one of four conditions. Two conditions involved a hypothetical situation of a skin cream treatment for a rash. Subjects in the two rash conditions (with identical numbers, but with the column names reversed) were given numerical data in a 2×2 matrix and had to discern whether the treatment was effective. These represented the control conditions (the conditions not involving myside bias).

In the two myside bias conditions, subjects were presented with 2×2 matrices of data (with the same numbers as the rash conditions) that involved a city government deciding whether to pass a law banning private citizens from carrying concealed handguns in public. Subjects were told that, to address this question, researchers had divided cities into two groups: one group consisting of cities that had recently enacted bans on concealed weapons and another group of cities that had no such bans. The two columns indicated the number of cities in which crime had increased and the number of cities in which crime had decreased. Two different conditions were created whereby the numbers in the 2×2 matrix were the same but the column labels (number of cities in which crime increased versus number of cities in which crime decreased) were simply reversed, thus creating one study in which the data indicated that gun control was effective and another study in which the data indicated that gun control was ineffective.

In the Kahan and colleagues 2017 study, the subjects' prior attitudes toward gun control were also assessed. Because subjects were randomly assigned to the conditions, some saw numerical data that supported their prior opinion and others saw data that contradicted their prior opinion about gun control. Still other subjects saw data about which they presumably had no prior opinion (the subjects assigned to the two rash conditions). The results clearly indicated that subjects were more accurate in their covariation assessments when the gun control data supported rather than contradicted their prior opinion, performing their assessments better than the subjects in the corresponding rash condition in the first instance and worse in the second instance.

Kahan and colleagues (2017) also observed that the myside bias was present in subjects on both sides of the issue in question. That is, it was observed in both pro–gun control and anti–gun control subjects. This demonstration of a myside bias in the evaluation of purely numerical data (rather than of a complicated experimental design, as in many previous myside studies) was extended by Anthony Washburn and Linda Skitka (2018) and by S. Glenn Baker and colleagues (2020) to a variety of other issues that trigger strong convictions—for example, immigration, health care, same-sex marriage, welfare, nuclear power, and carbon emissions. Matthew Nurse and Will Grant (2020) replicated the findings of these studies using the issue of climate change risk perceptions.

Myside Bias: From Laboratory to Real Life

In early to mid-2019, a study by Leaf Van Boven and colleagues with a particularly interesting myside bias research design appeared online. Its subjects were asked to process quantitative probabilistic information about two controversial issues: the Trump administration's ban on travel and immigration from seven countries, five of which were majority-Muslim countries (Syria, Iran, Libya, Somalia, and Yemen), meant to prevent potential terrorists from entering the United States, and an assault weapons ban, meant to reduce mass shootings. Contextualizing information was given to the subjects on the travel ban, including the fact that various other courts and organizations had questioned its legality, claiming that it was discriminatory. Subjects were then given the following statistics (M = Muslim; T = terrorist), which they were told were based on current and historical data:

p(M): The probability that an immigrant is from a Muslim country is 17 percent.

p(T): The probability that an immigrant is a terrorist is 0.00001 percent.

p(T|M): The probability that an immigrant from a Muslim country is a terrorist is 0.00004 percent.

p(M|T): The probability that a terrorist immigrant is from a Muslim country is 72 percent.

They were then asked which one of these probabilities was most important to them personally in deciding whether to support or oppose the travel ban policy (subjects had previously indicated whether they supported or opposed the policy on another questionnaire).

Most subjects chose one of the two conditional probabilities as the most important. Clearly, the "hit rate," p(M|T), of 72 percent seemed to support the travel ban policy more than the "inverse conditional probability," p(T|M), of 0.00004 percent did. Subjects who had expressed their support of the travel ban policy at the start of the experiment overwhelmingly chose p(M|T) as the most important probability, but subjects who had expressed their opposition to it, in contrast, overwhelmingly chose p(T|M) as the most important probability. The huge myside bias observed was roughly equivalent on both sides of this issue, and it was not attenuated by higher numeracy. In fact, the more numerate subjects displayed a greater myside bias, a finding we will discuss in greater detail in chapter 3.

One of the most interesting things about the 2019 Van Boven and colleagues experiment was that it tested exactly the same subjects who had responded to the travel ban issue on a second controversial issue of contemporary importance, an assault weapons ban, meant to reduce mass shootings. The subjects were given a definition of "assault weapon" (any of a number of semiautomatic rifles, and other semiautomatic weapons equipped with attachments—such as a scope, pistol grip, or grenade launcher—or high-capacity magazines), they were told that a comprehensive bill banning a number of assault weapons had been introduced in Congress, and they were given the following statistics (presented as frequencies in order to disguise the parallel with the experiment's other issue), based on current and historical data (S = mass shooting; A = assault weapon):

p(S): In the last few years, 6 out of 100 million American adults committed a mass shooting.

p(A): In last few years, 12 million out of 100 million American adults owned an assault weapon.

p(A|S): Out of 6 American adults who committed a mass shooting, 4 owned an assault weapon.

P(S|A): Out of 12 million American adults who owned an assault weapon, 4 committed a mass shooting.

They were then asked which one of these statistics was most important to them personally in deciding whether to support or oppose the assault weapons ban.

Most subjects chose one of the two conditional probabilities as the most important. Clearly, the hit rate, p(A|S), of 4 out of 6 (67 percent) seemed to support the assault weapons ban more than the inverse conditional probability, p(S|A) of 4 out of 12 million (0.000003 percent). Subjects who had supported the assault weapons ban overwhelmingly chose p(A|S) as the most important, but subjects who had opposed the assault weapons ban, in contrast, overwhelmingly chose p(S|A) as the most important. As on the previous issue, the huge myside bias observed was roughly equivalent on both sides of this issue, and it was not attenuated in those subjects high in numeracy (who in fact displayed a greater myside bias).

You have no doubt already intuited what is amazing about the results of the 2019 Van Boven and colleagues experiment. The subjects who opposed the travel ban tended to *support* the assault weapons ban (for simplicity, let's call them "the liberals")—and the subjects who supported the travel ban tended to *oppose* the assault weapons ban (for simplicity, let's call them "the conservatives"). That means that both liberals and conservatives were switching their preference for types of evidence depending upon the issue in question. The liberals did not like focusing on the hit rate when the issue was a travel ban, but they did when the issue was an assault weapons ban. Conversely, the conservatives liked focusing on the hit rate when the issue was a travel ban, but they did not when the issue was an assault weapons ban. The Van Boven and colleagues 2019 experiment provides a particularly good demonstration of how people pick and choose which statistic they view to be most important based on which is most consistent with their prior opinion on the issue at hand.

As I was pondering the implications of the Van Boven and colleagues (2019) experiment in the first half of 2019, I came across a *New York Times* article (Ward and Singhvi 2019) discussing the claim that there was an immigration crisis on the southern border of the United States. The entire thrust of the article was to present statistics rebutting the claim that the situation on our Mexican border was troubling. The three key statistics presented in the article were, first, that the number of arrests for illegally crossing the Mexican border had been decreasing since 2006; second, that most of the drugs seized on the southern border were seized at legal points of entry and not along the open border; and, third, that, although statistics were hard to come by, it appeared that the criminal conviction rate for undocumented immigrants in the United States was actually lower than that for native born citizens.[11] These statistics were clearly presented with the rhetorical purpose of refuting the views of those who were concerned about the southern border situation.

Prompted by reading the Van Boven and colleagues 2019 study, I began to wonder how people concerned with gun violence would react to statistics comparable to those presented by the *New York Times* on the illegal immigration issue. Imagine that there was legislation proposed to ban the AR-15 semiautomatic weapon. Imagine you are in favor of this legislation because you are a gun control advocate who is concerned about the large number of mass murders by firearms. Now imagine that a gun-rights advocate presents you with the following statistics: first, that the number of murders committed with firearms in the United States has been dropping fairly steadily since 1990; second, that the vast majority of firearm murders in the United States were committed with firearms other than the AR-15; and, finally, that the murder rate of AR-15s was lower per firearm than that of other firearms. The question that I asked myself after concocting this hypothetical was, if someone were a gun control advocate, would such statistics be any reason for that person not to support a ban on the AR-15 weapon? I think the answer is clearly not.

The thinking of the gun control advocate would be something like the following. A negative outcome is happening, and the advocate of the AR-15 ban wants it to stop. That the negative outcome is declining over time or that the AR-15 is implicated in only a small fraction of murders would seem to be of little concern to the gun control advocate who wants to bring the murder rate down. But surely the same can be said for the citizen who wants to decrease illegal immigration. That the negative outcome (illegal immigration) seen by this citizen has been declining over the years, or that some of the negative effects (illegal drug importation) are coming from policed borders and not unpoliced ones surely is irrelevant to such a citizen. Neither are relative rates of crime when the citizen's safety depends on the absolute numbers, not the relative rates, of crimes (just as global warming depends on the absolute not the per capita level of carbon dioxide). The *New York Times* reporters seem oblivious to the fact that their statistics on immigration—as congenial as they may seem to an open-borders advocate—would seem utterly irrelevant to citizens who want illegal immigration to end. They are as irrelevant as the parallel set of statistics listed in this section would be to the gun control advocate. The implications of the Van Boven and colleagues 2019 experiment offer a little taste of what is to come in later chapters, when we discuss some of the political and social policy implications of myside bias.

Why Is Myside Processing Such a Ubiquitous Tendency?

The brief and selective review of studies discussed so far was meant to suggest what is more comprehensively represented in table 1.1: that myside bias has been demonstrated in many different paradigms across many different behavioral and cognitive science disciplines. The extant literature also demonstrates that myside bias is not confined to any particular demographic group. It occurs across a wide range of ages. It is not limited to people of low intelligence—a fact that will be discussed at length in chapter 3. Myside bias is displayed by people holding all sorts of belief systems, values, and convictions. It is not limited to those with a particular worldview. Any belief that is held with conviction—any distal belief, to use Robert Abelson's (1986) term—can be the driving force behind myside thinking. In short, as an information processing tendency, myside cognition is ubiquitous.

Some might argue that something so ubiquitous and universal must be grounded in the evolution of our cognitive systems (either as an adaptation or as a by-product). Others, however, might argue that myside bias could not be grounded in evolution because evolutionary mechanisms would be truth seeking, and myside bias is not. In fact, evolution does not guarantee perfect rationality in the maximizing sense used throughout cognitive science—whether as maximizing true beliefs (epistemic rationality) or as maximizing subjective expected utility (instrumental rationality). Although organisms have evolved to increase their reproductive fitness, increases in fitness do not always entail increases in epistemic or instrumental rationality. Beliefs need not always track the world with maximum accuracy in order for fitness to increase.

Evolution might fail to select out epistemic mechanisms of high accuracy when they are costly in terms of resources, such as memory, energy, or attention. Evolution operates on the same cost-benefit logic that signal detection theory does. Some of our perceptual processes and mechanisms of belief fixation are deeply unintelligent in that they yield many false alarms, but if the lack of intelligence confers other advantages such as extreme speed of processing and the noninterruption of other cognitive activities , the belief fixation errors might be worth their cost (Fodor 1983; Friedrich 1993; Haselton and Buss 2000; Haselton, Nettle, and Murray 2016). Likewise, since myside bias might tend to increase errors of a certain type but reduce errors of another type, there would be nothing strange about such a bias from an evolutionary point of view (Haselton, Nettle, and Murray 2016; Johnson and Fowler 2011; Kurzban and Aktipis 2007; McKay and Dennett 2009; Stanovich 2004). What might be the nature of such a trade-off?

For many years in cognitive science, there has been a growing tendency to see the roots of reasoning in the *social* world of early humans rather than in their need to understand the natural world (Dunbar 1998, 2016). Indeed, Stephen Levinson (1995) is just one of many theorists who speculate that evolutionary pressures were focused more on negotiating cooperative mutual intersubjectivity than on understanding the natural world. The view that some of our reasoning tendencies are grounded in the evolution of communication dates back at least to the work of Nicholas Humphrey (1976), and there are many variants of this view. For example, Robert Nozick (1993) has argued that in prehistory, when mechanisms for revealing what is true about the world were few, a crude route to reliable knowledge might have been to demand reasons for assertions by conspecifics (see also Dennett 1996, 126–127). Kim Sterelny (2001) developed similar ideas in arguing that social intelligence was the basis of our early ability to simulate (see also Gibbard 1990; Mithen 1996, 2000; Nichols and Stich 2003). All of these views are, despite subtle differences between them, sketching the genetic-cultural coevolutionary history (Richerson and Boyd 2005) of the negotiation of argument with conspecifics.

The most influential synthesis of these views—and the most relevant to myside bias—was achieved by Hugo Mercier and Dan Sperber (2011, 2017),whose subtle, nuanced theory of reasoning is grounded in the logic of the evolution of communication. Mercier and Sperber's theory posits that reasoning evolved for the social function of persuading others through arguments. If persuasion by argument is the goal, then reasoning will be characterized by myside bias. We humans are programmed to try to convince others with arguments, not to use arguments to ferret out the truth. Like Levinson (1995) and the other theorists mentioned earlier, Mercier and Sperber (2011, 2017) see our reasoning abilities as arising from our need not to solve problems in the natural world but to persuade others in the social world. As Daniel Dennett (2017, 220) puts it: "Our skills were honed for taking sides, persuading others in debate, not necessarily getting things right."

In several steps, Mercier and Sperber's (2011, 2017) theory takes us from the evolution of reasoning to our ubiquitous tendency, as humans, to reason with myside bias. We must have a way of exercising what Mercier and Sperber call "epistemic vigilance." Although we could adopt the inefficient strategy of differentiating trustworthy people from untrustworthy people by simply memorizing the history of our interactions with them, such a strategy would not work with new individuals. Mercier and Sperber (2011, 2017) point out that argumentation helps us to evaluate the truth of communications based simply on content rather than on prior knowledge about particular persons. Likewise, we learn to produce coherent and convincing arguments when we wish to transmit information to others with whom we have not established a trusting relationship. These skills of producing and evaluating arguments allow members of a society to exchange information with other members without the need to establish a prior relationship of trust with them.

If, however, the origins of our reasoning abilities lie in their having as a prime function the persuasion of others through argumentation, then our reasoning abilities in *all* domains will be strongly colored by persuasive argumentation. If the function of producing an argument is to convince another person, it is unlikely that the arguments produced will be an unbiased selection from both sides of the issue at hand. Such arguments would be unconvincing. Instead, we can be expected to have an overwhelming tendency to produce arguments that support our own opinion (see Mercier 2016).

Mercier and Sperber (2011) argue that this myside bias carries over into situations where we are reasoning on our own about one of our opinions and that, in such situations, we are likely to *anticipate* a dialogue with others (see Kuhn 2019). The anticipation of a future dialogue will also cause us to think to ourselves in a mysided manner. Mercier and Sperber's (2016, 2017) theory makes differential predictions about our ability to *evaluate* the arguments of others. Basically, it predicts that, though we will display a myside bias in evaluating arguments if the issue in question concerns a distal belief, we will display much less of a myside bias when the issue in question is a testable belief.[12]

In short, Mercier and Sperber (2011, 2017) provide a model of how myside bias is inherent in the evolutionary foundations of reasoning. From their evolutionary story of origins, it is not hard to imagine how the gene-culture coevolutionary history (see Richerson and Boyd 2005) of argumentation abilities would reinforce the myside properties of our cognition (a subject of much speculation I can only allude to here). For example, in an early discussion of myside costs and benefits, Joshua Klayman (1995) suggests some of the gene-culture coevolutionary trade-offs that may have been involved. He discusses the cognitive costs of generating ideas outside the mainstream—"Just keeping an open mind can have psychic costs" (Klayman 1995, 411)—and the potential social disapproval of those who waffle. And he discusses the often-immediate benefits of myside confidence triumphing over the more long-term benefits of doubt and uncertainty. Anticipating Mercier and Sperber (2011) in some ways, Klayman (1995, 411) argues that "when other people lack good information about the accuracy of one's judgments, they may take consistency as a sign of correctness"; he points to the many characteristics of myside argumentation (e.g., consistency, confidence) that can bootstrap social benefits to the individual and group. Dan Kahan's discussions of his concept of identity protective cognition (Kahan 2013, 2015; see also Kahan, Jenkins-Smith, and Braman 2011; Kahan et al. 2017) likewise suggest other potential mechanisms for myside bias to confer evolutionary benefit by facilitating group cohesion. These possible social benefits must be taken into account when we assess the overall rationality of mysided thinking—a point I will explore at greater length in chapter 2.

2 Is Myside Processing Irrational?

In chapter 1, we established several basic things about myside processing: that it is easy to experimentally demonstrate in any number of laboratory paradigms; that it is ubiquitous, being neither limited to individuals with certain cognitive characteristics nor characteristic of only a minority of individuals; that it characterizes our thinking about real-life issues; and, finally, that it may have evolved as a basic human information processing characteristic. But the central issue we have not addressed so far is whether myside bias processing is irrational: Does it represent a thinking error? Or, to use the language of cognitive science, can we assume that it is not normative[1] to display myside bias?

In chapter 1, we also considered the two senses of the term "bias" used by Joshua Klayman (1995)—bias as an evaluatively neutral and as a fundamentally flawed reasoning process. Should the "bias" in "myside bias" be taken in the neutral sense of simply describing a general information processing *tendency* (without connoting whether that tendency is right or wrong)? Or should it be taken to mean an inherently flawed way of information processing that systematically leads to errors and to nonnormative responses?

First, because the many paradigms used to study myside thinking (see table 1.1) involve many different normative issues, I will begin our discussion here by considering the most common myside paradigm—evidence evaluation tasks, where subjects have to evaluate the quality of evidence provided by hypothetical experiments.

The case for considering myside bias to be a systematic source of nonnormative reasoning would, at first, seem to be clear cut. Myside bias clearly seems to violate the strictures of Bayesian belief updating. But, as we will see, such a conclusion would be premature. The normative issues surrounding myside bias turn out to be quite complex. Researchers now realize that the Bayesian formula has been too thoughtlessly applied in many myside paradigms in which its application calls for more nuance.

The critical thinking literature in psychology and education strongly emphasizes our ability to decouple prior beliefs and opinions from the evaluation of new evidence and arguments (Baron 2008; Lipman 1991; Nussbaum and Sinatra 2003; Perkins 1995; Sternberg 2001, 2003). From within the critical thinking framework, it seems natural to see myside bias as a dysfunctional thinking style that should be suppressed through instruction in balanced argumentation and balanced evidence evaluation. The literature on Bayesian reasoning (e.g., De Finetti 1989; Earman 1992; Fischhoff and Beyth-Marom 1983; Howson and Urbach 1993) would at least *seem* to justify the emphasis on unbiased evidence evaluation in the critical thinking literature.

For judgment and decision making, Bayes's theorem has special salience. The following Bayesian formula is often used as the formal standard for the important task of belief updating—how the belief in a particular hypothesis should be updated based on the receipt of new evidence that is relevant to the hypothesis. The formula contains two fundamental concepts: the focal hypothesis under investigation (labeled "H") and new data that are collected relevant to the hypothesis (labeled "D").

$$P(H/D)=\frac{P(H)*P(D/H)}{P(H)*P(D/H)+P(\sim H)*P(D/\sim H)}$$

In the formula, there is an additional symbol, ~H ("not H"), which simply refers to the alternative hypothesis: the mutually exclusive alternative that must be correct if the focal hypothesis, H, is false. Thus the probability of the alternative hypothesis, ~H, is one minus the probability of the focal hypothesis, H.

In the formula, P(H) is the probability estimate that the focal hypothesis is true *prior* to collecting the data, and P(~H) is the probability estimate that the alternative hypothesis is true *prior* to collecting the data. Additionally, a number of conditional probabilities come into play. For example, P(H/D) represents the probability that the focal hypothesis is true *after* collecting the data actually observed (this is sometimes termed the "*posterior* probability"). P(D/H) is the probability of observing that particular data pattern given that the focal hypothesis is true, and P(D/~H) is the probability of observing that particular data pattern given that the alternative hypothesis is true. It is important to realize that P(D/H) and P(D/~H) are *not* complements (they do not add up to 1.0). The data might be likely given the focal hypothesis *and* likely given the alternative hypothesis—or unlikely given the focal hypothesis *and* unlikely given the alternative hypothesis.

In order to facilitate our discussion of the normative appropriateness of myside bias, I will also present Bayes's theorem in a different form—one arrived at by simple mathematical transformation. The first formula was written in terms of the posterior probability of the focal hypothesis (H) given the new data (D), P(H/D). We could of course also write the formula in terms of the posterior probability of the nonfocal hypothesis (~H) given the new data (D), P(~H/D). By dividing the two formulas, we can arrive at the most theoretically transparent form of Bayes's formula (see Fischhoff and Beyth-Marom 1983)—one that is written in "odds form":

$$\frac{P(H/D)}{P(\sim H/D)} = \frac{P(H)}{P(\sim H)} * \frac{P(D/H)}{P(D/\sim H)}$$

In this ratio formula, from left to right, the three ratio terms represent the posterior odds favoring the focal hypothesis (H) after receipt of the new data (D); the prior odds favoring the focal hypothesis; and the likelihood ratio (LR)—the probability of the data given the focal hypothesis divided by the probability of the data given the alternative hypothesis; specifically:

Posterior odds = P(H / D) / P(~H / D)

Prior odds = P(H) / P(~H)

Likelihood ratio = P(D / H) / P(D / ~H)

This formula tells us that the odds favoring the focal hypothesis (H) after receipt of the data are arrived at by multiplying together the other two terms—the prior odds favoring the focal hypothesis and likelihood ratio:

Posterior odds favoring the focal hypothesis = Prior odds × LR

The key normative principle captured by Bayes's theorem is that the evaluation of the diagnosticity of the evidence (the extent to which the evidence can discriminate between a hypothesis and its alternatives or, more simply, the likelihood ratio) should be conducted *independently* of the assessment of the prior odds favoring the focal hypothesis. The point is *not* that prior beliefs should not affect the posterior probability of the hypothesis.

They most certainly should. A Bayesian analysis is an explicit procedure for factoring in such prior beliefs. The point, rather, is that they should not be factored in *twice*. Prior beliefs are encompassed in one of two multiplicative terms that define the posterior probability, but the diagnosticity of the evidence should be assessed *separately* from the prior beliefs. Thus the concern in the critical thinking literature for segregating prior beliefs from evidence evaluation receives support from the Bayesian literature (see Fischhoff and Beyth-Marom 1983).

Nevertheless, we should not jump to the conclusion that such a simple analysis means that any degree of myside bias—any indication that confidence in the focal hypothesis is being used to evaluate the likelihood ratio—is automatically nonnormative. The simple analysis we have done here would apply to some Bayesian reasoning experiments where subjects are given numerical information that allows the likelihood ratio to be mathematically calculated with precision (e.g., Beyth-Marom and Fischhoff 1983; Stanovich and West 1998b).

In most of the myside paradigms discussed in chapter 1, however, and in the myside literature generally, subjects are not given specific numerical information with which to calculate the likelihood ratio. Instead, they must evaluate either informal arguments or hypothetical experiments that produce data relevant to the focal hypotheses. This information is much more ambiguous than actual numerical values for the two components of the likelihood ratio in that it requires considerable interpretation and inference to derive a subjective likelihood ratio from it.

In such studies, subjects are asked not to estimate a numerical likelihood ratio but merely to evaluate the information provided (either informal arguments or hypothetical experiments). Myside bias is inferred when subjects give a higher quality rating to information that confirms than to information that contradicts their prior beliefs or opinions. It is usually assumed that the Bayesian stricture here is that subjects should give equal likelihood ratios to the same information regardless of whether it confirms or refutes their prior beliefs or opinions. Although this was the general assumption in the early heuristics and biases literature of the 1970s and 1980s, since the 1990s, there is growing agreement that this stricture does not apply in these paradigms.

The Knowledge Projection Argument and Koehler's Proof B

We have previously discussed examples of the experiment evaluation paradigm, which is much used in the myside literature. Often subjects are presented with flawed hypothetical experiments that lead to conclusions that are either consistent or inconsistent with their prior positions or opinions. Subjects rate studies whose results are inconsistent with their prior positions or opinions more harshly than they rate studies whose results are consistent with them. For example, Jonathan Koehler (1993) found that both parapsychologists and scientific critics of parapsychology gave lower ratings to studies that disagreed with their prior positions on extrasensory perception. But Koehler (1993) went on to analyze in detail whether it was really nonnormative for subjects to let their prior beliefs influence the evaluation of a study's quality, as the subjects in his experiments were doing. His analysis demonstrated that, in a paradigm like this one—where the reliability of the information presented is in question—some degree of myside bias can be normatively justified.

We now know that the Bayesian stricture that the prior belief probability not infect the evaluation of the likelihood ratio is considerably weakened in paradigms where subjects are presented with information whose source reliability has to be assessed (see Hahn and Harris 2014). This is true in paradigms like the one used by Koehler (1993), where subjects are presented with a hypothetical experiment but have no other contextual knowledge as they would have in actual science, such as the credibility and track record of the research lab in question. Absent other contextual information, it would seem natural for them to evaluate the credibility of the study in part by whether the results appear plausible in light of their prior beliefs about the hypothesis. This would seem to be especially true for the scientist subjects in Koehler's experiment who had years of methodological training and experience in assessing behavioral claims. The issue that Koehler analyzed was whether they were correct in using the size of the discrepancy between the outcome of the study and their prior beliefs as a basis for judging the quality of the study.

Koehler (1993) presented two formal proofs in an appendix demonstrating that such a projection of prior beliefs was justified under certain circumstances. For our purposes, the more relevant proof is proof B from the

Appendix. Without going into formal details, I will simply sketch out the gist of it. Koehler's proof B defines three propositions: A = "This study gives results that agree with the scientist's hypothesis or prior belief"; T = "This study gives results that are congruent with the true state of nature"; G = "This is a good-quality study." For simplicity in the proof, Koehler considers these to be 0/1 propositions, but nothing depends on that simplification. Proof B assesses the relative constraints on two conditional probabilities: the probability that the study is good given that it agrees with the scientist's prior belief, $P(G/A)$, and the probability that the study is good given that it disagrees with the scientist's prior belief, $P(G/\sim A)$. And, finally, it addresses the question whether scientists are ever justified in thinking that a study that agrees with their prior beliefs is more likely to be a good study than a study that disagrees with them—or, more formally, when they are justified in thinking that $P(G/A) > P(G/\sim A)$.

Koehler's equation 15 (Koehler 1993, 51) and his subsequent comments explicating this equation show that there are two conditions that must be met for $P(G/A)$ to always exceed $P(G/\sim A)$. First, $P(T/G)$ must be greater than $P(T/\sim G)$, which simply means that a good study is more likely to produce results congruent with the true state of nature than a bad one is. Because this should be true in all but the most anomalous scientific environments, it is safe to assume that it holds. And, second, $P(H)$ must be greater than .50—that is, the focal hypothesis, H, must be the one that the scientist deems more likely than the mutually exclusive alternative hypothesis, $\sim H$, to be true.

So what Koehler's proof B shows is that, in almost all cases, scientists are justified in rating studies that agree with their favored hypotheses as being better studies than those which disagree with them. Thus the proof shows that some degree of myside bias is justified in experiment evaluation studies of the type run by Koehler (1993) and discussed in chapter 1.

In fact, as I pointed out in *Who Is Rational?* (Stanovich 1999), although Koehler's 1993 paper was unusual in providing a formal proof, the argument that it can be normative to let prior beliefs affect the evaluation of new evidence has reappeared many times in the cognitive psychology literature, as well as in the philosophy of science literature (for a discussion of the latter, see Kornblith 1993, 104–105). Indeed, the argument was so common that, some twenty years ago, I named it the "knowledge projection argument" (Stanovich 1999).[2] The label provides a handle for the argument that it is sometimes appropriate to let prior beliefs become implicated in the process of evaluating new information.

The knowledge projection argument, basically, is that in natural environments where most of our prior beliefs are true, projecting our beliefs onto new information, will lead to faster accumulation of knowledge. For example, Lauren Alloy and Naomi Tabachnik (1984, 140) defend knowledge projection in their discussion of the covariation detection literature on humans and other animals: "When individuals' expectations accurately reflect the contingencies encountered in their natural environments . . . it is not irrational for them to assimilate incoming information about covariation between events to these expectations." Of course, Alloy and Tabachnik (1984) emphasize that we must project from a largely accurate set of beliefs in order to obtain the benefit of knowledge projection.

Jonathan Evans, David Over, and Ken Manktelow (1993) rely on a variant of this argument when considering the normative status of belief bias in syllogistic reasoning. Only when faced with unbelievable conclusions do subjects engage in logical reasoning about the premises. Evans, Over, and Manktelow (1993) consider whether such a reasoning strategy could be rational in the sense of serving to achieve the reasoner's goals, and they conclude that it could. Again, their strategy works only when it is applied using a subset of beliefs that are largely true in the relevant domain (see Edwards and Smith 1996 for a similar argument). Knowledge projection is only efficacious in domains where most of a reasoner's prior beliefs are true. When, however, the subset of beliefs that the reasoner is projecting contains substantial false information, knowledge projection will delay the assimilation of the correct information.

Imagine two scientists, A and B, working in domain X. Most of the hypotheses in domain X held by scientist A are true, whereas most of the hypotheses in domain X held by scientist B are false. Imagine that they both then begin to project their prior beliefs onto the same new evidence in the way demonstrated experimentally by Koehler (1993)—with stronger tendencies to discount the evidence when it contradicts their prior beliefs. It is clear that scientist A—who already exceeds B in the number of true beliefs—will increase that advantage as new evidence comes in. Knowledge projection from differing prior beliefs is the mechanism generating the belief polarization effect demonstrated in the famous Charles Lord, Lee Ross, and Mark Lepper 1979 study discussed in chapter 1 (see Cook and Lewandowsky 2016; Hahn and Harris 2014; Jern, Chang, and Kemp 2014).

The knowledge projection tendency, efficacious in domains where most of a reasoner's prior beliefs are true, may have the effect of isolating certain individuals on "islands of false beliefs" from which—because of the knowledge projection tendency—they are unable to escape. In short, there may be a "knowledge isolation effect" when projection is used in particularly ill-suited circumstances. Thus knowledge projection, which in domains where most of the reasoner's prior beliefs are true, might lead to more rapid acquisition of new true beliefs, may be a trap in a minority of cases where a reasoner, in effect, keeps reaching into a bag of beliefs that are largely false, using these beliefs to structure the reasoner's evaluation of evidence, and hence more quickly adding incorrect beliefs to the bag for further projection. Knowledge projection from an island of false beliefs might explain the phenomenon of otherwise intelligent people who get caught in a domain-specific web of falsity from which they cannot escape (e.g., otherwise competent physical scientists who believe in creationism). Indeed, such individuals often use their considerable computational power to rationalize their beliefs and to ward off the arguments of skeptics (Evans 1996, 2019; Evans and Wason 1976; Nisbett and Wilson 1977; Wason 1969).

In summary, on an overall statistical basis, knowledge projection may well increase the rate of acquisition of true beliefs. But this does not prevent particular individuals with particularly ill-formed prior beliefs from projecting them and developing beliefs that are even less in correspondence with reality. Koehler's proof B reinforces a range of scholarship showing that, when the likelihood ratio is not quantitatively specified, the prior probability can also, validly, be used in estimating the likelihood ratio, especially when issues of source credibility and trust are at stake (Druckman and McGrath 2019; Gentzkow and Shapiro 2006; Hahn and Harris 2014; Kim, Park, and Young 2020; O'Connor and Weatherall 2018; Tappin and Gadsby 2019; Tappin, Pennycook, and Rand 2020).[3]

The Local versus Global Rationality of Myside Bias

In this section, we will dig a little deeper into just what kind of inferential behavior has been deemed normative by Koehler's proof B. Recall that, when two mutually exclusive alternative hypotheses hold, Koehler's proof B shows that we are justified in using our prior beliefs to help evaluate the likelihood ratio—that we are justified in judging $P(G/A) > P(G/\sim A)$. One of the two key stipulations is that P(H) must be greater than .50—that is, the focal hypothesis, H, must be the hypothesis that prior experience and evidence deems more likely than the mutually exclusive alternative hypothesis, ~H, to be true.

The ambiguity in "more likely to be true" covers up the fact that Koehler's proof B really does not show that myside bias is normative in all cases; or, rather, that it does so only in a narrow, very local sense—the restricted case of the new evidence that a reasoner is currently assimilating. Koehler's proof does not address at all the myside bias that may have determined the prior belief the reasoner is now about to project. When the present prior belief is not itself determined by myside bias, I am calling the situation *"globally* rational." That is, a reasoner is globally rational in projecting the prior belief *only* if the reasoner has arrived at the prior probability through a procedure that is not itself myside biased. In cases where we have no knowledge of how the reasoner's prior probability was determined, then Koehler's proof B only shows that it is not irrational to project the prior onto this new evidence, but these cases are only *"locally* rational."

To achieve global rationality, we require that P(H) contain prior knowledge that validly reflects on the credibility of new evidence, rather than on a myside preference for the focal hypothesis. Of course, global rationality is on a continuum and, in a particular instance, we may not be completely aware of how much our prior probability has been based on true evidence and how much of it derives from the mysided projection of our worldviews. And individual differences in how metacognitively aware we are of myside bias create some interesting ironies. For example, we would not want people who are *least* aware of the standards of global rationality to blithely project their prior beliefs in local instances by Koehler's proof B. But the ambiguity surrounding the phrasing of what H is introduces precisely this potential for mischief into the proof: the proof itself contains no constraints on a reasoner's attitude toward H—the hypothesis deemed "more likely to be true."

How we conceive of H determines everything subsequent in the Koehler proof because it is critical in defining A (whether evidence agrees with the focal hypothesis deemed more likely). Agreement (A) is the thing that determines whether a study is deemed to be well conducted (G, that is, a good study in the Koehler analysis), the probability of G depending critically on whether A or ~A is the final result of the study in question. To achieve global rationality, H must be the hypothesis that a reasoner thinks more likely based on an *accurate* view of previous evidence. H is not the hypothesis that the reasoner *wants* to be true; neither is it a hypothesis saturated with the effects of previous myside bias in evaluating evidence, nor the one that comports with the reasoner's worldview. Global rationality requires that H must be what I am calling the "evidence-favored hypothesis," rather than the "personally favored hypothesis." But the local rationality of Koehler's proof B does not require this.

An example might help here. Imagine a psychology professor who was asked to evaluate the quality of a typical study on the heritability of intelligence and to structure prior and posterior probabilities around the hypothesis that the heritability of human intelligence is either zero or not equal to zero. Suppose she knows the evidence on the substantial heritability of intelligence (Deary 2013; Plomin et al. 2016; Rindermann, Becker, and Coyle 2020), but because of personal affinities with the blank-slate view of human nature, she wishes that it were not true—in fact, wishes it *were* zero. The question is what is the H that the professor uses to approach new evidence with the justified strategy of considering $P(G/A) > P(G/{\sim}A)$? What is the H that the professor uses to compare with the new evidence to determine whether it agrees with the prior hypothesis (A) or not (~A)?

We will call this professor "Kelly," and we will assume that she is meta-aware and mentally disciplined. Kelly knows that the hypothesis more likely to be true ("The heritability of human intelligence is not zero") is not the hypothesis that she *wants* to be true ("The heritability of human intelligence is zero"). Kelly exerts the mental discipline to insert the hypothesis that she knows is more likely—"The heritability of human intelligence is not zero"—as $P(H) > .50$. When she then proceeds to project this prior hypothesis onto new evidence, Kelly will be both locally and globally rational.

We can see the limitations of Koehler's proof B by noting that, if we are confined to assessing local rationality, we will have no way of differentiating this self-aware professor from another psychology professor who embraces the blank-slate view (see Pinker 2002) that the variability in human intelligence is not driven by any genetic causes. This second professor, whom we will call "Dale," knows from his colleagues that there is evidence on substantial heritability of intelligence, but avoids it. Assume that this mentally undisciplined professor chooses as the focal hypothesis, H, the proposition "The heritability of human intelligence is zero" and that he assumes $P(H) > .50$. We would suspect that Dale is substituting a myside hypothesis for a true view of the evidence. And we would be queasy when he then proceeded to project this prior belief in evaluating the credibility of the new evidence—when he used this H to determine whether the new evidence was A or ~A. But there is nothing within Koehler's proof itself to aid us in arguing that Dale is wrong.

In short, Kelly knows that the more probable hypothesis, H, is not always the one she would want to be true. She knows that the evidence-favored hypothesis and the personally favored hypothesis are not always the same. In contrast, Dale thinks that the hypothesis he *wants* to be true is *more likely* to be true. In noting that Koehler's proof B does not distinguish Kelly from Dale—both behave normatively if they project their prior beliefs—we see that the reach or scope of the proof is quite limited. It only establishes that myside bias is *locally* normative but says nothing about its global normativity. I use the term "locally" because all of the heavy lifting is done before the new evidence arrives. For projection of prior beliefs in evaluating new evidence to be globally rational, evidence-based priors must at least predominate over personally favored priors in belief updating *before* receipt of the new evidence. And if people with differing prior beliefs do not achieve this more global type of rationality, they will not reach Bayesian convergence: they will not eventually converge in their posterior beliefs after seeing enough of the same evidence (although convergence itself has many unacknowledged complexities, see Bullock 2009).

Although Koehler's proof B allows both Kelly and Dale to project their current prior beliefs when they evaluate the credibility of a new experiment, it neither affirms nor prohibits anything that may have *led* to their differing P(H)s. Specifically, it is silent on the issue of Dale's ignoring the previous evidence on this issue and inserting a desired hypothesis as the focal hypothesis rather than one based on evidence. Koehler's proof B sanctions (in the sense of *allowing*) local knowledge projection but not global knowledge projection. The local knowledge projection of both Kelly and Dale may well be normative, but, at a global level, Dale's is less rational.[4]

Globally Justified Myside Thinking: Projecting Testable Beliefs versus Distal Beliefs

Global rationality requires that the focal hypothesis, H, be properly chosen.[5] By "properly chosen," I mean chosen so that $P(H) > .50$ is based on previous evidence, not simply on a worldview. The great limitation of Koehler's proof B is that it is subject to what might be called "serial abuse."

It does not assess where the prior belief has come from—that is, whether the belief has a strong basis in evidence. It allows people like Dale to bring a prior belief built not on evidence, but simply on a worldview. An abuser of proof B is someone who chooses a starting prior belief associated with a worldview rather than a testable belief that is based on evidence.

It is possible to make some generalizations about the types of situations that lead to focal hypotheses that should be projected and those which should not. I will again make use of Robert Abelson's (1986) distinction between testable belief and distal belief, using distal belief synonymously with conviction or worldview.[6]

In inquiring about whether myside bias is not just locally but also globally rational, we have to ask how a reasoner is deriving H, the focal hypothesis that the reasoner deems more likely than the mutually exclusive alternative hypothesis, ~H, to be true. If a reasoner's prior probability comes from subjecting a testable belief to epistemologically warranted updating before using it in knowledge projection (as in the case of Kelly), then the reasoner's knowledge projection would be both locally and globally rational. Dale's case is different, however. Dale's worldview, rather than evidence, leads to the prior belief of zero heritability of human intelligence as the focal hypothesis (the hypothesis more likely to be true, from the reasoner's perspective).

Of course, this situation is really one of a continuum—with most people's prior beliefs being conditioned partly by evidence-based knowledge and partly by association with untestable convictions and worldviews. Most people's prior beliefs are each some unknown combination of worldview and evidence. Figure 2.1 displays three examples, the first two corresponding to our previously discussed professors, Dale and Kelly. The specific issue in question is how to evaluate new data on whether private school vouchers are efficacious in raising educational achievement. Dale must generate a prior belief (arrow B) to mesh with the diagnosticity of the evidence (arrow C) and, following Koehler's proof, to also use in evaluating the evidence itself (arrow A). Dale knows very little about schooling or educational debates, so has very little actual testable knowledge to bring to bear in forming a prior probability, However, the worldview that Dale holds has a long-standing association with a position on the efficacy of private school vouchers, so he relies heavily on that in forming his prior belief. The thickness of the arrows reflects the relative weighting of evidence and worldview. When Dale projects the prior belief (arrow A), he is projecting a worldview, not evidence-based knowledge.

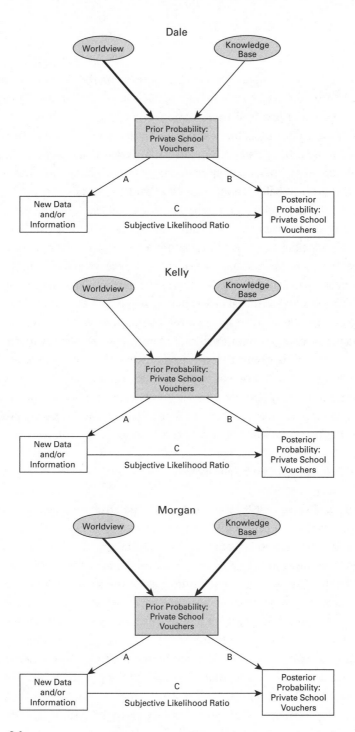

Figure 2.1
Three different weightings of worldview and actual knowledge in determining a prior probability

Kelly, on the other hand, has read extensively on the issue of the efficacy of private school vouchers in quality media sources and knows a great deal about the issues involved in education. She brings all of this to bear on developing a prior probability and relies little on a worldview that is connected to a particular stance on this issue. When Kelly projects the prior belief (arrow A), she is largely projecting evidence-based knowledge. Her myside bias is globally rational in a way that Dale's is not.

Our third psychology professor, whom we will call Morgan, shows how this trade-off between worldview and testable knowledge is really continuous. Approaching the task of evaluating a study of the efficacy of private school vouchers, Morgan has more testable knowledge to use in forming her prior belief than Dale has, but less than Kelly has, and, in addition, she relies more on a worldview (distal belief) than Kelly does, but less than Dale.

Figure 2.1 allows us to imagine the continuum on which we find ourselves when we draw on information to form a prior probability for the focal hypothesis. To the extent that a reasoner is like Kelly in forming the prior probability, and then proceeds to project that prior probability in evaluating evidence in the way Koehler shows is normatively appropriate, the reasoner is not abusing the license that proof B provides to project the prior probability in this particular case. The reasoner is both locally and globally rational.

Belief Polarization Can Be Normative

Koehler's (1993) proof B explains the belief polarization effect observed in the Lord, Ross, and Lepper 1979 study discussed in chapter 1 (see also Taber and Lodge 2006). Recall that Lord, Ross, and Lepper (1979) presented their subjects with two studies on the effects of capital punishment that provided conflicting evidence because the outcomes of the studies were in opposite directions. Nevertheless, after viewing the mixed evidence, the pro- and anti–capital punishment groups reported being even farther apart than they had been at the beginning of the experiment, thus demonstrating the belief polarization effect—when subjects with opposing views see the same mixed evidence and diverge rather than converge in their posterior probabilities.

Using Koehler's analysis, we can assume that the conditions for knowledge projection held for both groups of subjects in the Lord, Ross, and Lepper 1979 study and that both were justified in assuming $P(G/A) > P(G/\sim A)$. Thus it was not *functionally* the case that the two studies the groups received—one study on each side of the issue—were equally strong. In fact, in assuming that $P(G/A) > P(G/\sim A)$, each group found the study that was consistent with its central beliefs to be a little bit better than the study that was not. Thus, too, both the pro– and the anti–capital punishment groups had a likelihood ratio greater than one. Each group's ratio then moved the probability of its focal hypothesis in a more extreme direction, hence increasing the polarization between the two.

A more comprehensive, formal analysis of the conditions under which belief polarization is in fact normatively appropriate was conducted by Alan Jern, Kai-min Chang, and Charles Kemp (2014). The take-home message from their analysis is that belief polarization tends to occur, and indeed is not irrational, when different subjects have different ways of framing how the focal hypothesis relates to the evidence they receive.

To illustrate their point, I will modify one of the simplest examples in the Jern, Chang, and Kemp 2014 paper. Imagine that two chess players, Bobby and Boris, are facing off and they leave the chessboard in the middle of the game to take a break. And imagine, too, that you and I are two spectators who enter the room at that point, having not seen the beginning of the match. You think that Bobby is the better player by a clear margin, and I think that Boris is, also by a clear margin. We both look at the board and see that white has a substantial advantage. Given our prior beliefs about these players, you think that Bobby is more likely white, and I think that Boris is. If we both now update our prior probabilities of who will win the match, Bobby or Boris, and if we are perfect Bayesians, our posterior probabilities will now be even farther apart. We have brought different assumptions to the interpretation of the evidence (board positions for an incomplete match), and we show belief polarization even though neither of us has acted irrationally.

The remaining examples in Jern, Chang, and Kemp (2014) are far subtler than this, however, and many are analyses of actual experiments where a milder version of my hypothetical seems to be producing belief polarization. Thus the three coauthors discuss an experiment by Scott Plous (1991) where nuclear power supporters and opponents are presented with a balanced and fair description of the 1979 nuclear reactor accident at Three Mile Island, Pennsylvania. After reading the description, the supporters and opponents ended up even farther apart regarding the usefulness and safety of nuclear power: their opinions did not converge as would be expected under a simplified Bayesian model.

Jern, Chang, and Kemp (2014) discuss how the description of the Three Mile Island incident, where a reactor broke down but its breakdown was safely contained, might have reinforced the two differing worldviews of the supporters and the opponents. Jern, Chang, and Kemp (2014) point out that the pro–nuclear power subjects might have had a "fault-tolerant" worldview, in which breakdowns are bound to happen but are likely to be safely contained. Plous (1991) himself mentions that in the free-response part of his experiment, the pro–nuclear power students tended to view the breakdown as a successful test of system safeguards for nuclear power. The anti–nuclear power students, on the other hand, might have had a "fault-free" worldview, in which any breakdown at all is viewed as unacceptable. Thus both groups of subjects might have viewed the description of the incident as reinforcing their previous worldviews—resulting in belief polarization. They interpreted the very same evidence as having different implications because of the way the evidence interfaced with their previous worldviews.

Both the Koehler (1993) and the Jern, Chang, and Kemp (2014) analyses show that the simple Bayesian stricture that the prior probability should not be implicated in the assessment of the likelihood ratio holds only when the probabilities in the likelihood ratio are stipulated or directly observed, as in the classic bookbag and poker chips experiments (Edwards 1982). There the likelihood ratio can be calculated with certainty, and the reliability of the source of the new evidence is not in doubt. But both the Koehler (1993) and the Jern, Chang, and Kemp (2014) analyses exemplify a point covered in depth by Ulrike Hahn and Adam Harris (2014)—that Bayesian inference becomes more complex when the reliability or credibility of the source of the new evidence is in doubt.[7] One of the most important conclusions from Hahn and Harris's subtle and nuanced 2014 review is that the actual content of the new evidence presented for Bayesian updating can affect our assessment of the *diagnosticity* of the new evidence. It can do this by affecting our judgment of the credibility of the source of the evidence, depending upon the magnitude of the gap between our prior probability and the magnitude and direction of the likelihood ratio. The larger the gap, the more surprising the evidence is, and the more we will question the reliability of its source and thus reduce the implicit diagnosticity of the evidence. Hahn and Harris (2014, 90) argue that "the content of the testimony itself may provide one indicator (and in many contexts our only indicator) of the source's reliability" and they discuss other analyses showing that it is appropriate to condition our beliefs about source reliability based on message content (Bovens and Hartmann 2003; Gentzkow and Shapiro 2006; Olsson 2013).

The defense of belief polarization as normative in certain cases by Jern, Chang, and Kemp (2014; see also Gershman 2019; Kahan 2016) shares many similarities with Koehler's (1993) defense of the normativity of using the prior probability to evaluate the quality of the study. In both cases, the defense is a local and not a global one. Koehler's normative analysis does not critique the steps leading up to the development of the prior probability. From a more global perspective, however, if the prior probability is irrational (that is, derived from previous nonnormative myside processing), then projecting the prior probability will lead to a globally irrational posterior probability. Likewise, the Jern, Chang, and Kemp (2014) analysis does not evaluate the rationality of the framing used to interpret the evidence (see Andreoni and Mylovanov 2012; Benoit and Dubra 2016) or the rationality of the auxiliary assumptions linked to the framing (Gershman 2019). If the framing used by one of the parties in a belief polarization experiment is seriously irrational, the posterior probability of at least one of the parties in the polarization will be globally irrational.

Differentiating the "Good" Myside Bias from the "Bad" Myside Bias

For the first several decades of work in the heuristics and biases tradition (Kahneman and Tversky 1973; Tversky and Kahneman 1974), from the 1970s to the 1990s, myside bias (often termed confirmation bias; see Mercier 2017) was treated as simply another on a growing list of biases (anchoring bias, hindsight bias, availability bias, and so on), and its occurrence in the laboratory paradigms designed to study it was deemed nonnormative, without much discussion in most papers. The appearance of the knowledge projection argument throughout the 1990s (see studies cited here and Stanovich 1999) led heuristics and biases researchers to realize that they had thrown out the baby with the bathwater. Wanting to curb what they saw as the clearly dysfunctional behavior of using a distal worldview to structure the search and evaluation of all evidence, these early researchers did not see the efficacy of a scientist using extremely well thought out and evidence-based prior beliefs to evaluate the credibility of new experimental evidence. The researchers had not seen that projecting prior knowledge in this manner was normatively appropriate. This is actually what the trained scientists in Koehler's 1993 empirical study did with the evidence and experiments they were presented on extrasensory perception. Koehler in fact found that it was the skeptical scientists who showed some of the largest myside biases.

As outlined here, Koehler's proof B showed that the behavior of the scientists was normatively appropriate, at least qualitatively. The problem with Koehler's proof, however, is that it still applies even if the prior probability was derived from a distal belief—from a conviction not supported by evidence. The proof itself has no way of differentiating a conviction-based from an evidence-based prior probability. The Jern, Chang, and Kemp (2014) normative justification for belief polarization likewise fails to differentiate framing based on legitimate scientific differences from framing based on untestable distal beliefs or worldviews.

Thus we seem to have moved from one unsatisfactory situation to another. The old heuristics and biases literature called too much myside thinking irrational. By too rigidly applying the rule that the prior probability should *never* be implicated in the evaluation of the likelihood ratio, this literature ruled out some very reasonable inferential behavior. And, in targeting what we might informally call the "bad" type of myside bias (letting an untested conviction influence the interpretation of new evidence), it also mistakenly condemned a "good" type of myside bias (using an evidence-based prior probability to evaluate the credibility of new evidence). But in correcting this mistake with the insights from Koehler (1993) and Jern, Chang, and Kemp (2014), we now have a problem of the opposite type.[8] These new analyses, while normatively approving of the good type of myside bias, fail to rule out the bad type.

So it might seem that we are at an impasse. Looking at philosophical discussions of the epistemic rationality of myside bias, we cannot seem to get what we intuitively want: a philosophical analysis that deems the good type of myside bias normatively appropriate, but judges the bad type to be irrational. As is often the case in cognitive science, this kind of impasse might be a signal for us to reexamine our intuitions. Unable to get a theory that will normatively condemn the projection of worldviews onto the evaluation of evidence, perhaps we should explore more thoroughly, and with a broader conception of rationality, whether our intuition that projecting worldviews onto the evaluation of evidence is wrong—or at least in what sense it may be wrong.

Is Projecting a Worldview onto Evidence Necessarily Irrational?

Up until now, we have been treating myside bias exclusively as an issue of epistemic rationality, but a comprehensive discussion of its normative status needs to consider instrumental rationality as well. The distinction between the two is captured in the contrast between what is true (the purview of epistemic rationality) and what to do (the purview of instrumental rationality; see Manktelow 2004).

For our beliefs to be epistemically rational, they must correspond to the way the world is—they must be true. In contrast, for our actions to be instrumentally rational, they must be the best means toward our goals—they must be the best things to do. Somewhat more technically, instrumental rationality is the optimization of the individual's goal fulfillment, which economists and cognitive scientists have refined into the technical notion of expected utility.

The normative analyses we have discussed so far—analyses like those of Koehler (1993) and Jern, Chang, and Kemp (2014)—examine myside bias solely from the standpoint of epistemic rationality, whether a person's beliefs have the right probabilities attached for successful information processing. But these analyses totally ignore factors on the instrumental side of the ledger, a significant omission because, as philosopher Richard Foley (1991, 371) points out, "There is nothing in principle wrong with evaluating the rationality of your beliefs in terms of how well they promote your non-intellectual goals." Russell Golman, David Hagmann, and George Loewenstein (2017) show how it may also be instrumentally rational to *avoid* information that might disrupt beliefs.

Epistemic rationality and instrumental rationality can come into conflict, particularly in an organism as complex as a human. There may be costs in goal achievement paid when we too avidly pursue the truth. Likewise, there may be instrumental benefits in adopting beliefs that are inaccurate. For example, Nick Chater and George Loewenstein (2016) discuss why belief change might exhibit considerable inertia because it incurs many costs. The search for a better model to accommodate the new information might be difficult and cognitively taxing. Chater and Loewenstein (2016) point out that the easiest way to find a better explanation for information requiring change in a belief network is to make the fewest possible local adjustments to the current explanation. They point out that many computer models in the cognitive sciences accommodate new information by conducting highly local searches for better cognitive models. Chater and Loewenstein (2016) also note that the accommodation of new information often necessitates the restructuring of other information in the network.

In short, an efficient cognitive agent should make the fewest possible changes in extant models, and those changes should be as local as possible. That very efficiency will entail a myside bias: there will be a disinclination to process and accommodate to information that conflicts with resident beliefs. The costs of belief change may also explain the many documented instances where true beliefs are explicitly *avoided* (Golman, Hagmann, and Loewenstein 2017).

Thus achieving instrumental rationality might sometimes require that epistemic rationality be sacrificed. A complement to an analysis of the costs of belief change is an analysis of the possible instrumental *gains* from adopting beliefs that do not exactly track the truth, for example, in the motivational domain (Golman, Hagmann, and Loewenstein 2017; McKay and Dennett 2009; Sharot 2011; Sharot and Garrett 2016). Likewise, there could be gains in the domain of personal relationships. For example, Richard Foley (1991) describes the case of a person, a man, say, believing that his lover is faithful despite substantial evidence to the contrary. Because believing that the lover is faithful satisfies a number of his desires (that the relationship continue; that domestic living arrangements not be disrupted), it would not be surprising that, were you in such a situation, you may "find yourself insisting on higher standards of evidence, and as a result it may take unusually good evidence to convince you of infidelity" (Foley 1991, 375). Although, without knowing that there were goals or desires involved, an outside observer might view the criterion for belief as irrationally high, consideration of epistemic *and* instrumental goals would make the setting of a high epistemic criterion here seem rational.

Generally, our goals will be best served by having a network of beliefs containing many truths and few falsehoods. Truthful beliefs will facilitate the attainment of our goals in most cases—but not always, as in the Foley (1991) example, where epistemic and practical reasons for belief have come into conflict. In such cases, it is at least not irrational to let instrumental goals take precedence over epistemic ones.

The social domain is one that often makes epistemic accuracy subordinate to instrumental rationality. Group cohesion often necessitates that group members hold beliefs that exhibit considerable inertia. Being a good group member almost by definition requires that the members display considerable myside bias when encountering ideas that contradict group beliefs. It is almost always the case, however, that the costs of the inaccuracies introduced into a particular member's belief network by that myside bias are outweighed by the considerable benefits provided by group membership (Boyer 2018; Clark et al. 2019; Clark and Winegard 2020; Dunbar 2016; Greene 2013; Haidt 2012; Kim, Park, and Young 2020; Sloman and Fernbach 2017; Van Bavel and Pereira 2018).

Studies in political science would seem to reinforce the importance of group membership in fostering mysided thinking. Lilliana Mason (2018a) found that the degree of affective polarization between groups of political partisans was driven much more by group identity than by issue-based ideology. Statistically, partisan identification was a much stronger predictor than actual differences on specific issues (see Cohen 2003 and Iyengar, Sood, and Lelkes 2012 for converging findings). Mason (2018a, 885) concluded: "The power behind the labels 'liberal' and 'conservative' to predict strong preferences for the ideological in-group is based largely in the social identification with those groups, not in the organization of attitudes associated with the labels." And to highlight this point, Mason (2018a) titled her article "Ideologues without Issues."

Many different theorists have posited dueling motivations in the psychology of belief: a drive for epistemic accuracy and a drive to embrace beliefs that serve social or group ends (Chen, Duckworth, and Chaiken 1999; Flynn, Nyhan, and Reifler 2017; Golman, Hagmann, and Loewenstein 2017; Haidt 2001, 2012; Kunda 1990; Loewenstein and Molnar 2018; Petty and Wegener 1998; Taber and Lodge 2006; Tetlock 2002; West and Kenny 2011). Some instances of myside bias may result from a person sacrificing epistemic accuracy to serve instrumental social goals. It is thus wrong to automatically consider any nonnormative response on an epistemic task to be irrational because the person might be pursuing rationality at the instrumental level. The subjects in our German car experiment described in chapter 1 (Stanovich and West 2008b) might have been displaying myside bias, but, in that particular context, it is wrong to consider such a bias irrational. There is nothing inherently irrational about people preferring regulatory and economic decisions that benefit their own country. As Cory Clark and colleagues (2019, 590) note: "A bias toward viewing one's own tribe in a favorable light is not necessarily irrational." Thus group identities are a key source of myside bias (Clark and Winegard 2020; Clark et al. 2019; Haidt 2012; Tetlock 2002).

Dan Kahan (2013, 2015; see also Kahan et al. 2017) has a research program strongly focused on this group identity source of myside bias—what he terms "identity protective cognition." According to Kahan (2013, 2015), it arises when we have a defining commitment to an affinity group that holds certain beliefs as central to its social identity. The ebb and flow of the information that we are exposed to may contain evidence that undermines one of these central beliefs. If we accurately update our beliefs on the basis of this evidence, we may subject ourselves to sanctions from a group that defines our identity. Hence we will quite naturally have a myside bias toward the group's central beliefs—adopting a high threshold for accommodating disconfirming information and a low threshold for assimilating confirming information (Johnston, Lavine, and Federico 2017).

It is difficult to know whether myside bias is irrational without properly assessing the epistemic costs and the group identity gains. As a result, myside bias that is driven by identity protective cognition is not necessarily irrational. As Kahan (2012, 255) notes: "If anything, social science suggests that citizens are culturally polarized because they are, in fact, too rational—at filtering out information that would drive a wedge between themselves and their peers." Kahan's (2013, 2015) identity protective cognition belongs to a class of symbolic behavior that has been discussed using a variety of conceptual labels (symbolic utility, ethical preferences, protected values, and so on), behaviors I have previously grouped under the generic term expressive rationality (see Stanovich 2004).

Expressive Rationality and Myside Bias

Many of our communications are not aimed at conveying information about what is true (Tetlock 2002). Instead, as signals to others and sometimes signals to ourselves, they are *functional* communications because, when sent to others, they bind us to a group that we value, and, when sent to ourselves, they serve motivational functions. These signals are sometimes termed exemplars of expressive rationality to reflect that they are not aimed at maximizing first-order desires or immediate consumption utility (see Abelson 1996; Akerloff and Kranton 2010; Anderson 1993; Golman, Hagmann, and Loewenstein 2017; Hargreaves Heap 1992; Stanovich 2004, 2013).

Robert Nozick's (1993) alternative term—symbolic utility—serves to differentiate expressive sources of utility from other more tangible sources. Nozick (1993, 27) defines symbolic utility as an action that "symbolizes a certain situation, and the utility of this symbolized situation is imputed back, through the symbolic connection, to the action itself." Nozick notes that we are apt to view a concern for symbolic utility as irrational in cases where the lack of a causal link between the symbolic action and the actual outcome has become manifestly obvious, yet the symbolic action continues to be performed. Nozick (1993) points to several antidrug measures that may fall in this category. In some cases, evidence has accumulated to indicate that an antidrug program does not reduce actual illegal drug use, but the program is continued because it has become the symbol of our concern for stopping such illegal use. In the present day, many actions signaling a concern for global warming have this logic (their immediate efficacy is less important than the meaning of the signal being sent by the signaler). The buying of books that we know we will never read is perhaps another example. Behavioral economics also provides examples of people treating beliefs as investments and thus gaining utility from signaling that their identities encompass such "epistemic assets" (Bénabou and Tirole 2011; Golman, Hagmann, and Loewenstein 2017; Sharot and Sunstein 2020).

Many acts of expressive rationality are done out of concern for our "being a certain type of person" or for signaling to social groups that we are. The act of voting serves a symbolic function for many of us. We are aware that the direct utility we derive from the influence of our vote on the political system (a weight of less than one one-millionth or less than one one-hundred-thousandth depending on the election) is less than the effort that it takes to vote (Baron 1998; Brennan and Hamlin 1998). All the same, many of us would still never miss an election. Even after recognizing that our feeling of efficacy is misplaced, we still feel a sense of warmth when voting.

But in the example just described, performing the act of voting might enable people to maintain an *image* of themselves. In this manner, expressive actions might serve a motivational function. A reinforced image of themselves as "that kind of person" might make it easier, at a later date, for such people to perform the acts that *actually are* causally efficacious in making them "that type of person."

The concept of ethical preferences in the economics literature (see Anderson 1993; Hirschman 1986; Hollis 1992) illustrates another example of expressive rationality. The boycott of nonunion grapes in the 1970s, the boycott of South African products in the 1980s, and the interest in fairtrade products that emerged in the 1990s are examples of ethical preferences. Likewise, analyses of voting as an expressive act de-emphasize the instrumental utility of the voting and emphasize the signaling and psychological benefits (Brennan and Lomasky 1993; Johnston, Lavine, and Federico 2017; Lomasky 2008).

Expressive responding partly explains a well-known myside finding in political science: that people learn and retain facts that are favorable to their party better than facts that are not (Bartels 2002; Gerber and Huber 2010; Jerit and Barabas 2012). On the other hand, John Bullock and colleagues. (2015) have found that rather modest incentives for correct responding can vastly reduce, if not entirely eliminate, this myside gap. The research of Bullock and colleagues (2015) and other related studies (Bullock and Lenz 2019; McGrath 2017) suggest that, when it is cost free to provoke partisan opponents by denying facts supportive of their opponents' position, some people will do so. But such denials represent expressive "support for the home team," not an actual epistemic error of misapprehension.

Expressive acts often spring from protected, or sacred, values that were discussed in chapter 1—those which resist trade-offs with other values, particularly economic ones (Baron and Spranca 1997; Tetlock 2003). Douglas Medin and Max Bazerman (1999; see also Medin et al. 1999) discuss a number of experiments in which subjects are shown to be reluctant to trade or compare items when protected values are at stake. For example, people do not expect to be offered market transactions for their pet dog or for their wedding rings.

Thus the belief in a protected value will not be easily altered by any kind of evidence. New information concerning a sacred value will be subject to massive myside bias—confirming evidence assimilated readily into existing belief networks and disconfirming evidence subject to severe scrutiny. And none of this should be considered irrational, at least not without a cost-benefit analysis that acknowledges the possible benefits of expressive acts.

Rational Myside Bias and the Tragedy of the Communications Commons

We seem to have reached an unexpected juncture in our discussion of the normative appropriateness of myside bias. Only when a reasoner has a pre-specified numerical likelihood ratio is it nonnormative for the reasoner to use the prior probability in the evaluation of new evidence. When the reasoner must instead make a credibility judgment about the evidence, it is *not* always nonnormative to use the distance between the evidence and the prior probability as part of this credibility assessment.

Perhaps this is less surprising in the case of an evidence-based prior probability. We might have thought, before this discussion, that a prior probability derived not from evidence, but from a distal belief or worldview should surely not be projected onto new evidence. But we have seen no argument that rules this out entirely, especially when we go beyond epistemic rationality to bring in issues of instrumental and expressive rationality as well. It seems that our intuition that myside bias is a cognitive error—similar to the many other reasoning faults in the rest of the heuristics and biases literature—is unwarranted.

Recall that it is common in that literature to say that a particular bias or heuristic is "useful overall"—and indeed resides in our brains for clear evolutionary reasons—but that occasional mismatches between the evolutionary environment in which the heuristic developed and the modern environment sometimes make us inclined to error (Kahneman 2011; Li, van Vugt, and Colarelli 2018; Stanovich 2004). This argument may be less true for myside bias, particularly when we are talking about the individual as opposed to societal negative effects of the bias. Perhaps myside bias is an odd bias (a theme I will develop in greater depth in chapter 3) in that most of its negative effects fall on others rather than on ourselves. Society seems to suffer the negative consequences of myside bias, even though it is not at all clear that particular people do, an idea explored by law professor Dan Kahan (2013).

The title of this section is derived from Kahan and colleagues' phrase "tragedy of the science communications commons" (Kahan 2013; Kahan,

Peters, et al. 2012; Kahan et al. 2017) for the conundrum that results from a society full of people gaining utility from rationally processing evidence with a myside bias, but ultimately losing more than they gain because society overall would be better off if public policy were objective and based on what was actually true. When everyone processes with a myside bias, the result is a society that cannot converge on the truth.

Kahan and colleagues' phrase derives from Garrett Hardin's (1968) famous "tragedy of the commons" argument, which itself derives from the much-studied prisoner's dilemma paradigm (Colman 1995, 2003; Komorita and Parks 1994). In this game-theory classic, two criminals commit a crime together and are segregated in separate cells. The prosecutor has proof of a joint minor crime but does not have enough evidence to prove a joint major crime. Each prisoner is asked separately to confess to the major crime. If either confesses and the other does not, the confessor goes free and the other gets the full penalty of twenty years for the major crime. If both confess, both are convicted and get ten-year sentences. If neither confesses, they are both convicted of the minor crime and are both sentenced to two years.

Each prisoner will notice that no matter what the other does, they are both better off confessing. Thus each does the narrowly rational thing and confesses (the defection response), and they are both convicted of the major crime and given ten-year sentences—a much worse outcome than if neither of them had confessed (the cooperative response) and both received two-year sentences. The generic situation is one in which, from an individual perspective the defection response dominates the cooperative response, but if both players make the individually rational response, the payoff for both is low. The multiple-player version of the prisoner's dilemma is known as a "commons dilemma" (Hardin 1968) and has a similar logic. Collective action problems like pollution control, population control, and combating global warming exemplify this logic.

Kahan and colleagues (Kahan 2013; Kahan et al. 2017) saw that the same logic applied in the domain of the communication of relevant public policy information and called it "the tragedy of the science communications commons." The analyses we have reviewed in this chapter confirm the individual rationality of using prior beliefs to aid in the evaluation of new evidence (Koehler 1993). They support the natural tendency to use one's own perspective in interpreting the meaning of new evidence (Jern, Chang, and Kemp 2014). They confirm the rationality of our epistemic activities being in part determined by our larger instrumental goals. And finally, they confirm the rationality of taking meaningful group affinities into account when we update and express beliefs. Yet all of this normatively appropriate individual epistemic behavior has resulted in a fractious and politically divided society that can't seem to agree on the truth (Clark and Winegard 2020; Kahan 2012; Kronman 2019; Lukianoff and Haidt 2018; Pinker 2002)—indeed, one that can't agree on the most basic facts about a host of public policy issues.[9] As Charles Taber, Duncan Cann, and Simona Kucsova (2009, 138) have lamented: "If societies polarize in response to a common stream of information, then it is hard to imagine the marketplace of ideas operating as an efficient arbiter of policy differences."

The Bias That Divides Us offers no simple solution to the tragedy of the communication commons. It would have been simpler if the analysis of normative considerations had pointed to myside bias as a clearly irrational processing tendency—one that was suboptimal at the level of the individual. We then would have the rationale for mounting educational programs to rid people of the bias. It would also have been easier even if, like most biases, myside bias as a processing tendency had been appropriate in some situations and not in others. We then could teach people which situations to treat as inappropriate for myside processing.

Instead, myside bias seems to hurt us, but more at the societal than the individual level. I will reserve my systemic recommendations for remedying the tragedy of the communications commons for later chapters. Before outlining those recommendations, however, I need to describe how myside bias is an "outlier bias"—quite different from other biases in the heuristics and biases literature.

3 Myside Thinking: The Outlier Bias

When Richard West and I began examining individual differences in cognitive biases in the late 1990s, one of the first consistent results from our earliest studies in these years was that the biases tended to correlate with one another (Stanovich and West 1997, 1998a, 1998b; Sá, West, and Stanovich 1999). The correlations were usually quite modest but, then again, they derived from tasks measured with just a few items and hence were of fairly low reliability. Another consistent result from our earliest studies was that almost every cognitive bias was correlated with intelligence as measured with a variety of cognitive ability indicators. Individual differences in most cognitive biases were also predicted by several well-studied thinking dispositions, most notably, by an actively open-minded thinking (AOT) scale, inspired by the work of Jonathan Baron (1985, 1988) and first developed in our lab (Stanovich and West 1997, 2007; Stanovich and Toplak 2019).

Our finding that the tendency to override various cognitive biases was correlated with individual differences in cognitive ability and thinking dispositions has stood the test of time. We have repeatedly observed this tendency in our lab for over two decades now (see Stanovich, West, and Toplak 2016 for a review of the evidence), and our finding has been replicated in numerous experiments conducted by other researchers (Aczel et al. 2015; Bruine de Bruin, Parker, and Fischhoff 2007; Finucane and Gullion 2010; Klaczynski 2014; Parker and Fischhoff 2005; Parker et al. 2018; Viator et al. 2020; Weaver and Stewart 2012; Weller et al. 2018). The finding has also held for some of the most-studied biases in the heuristics and biases tradition (Kahneman 2011; Tversky and Kahneman 1974): anchoring biases, framing biases, hindsight bias, overconfidence bias, outcome bias, conjunction fallacies, representativeness errors, the gambler's fallacy, probability matching, base rate neglect, sample size neglect, ratio bias, covariation detection errors, pseudo-diagnosticity effects, among others.

To illustrate the nature of these relationships, I will give some examples from the largest study we conducted to examine the structure of our Comprehensive Assessment of Rational Thinking (CART; see Stanovich, West, and Toplak 2016, chapter 13). The CART contains twenty subtests that measure the ability to avoid many of the biases that have been studied by cognitive psychologists. For example, the ability to avoid framing effects was correlated .28 with cognitive ability, and the ability to avoid overconfidence bias was correlated .38 with cognitive ability. The probabilistic reasoning subtest of the CART, which assesses the ability to avoid many biases and processing errors (e.g., the gambler's fallacy; conjunction errors; base rate neglect; sample size neglect), was found to be correlated .51 with cognitive ability. In fact, all of the subtests of the CART that examine cognitive biases show significant correlations between the ability to avoid these biases and cognitive ability.

There is no doubt that, based on previous work, the clear expectation is that any new cognitive bias studied will show the same correlations with individual difference variables. This body of previous work sets the context for the startling finding about the individual difference predictors of myside bias: *There aren't many!*

The Strange Case of the Missing Individual Difference Predictors

Some years ago, David Perkins, Michael Farady, and Barbara Bushey (1991) reported that, even though intelligence was moderately correlated with the *total* number of ideas produced in an argument generation task, it was virtually *un*correlated with the number of arguments generated that ran *counter* to the subjects' own positions. The Perkins, Farady, and Bushey (1991) finding lay all but unnoticed for more than a decade until a flurry of more recent studies showed that it was replicable and generalizable.

In a paradigm similar to that of Perkins, Farady, and Bushey (1991), Maggie Toplak and I (Toplak and Stanovich 2003) had subjects generate arguments relevant to controversial issues (e.g., "Should people be allowed to sell their organs?"). We found that, although subjects displayed a substantial myside bias in the task (they tended to give more arguments in favor of their position than against), the degree of myside bias was not correlated with cognitive ability. Robyn Macpherson and I (Macpherson and

Stanovich 2007) replicated the main finding that cognitive ability was not correlated with myside bias in an argument generation task, and we found that it was also not correlated with myside bias in an experiment evaluation task.

In the "Ford Explorer" study described in chapter 1, Richard West and I found absolutely no correlation between the magnitude of the myside bias displayed by subjects and their level of intelligence (Stanovich & West, 2008b). In Chapter 1, I also mentioned studies by my own research group (Stanovich & West, 2008a) using an argument evaluation paradigm in which a strong myside bias was observed. That is, subjects rated the arguments consistent with their own positions as better than the arguments not consistent with their own positions. However,, the myside bias was not any stronger in the subjects in the sample of lower cognitive ability than it was in those of higher cognitive ability.

In a series of experiments, Paul Klaczynski and colleagues (Klacynski 1997; Klaczynski and Lavallee 2005; Klaczynski and Robinson 2000) presented subjects with flawed hypothetical experiments and arguments that led to either opinion-consistent or opinion-inconsistent conclusions. Evaluating the quality of the subjects' reasoning when they critiqued the flaws in the experiments, Klaczynski and colleagues found that verbal ability was correlated with the overall quality of the subjects' reasoning in both the opinion-consistent and opinion-inconsistent conditions, but was *not* correlated with the magnitude of the myside bias effect—the tendency to critique opinion-inconsistent experimental results more harshly than opinion-consistent ones.

This finding of independence between intelligence and myside reasoning also occurs in more naturalistic reasoning paradigms, where the subjects are not cued by the nature of the task or the instructions that there is an evaluative component to the experiment. For example, Richard West and I studied a variety of biased beliefs based on societal and demographic status (Stanovich and West 2007, 2008a). Subjects simply had to agree or disagree with facts that put their status in a positive or negative light. Myside biases were prominently displayed by the subjects in our two studies: subjects who smoked were less likely than those who did not to acknowledge the negative health effects of secondhand smoke; subjects who were religious were more likely than those who were not to think that religious people were more honest than people who were not religious; subjects who voted for

George Bush were more likely than those who voted for John Kerry to think that the invasion of Iraq made us safer from terrorists; and so on. When, however, we examined not just whether these biases were present but also whether intelligence served to attenuate them, the results were clear cut. Of the fifteen different myside biases examined (Stanovich and West 2008a), not one was attenuated by high intelligence.

The failure of intelligence to attenuate myside bias extends to variables that are closely related to intelligence such as numeracy, scientific literacy, and general knowledge. For example, Caitlin Drummond and Baruch Fischhoff (2019) tested subjects who were either supporters or critics of the Affordable Care Act (ACA). Their individual difference variable was not intelligence but was a test of scientific reasoning skills. Subjects read and evaluated a description of one scientific study finding positive effects of the ACA and another study finding negative effects. Not surprisingly, the researchers observed a myside bias effect. But just as Klaczynski and colleagues and West and I had, Drummond and Fischhoff (2019) found that the level of scientific reasoning skills did not correlate with the magnitude of myside bias displayed. Indeed, in some of their experiments, there was a slight tendency for subjects with *higher* levels of scientific reasoning skills to show even greater myside bias than subjects with lower levels did. This counterintuitive finding occasionally appears in the myside literature,[1] most notably in the work of Dan Kahan and colleagues (Kahan 2013; Kahan, Peters, et al. 2012; Kahan et al. 2017).

Dan Kahan, Ellen Peters, and colleagues (2012) found that, not surprisingly, left-leaning subjects thought that climate change posed more risks to health and safety than right-leaning subjects did.[2] What was surprising was that this difference between groups was larger among subjects who were rated high in measured numeracy than among those who were rated low. Along the lines of the simplified Bayesian thinking discussed in chapter 2, most people expect that higher levels of general intelligence, numeracy, scientific literacy, and general knowledge will bring subjects together in their views of the facts, but this was not the case in the Kahan, Peters, and colleagues 2012 study. Indeed, higher numeracy was associated with greater belief polarization between the groups.

Using a paradigm that more directly measured myside bias, Kahan (2013) again found belief polarization between groups based on a different individual difference indicator—the Cognitive Reflection Test (CRT;

Frederick 2005). The psychometrically complex CRT displays associations with thinking dispositions and numeracy, as well as cognitive capacity (see Liberali et al. 2012; Sinayev and Peters 2015; Toplak, West, and Stanovich 2011, 2014a)—but this just makes Kahan's (2013) finding even more fascinating. He measured myside bias by assessing how much subjects tended to endorse the validity of an indicator when it yielded an outcome consistent versus inconsistent with their beliefs. The myside bias displayed was again statistically greater among subjects who scored higher on the CRT.

Kahan and colleagues (2017) observed the same thing using the 2×2 covariation detection paradigm discussed in chapter 1, which involves direct processing of numerical information. The polarizing issue in their experiment was gun control, with half of the sample subjects being in favor of and half opposed to gun control, and the individual difference variable was numeracy. Subjects on both sides of the issue evaluated the gun control information more inaccurately than they did information on a neutral second issue (treatment for a rash), but higher numeracy was associated with *greater* myside bias for each of the groups on either side of the gun control issue.

The study by Van Boven and colleagues (2019) discussed in chapter 1 provides one further example of this trend. They asked their subjects to choose which of two conditional probabilities (the hit rate or the inverse conditional probability) was the more relevant in evaluating information on two politically charged issues: the Trump administration's ban on travel and immigration from seven countries (five of which had Muslim majorities) and a proposed ban on assault weapons. Despite the similar logic of the two issues, the subjects picked totally different conditional probabilities for the two issues because subjects who were pro-ban on one issue were anti-ban on the other. The myside bias displayed was actually greater for the subjects who were more highly numerate, but who apparently used their superior numerical reasoning skills not to reason in an unbiased manner across the different conditions, but to figure out which probability was more favorable to their side of the issue.

Converging with the results of studies by Kahan (2013) and Van Boven and colleagues (2017) are political science studies showing that various indices of cognitive sophistication such as educational level, knowledge level, and political awareness not only do not attenuate partisan myside bias but often increase it. For example, Mark Joslyn and Donald Haider-Markel (2014) found that highly educated partisan survey respondents were in greater disagreement about policy-relevant facts than less-educated partisan respondents were. To take two of their examples, Democratic respondents were more accurately informed about the Earth's getting warmer because of human activities, but Republican respondents (at the time the study was run) were more accurately informed about the success of President George Bush's 2006–2007 troop surge into Iraq in reducing US military casualties there. Although many might have thought that these differences would be smaller among the more educated respondents, partisan disagreement on both issues was instead greatest among the highly educated.

The trend observed by Joslyn and Haider-Markel (2014) has been found in other political science work on partisan attitudes. Philip Jones (2019) found that political perceptions about policy-relevant conditions such as the state of the economy were more polarized among the more informed and politically aware partisan survey respondents. Multiple measures of cognitive sophistication show that cognitive elites display more polarization on a variety of political issues (Drummond and Fischhoff 2017; Ehret, Sparks, and Sherman 2017; Hamilton 2011; Henry and Napier 2017; Kahan and Stanovich 2016; Kraft, Lodge, and Taber 2015; Lupia et al. 2007; Sarathchandra et al. 2018; Yudkin, Hawkins, and Dixon 2019).

The survey responses in these political science studies are not direct measures of myside bias, and they involve a host of other complexities. Political polarization is far from a pure measure of the myside processing tendency that we reviewed in chapter 1. But these responses are mentioned here because of the interesting convergence between political science survey research findings and myside bias laboratory findings. The convergence I wish to draw attention to in this chapter concerns the *weak* conclusion that intelligence and other related measures of cognitive sophistication do not inoculate the reasoner against myside bias. The *strong* conclusion, drawn by Kahan and many political science researchers—that cognitive elites may actually show a larger myside bias—is not necessary for my argument going forward. Thus, I prefer to view that research as simply bolstering confidence in the weaker conclusion that we cannot look to education or intelligence as a way out of the tragedy of the communication commons discussed in chapter 2.

In summary, well-controlled laboratory studies of myside bias converge with political science survey research and polling data in showing that intelligence and education do not inoculate us against myside bias or polarizing tendencies. As Peter Ditto and colleagues (2019b, 312) note, "What if bias is not the sole province of the simpleminded? . . . A growing body of research suggests that greater cognitive sophistication and expertise often predict greater levels of political bias, not less. . . . Cognitive sophistication may allow people to more skillfully argue for their preferred conclusions, thus improving their ability to convince others—and themselves—that their beliefs are correct."

Other Individual Difference Anomalies

From an individual difference point of view, myside bias displays other curious tendencies. Most of the other biases in the heuristics and biases literature display correlations not only with intelligence, but also with thinking dispositions that should be related to rational thinking such as actively open-minded thinking (AOT) and need for cognition (Bruine de Bruin, Parker, and Fischhoff 2007; Finucane and Gullion 2010; Kokis et al. 2002; Macpherson and Stanovich 2007; Parker and Fischhoff 2005; Stanovich and West 1997, 1998a; Toplak et al. 2007; Toplak and Stanovich 2002; Toplak, West, and Stanovich 2011, 2014a, 2014b; Viator et al. 2020; Weller et al. 2018).

We can again turn to some examples from the Comprehensive Assessment of Rational Thinking (CART; see Stanovich, West, and Toplak 2016, chapter 13), which contains twenty subtests that measure the ability to avoid many important cognitive biases and processing errors. For example, the ability to avoid framing effects was correlated .20 with actively open-minded thinking, and the ability to avoid overconfidence bias was correlated .29 with actively open-minded thinking. The probabilistic reasoning subtest of the CART shows a correlation with actively open-minded thinking of .43. Similarly, all of the subtests of the CART that examine cognitive biases show significant correlations with thinking dispositions.

Despite these consistent findings involving almost every other cognitive bias, myside bias has failed to correlate with relevant thinking dispositions, just as it has failed to correlate with intelligence (Kahan 2013; Kahan and Corbin 2016; Kahan et al. 2017; Stanovich and West 2007; Stenhouse et al. 2018).[3] For example, in our study using Perkins's (1985) argument generation paradigm (Toplak and Stanovich 2003), we found substantial myside biases on several issues (subjects tended to give more arguments in favor of their position than against), but the degree of myside bias was not correlated with several thinking dispositions, including actively open-minded thinking, dogmatism, and need for cognition. In Robyn Macpherson's and my 2007 study (Macpherson and Stanovich 2007), we examined myside bias in both argument generation and evidence evaluation, and we measured three different thinking dispositions: actively open-minded thinking, need for cognition, and avoidance of superstitious thinking. None of the six resulting correlations indicated that a higher level of sophisticated thinking was significantly associated with avoiding myside bias.

This lack of association with thinking dispositions was also found in one of our studies of naturalistic myside bias (Stanovich and West 2007) that employed four status variables (alcohol use, smoking, religious belief, sex). Myside biases were present on all the variables: smokers were less likely to acknowledge the negative health effects of secondhand smoke; the more alcohol a subject consumed, the less likely the subject was to acknowledge the health risks of alcohol consumption; subjects who were more religious were more likely than those who were less religious to think that being religious led to honesty; and women were more likely than men to think that females were paid unfairly (effect sizes: .35 to .67). We looked at two different individual difference variables (actively open-minded thinking and need for cognition) across all four of the status variables and analyzed the status variable by thinking disposition interaction in two different ways (dichotomously and with regression analyses). Across the sixteen different analyses (four status variables by two thinking dispositions by two types of analyses), in only three was there a significant interaction. Although in the expected direction, the interactions were quite small (about 1 percent variance explained) and were significant primarily because of the large sample size (more than 1,000 subjects).

In the course of our research, we occasionally do get correlations between actively open-minded thinking and avoidance of myside bias, but they are usually small and are significant only in studies with large sample sizes. For example, in our argument evaluation paradigm (Stanovich and West 2008a), subjects rated the arguments consistent with their own position on two issues (abortion and lowering the drinking age) higher than those that were inconsistent with their own position. Myside bias was not correlated with intelligence or need for cognition, but it did exhibit small negative correlations with actively open-minded thinking (−.17 and −.13, respectively, across the two issues) that were significant because of the large sample size (more than 400 subjects).

Finally, even personality dispositions that would seem to be most directly related to the avoidance of myside bias fail to correlate with it. For example, Elizabeth Simas, Scott Clifford, and Justin Kirkland (2019) suggested that lack of empathy would seem to be a key mechanism in the development of political polarization, partisan bias, and ideological conflict but, in two of their experiments, they found that the differences in empathic concern did not predict the degree of partisan bias in evaluating a contentious public event, and that high empathic concern did not attenuate the degree of affective polarization among partisans. Simas, Clifford, and Kirkland (2019) explain their findings by positing that empathy itself is biased toward one's own in-group and thus does not inoculate against myside bias.

Belief Bias—but Not Myside Bias—Correlates with Cognitive Ability

If you are familiar with our lab's previous work, you might be surprised at this point at the paucity of correlations between individual difference variables and myside bias, and you might think to yourself, "surely I remember some studies going back to the beginning of the Stanovich and West work in the 1990s in which intelligence and thinking dispositions correlated with belief bias." If you thought this, you would be right. But it is worth repeating here that myside bias and belief bias are not the same (see discussion in chapter 1). Indeed, looking at the correlations exhibited by the two biases will give a clearer sense of just how different they are.

Belief bias occurs when real-world knowledge interferes with subjects' reasoning. Most often assessed with syllogistic reasoning tasks in which the believability of the conclusion conflicts with the logical validity of the syllogism, belief bias can also be assessed using other tasks (Thompson and Evans 2012). Most important, belief bias tasks employ testable beliefs. In contrast, people display myside bias when they evaluate evidence or generate evidence in a manner biased toward their own opinions or convictions. When the belief in question goes from being a testable belief to becoming a distal belief—when it becomes a conviction—then we have moved from belief bias to myside bias.[4]

It is important to note that belief bias has been just as consistent as most other cognitive biases in exhibiting substantial and significant correlations with the same individual difference variables that *fail* to predict the degree of myside bias. In our very earliest studies, we observed correlations with intelligence and the avoidance of belief bias in the range of .35 to .50 (Sá, West, and Stanovich 1999; Stanovich and West 1998a). Across the years, the intelligence measures varied from study to study, but we continued to observe correlations in the range of .35 to .50 (Macpherson and Stanovich 2007; Stanovich and West 2008a). In developmental studies with children, we have obtained correlations in the range of .30 to .45 (Kokis et al. 2002; Toplak, West, and Stanovich 2014b). In our book discussing the CART (Stanovich, West, and Toplak 2016, table 7.3), we presented twenty-one correlations that we have obtained between belief bias and various intelligence measures in nearly twenty years of work on this issue. The median correlation was .42, and nineteen of those correlations were between .30 and .50. Other research labs have also found belief bias to be correlated with cognitive ability differences (De Neys 2006, 2012; Ding et al. 2020; Gilinsky and Judd 1994; Handley et al. 2004; Newstead et al. 2004).

The story is much the same with respect to the correlations between thinking dispositions and the magnitude of the belief bias effect, except that those correlations are lower (but almost always statistically significant). In our very earliest studies, we observed correlations between thinking dispositions and the avoidance of belief bias in the range of .25 to .35 (Sá, West, and Stanovich 1999; Stanovich and West 1998a). Across the years, the thinking disposition measures varied from study to study, but we continued to observe correlations with the avoidance of belief bias in the range of .20 to .30 (Macpherson and Stanovich 2007; Stanovich and West 2008a). In developmental studies with children, we have observed correlations in the same range of .20 to .30 (Kokis et al. 2002; Toplak, West, and Stanovich 2014b). In our 2016 book (Stanovich, West, and Toplak 2016, table 7.4), we presented twenty-six correlations between belief bias and various thinking dispositions. The median correlation was .24, and nineteen of those correlations were between .15 and .35.

In short, the degree of belief bias displayed by subjects, like that displayed by virtually all the other biases in the heuristics and biases literature (see previous citations) is predictable from the subjects' cognitive ability and rational thinking dispositions. In contrast, myside bias—occurring when the interfering belief is a conviction (distal belief) rather than a testable belief—is not predictable from the same psychological variables as all the other biases in the literature are. In terms of individual differences, myside bias is a curiously free-floating bias—seemingly unconnected to personal characteristics.

Convergence with the Normative Arguments in Chapter 2

Although the failure of a potent individual difference variable like intelligence to correlate with myside bias avoidance might at first seem puzzling, it actually converges with the analysis in chapter 2 that found it difficult to show that displaying myside bias is nonnormative. Two decades ago, Richard West and I (Stanovich and West 2000) suggested that individual difference findings could be used to help adjudicate the normative disputes in the heuristics and biases literature—particularly in cases where researchers were championing alternative responses as normative.

We (Stanovich and West 2000) suggested that the directionality of individual difference correlations could have at least some probative value in indicating which response was normative and that Charles Spearman's (1904, 1927) positive manifold could serve as a useful device toward that end. For a number of classic tasks in the literature, we demonstrated that the traditional response considered by Tversky and Kahneman (1974; Kahneman and Tversky 1973; see also Kahneman 2011) to be normative was positively correlated with intelligence, but that, in contrast, the response championed by critics of the heuristics and biases tradition was negatively correlated with intelligence. We pointed out that the direction of the correlations with intelligence are embarrassing for critics who argue for an alternative normative response. Surely, we would want to avoid the conclusion that individuals with greater computational ability were systematically computing the *non*normative response. Such an outcome would be an absolute first in a psychometric field that is more than one hundred years old, with thousands of studies. It would mean that Spearman's positive manifold for cognitive tasks—virtually unchallenged for one hundred years—had finally failed.

Our argument was essentially that the response that preserves positive manifold is at least statistically more likely to be a more optimal response.[5] Conversely, given that positive manifold is the norm among cognitive tasks, a negative correlation or a zero correlation between the response traditionally considered normative and standard cognitive ability measures might be taken as a signal that the wrong normative model is being applied or, at least, that there are alternative models that are equally appropriate.

We have in fact observed the latter to be the case with some tasks in the heuristics and biases literature (Stanovich 1999; Stanovich and West 1998a). For example, some noncausal base rate problems failed to correlate with cognitive ability, as did the false consensus effect in social psychology (Ross, Greene, and House 1977). Indeed, there were independent reasons for thinking that the wrong normative model had been applied to the false consensus effect (Dawes 1989, 1990; Hoch 1987) and thus the individual difference correlations converged with theoretical analyses. This seems to also have occurred with respect to myside bias. The analyses in chapter 2 concluded that it is wrong to view any degree of myside bias displayed in a task as necessarily nonnormative or irrational. In this chapter, we have seen that individual difference analyses converge with that conclusion in showing no correlation between cognitive ability or thinking dispositions and the degree of myside bias displayed.

The Domain Specificity of Myside Bias

Another way in which myside bias is an outlier bias is that, in most circumstances, it shows very little domain generality and appears to be highly content dependent. Subjects who display high myside bias on one issue do not necessarily display it on another, unrelated issue. This was apparent in the 2003 study conducted by Maggie Toplak and me (Toplak and Stanovich 2003), where subjects showed large myside biases in generating arguments about three issues ("Should students pay the full cost of their university education?"; "Should people be allowed to sell their organs?"; and "Should the cost of gasoline be doubled to discourage people from driving?"). In contrast, however, there were no significant correlations across issues between the degree of myside bias displayed on one issue and that displayed on another. These results are unlike those reported by studies of other biases such as framing effects, where we and other researchers observed internal consistency reliabilities in the range of .60 to .70 across a dozen or so different items (Bruine de Bruin, Parker, and Fischhoff 2007; Stanovich, West, and Toplak 2016). In fact, there is a substantial degree of domain generality in most biases in the literature (Bruine de Bruin, Parker, and Fischhoff 2007; Dentakos et al. 2019; Parker et al. 2018; Stanovich and West 1998a; Stanovich, West, and Toplak 2016; Weaver and Stewart 2012; Weller et al. 2018)—but *not* in the case of myside bias.

Maggie Toplak and I (Toplak and Stanovich 2003) found that individual difference variables (both cognitive ability and thinking dispositions) could not predict the myside bias displayed by subjects on any of the three issues examined in that study. However, another variable, the strength of a subject's opinion on a specific issue consistently predicted the degree of myside bias shown by the subject on that issue. Strength of opinion was coded independently of agreement or disagreement with the issue proposition. So, on each particular issue, subjects who strongly agreed or disagreed with the issue proposition received a score of 3; those who moderately agreed or disagreed, a score of 2; and those who slightly agreed or disagreed, a score of 1. This strength of opinion variable was positively correlated with the myside bias displayed on all three issues examined in our study (Toplak and Stanovich 2003).

Our subsequent studies using an argument evaluation paradigm (Stanovich and West 2008a) had a larger sample size and investigated the strength of opinion variable more thoroughly. As previously mentioned, intelligence did not predict myside bias at all across issues in two experiments. The much-studied thinking disposition need for cognition also failed to correlate with the degree of myside bias. But, in contrast, actively open-minded thinking exhibited a negative correlation with the degree of myside bias displayed across two issues: –.17 on an abortion proposition and –.13 on a lowering the drinking age proposition. Unlike the case in the Toplak and Stanovich (2003) study, myside bias across the two propositions did show a significant .21 correlation. However, across both issues, the strength and direction of the opinion accounted for more variance in myside bias than did all of the individual difference variables combined.

We can see the effects of strength of opinion in somewhat greater detail in table 3.1. The top half of the table shows the mean myside bias on the abortion issue as a function of how subjects responded to the prior opinion question. The table shows a tilted U-shaped function, where myside bias increases with the strength of opinion for both the pro-choice and pro-life groups, although the pro-life group tends to display greater myside bias. The bottom half of the table shows a similar set of means across the responses to the drinking age issue. Here again, although myside bias increased with strength of opinion for both groups, those opposed to lowering the drinking age displayed greater myside bias at each level of opinion strength.

Richard West and I (Stanovich and West 2008a) conducted a regression analysis to examine the effects of opinion content (pro-choice versus pro-life; 0/1) and strength (1,2,3) on the degree of myside bias on the abortion issue and whether cognitive ability could account for any variance after

Table 3.1

Mean Myside Bias on the Abortion Issue as Function of Level of Agreement with Issue Statement[a]

	Mean (SD)
Strongly disagree ($n=86$)	4.86 (4.68)
Moderately disagree ($n=33$)	2.15 (4.44)
Slightly disagree ($n=41$)	0.83 (3.50)
Slightly agree ($n=74$)	0.82 (3.61)
Moderately agree ($n=75$)	1.07 (3.31)
Strongly agree ($n=111$)	2.74 (3.92)

Mean Myside Bias on the Lowering the Drinking Age Issue as Function of Level of Agreement with the Issue Statement[b]

	Mean (SD)
Strongly disagree ($n=61$)	3.16 (4.61)
Moderately disagree ($n=51$)	0.90 (3.31)
Slightly disagree ($n=42$)	0.55 (3.78)
Slightly agree ($n=104$)	−1.15 (3.80)
Moderately agree ($n=92$)	0.50 (3.30)
Strongly agree ($n=70$)	1.61 (4.46)

[a] "I believe that abortion should be legal in this country" in Stanovich and West 2008a, experiment 3.

[b] "Eighteen-year-olds should have the legal right to drink alcoholic beverages" in Stanovich and West 2008a, experiment 3.

valence and strength had been partialed out. In a simultaneous regression analysis, the beta weights of the valence variable and the strength variable were both significant ($p < .001$ in both cases), but the beta weight for cognitive ability was not significant. The analysis for the drinking age proposition resulted in an identical pattern: the valence variable and the strength variable were both significant ($p < .001$ in both cases), but the beta weight for cognitive ability was not significant. On their own, the strength and direction of the prior opinion variable predicted the degree of myside bias on both the abortion and the drinking age issues to a moderate degree (multiple R of .336 and .328, respectively; $p < .001$ in both cases).[6]

A more comprehensive analysis revealed the relative potency of the content of opinion variable versus all of the individual difference variables in the study. For the abortion issue, once direction and strength of opinion variables were entered as predictors of myside bias, the three individual difference factors (cognitive ability, actively open-minded thinking, and need for cognition) accounted for 2.7 percent additional variance. In contrast, after cognitive ability and the two thinking dispositions were entered into the equation, direction and strength of opinion variables accounted for almost four times more additional variance (10.6 percent unique variance). A similar pattern held for the drinking age issue (1.8 percent unique variance for the individual difference variables and 10.5 percent unique variance for the opinion content variables).

Other studies have converged with the suggestion in our 2008 study (Stanovich and West 2008a) that belief content rather than personal psychological characteristics predicts the degree of myside bias. Philip Tetlock (1986) studied the complexity of subjects' reasoning about important issues such as environmental protection, crime control, and health care. The differentiation complexity measure in this study is closely related to the concept of myside bias because it measures how well subjects consider alternative viewpoints and recognize complex trade-offs when reasoning about issues. That it operationalizes the processes that enable subjects to *avoid* myside bias makes it an inverse measure. Subjects received an overall differentiation complexity score averaging across the six issues tested, but when predicting differentiation complexity for a *particular* issue, the average score was a less potent predictor than the degree of conflict between the values implicated by each *particular* issue (for example, freedom versus national security on a question about surveillance).

Kaitlin Toner and colleagues (2013) employed a paradigm that investigates myside thinking in a most interesting way. They examined nine issues on which liberals and conservatives in the United States tend to disagree (health care, illegal immigration, abortion, affirmative action, government help for the needy, requiring voter identification, taxes, use of torture on terrorists, and laws based on religion). After assessing their subjects' opinions on these issues, they had them directly rate how much more correct they thought their viewpoints were compared with other people's. The scale ranged from the modest "no more correct than other viewpoints," to "slightly more correct than other viewpoints" or "somewhat more correct than other viewpoints," to "much more correct than other viewpoints," and, finally, to "totally correct—Mine is the only correct view." Thus Toner and colleagues (2013) measured both the opinion on each of the nine issues along with what they termed the "degree of belief superiority" for each: the degree to which subjects thought their opinions were superior to those of others.

For each of the nine issues, Toner and colleagues (2013) observed a very large strength of belief effect (exemplified as a very strong quadratic effect in their regression analysis). The more extreme a subject's viewpoint was (in either direction), the more the subject tended to believe that his or her viewpoint was better than that of others. The strength of opinion variable was a more potent predictor than the direction of opinion variable in all cases. Subjects displayed linear effects in addition to quadratic ones on only four of the nine issues—effects indicating that one end of the ideological spectrum displayed more belief superiority than the other. On two of the four issues (government help for the needy and making laws based on religion) liberal subjects displayed greater belief superiority than conservative subjects did, whereas on the other two issues (requiring voter identification and affirmative action), conservative subjects displayed greater belief superiority than liberal subjects did. As we did in our 2008 study (Stanovich and West 2008a), Toner and colleagues (2013) found that the strength of opinion variable was a stronger predictor than the individual difference variable of dogmatism.

It is interesting that, decades ago, in his classic papers on how mere beliefs are different from convictions, Robert Abelson (1986, 1988) reported several results that converge with the findings about myside bias that we examined in the first three chapters of this book. Based on subjects' answers to a series of survey questions, Abelson (1988) constructed a "conviction score" for each of several social issues that were current in the 1980s (nuclear power, belief in God, divestment from South Africa, abortion, welfare, the Strategic Defense Initiative, AIDS). Given the results we have just reviewed about the strength of belief variable, it is safe to assume Abelson's conviction scores would have correlated highly with the degree of myside bias displayed on each issue. Yet consistent with the results reviewed here, Abelson (1988) found no correlation between level of education and conviction on any of the issues and only modest degrees of domain generality for conviction (a median correlation of .25). He concluded that his results suggest a "lack of a powerful individual difference variable representing the proclivity to have convictions on social issues" (Abelson 1988, 271).

Predicting Myside Bias versus Predicting Proposition Agreement

It is important to understand what is meant when we say that myside bias has a low degree of domain generality. What is being correlated is not the degree of *agreement* with a particular proposition, but the degree of *myside bias* displayed when reasoning about the proposition. The two are not the same. Of course, a host of opinions are predictable from a broad individual difference variable such as political ideology. There certainly would be a close association between liberalism and belief in higher health care spending and a higher minimum wage—just as there would be a close association between conservatism and belief in higher military spending and greater school choice. There will definitely be a close association between ideology and which attitudinal direction of a proposition (e.g., "Military spending should be increased") a subject will endorse. What can be predicted from a particular subject's ideology is the valence on the proposition, and thus what that subject's "side" will be—but this is *not* the same as predicting the degree of *myside* bias a subject will display from that subject's ideology.

Imagine two propositions, one on raising the minimum wage and the other on raising the level of military spending. It will be highly predictable that if the prior opinion of a particular subject A is pro–higher minimum wage, then the prior opinion of person A will also be anti–higher military spending. The counterpart prediction would be that if the prior belief of person B is anti–higher minimum wage, then the prior belief of person B will also be pro–higher military spending. But these predictions are about which *opinions* will go together, not about whether the levels of myside bias displayed will go together. Although *opinion direction* has a high degree of predictability, this does not necessarily follow for the degree of *myside bias* displayed. Indeed, in the studies reviewed, the degree of myside bias displayed is not predictable from ideological direction.

Table 3.2 will let us see the difference, numerically and statistically, for a six-subject simulation. The subjects are assumed to differ widely on a worldview variable such as political ideology (measured on a 1 to 10 scale). Three of the subjects are of a distinctly different ideological persuasion than the other three. The subjects are assessed on two different opinions related to their political ideology, labeled here as simply "opinion 1" and "opinion 2" (also measured on a 1 to 10 scale) on two issues about which the different ideological groups in this sample would be expected to cluster in their opinions—higher spending for public schools and single-payer governmental health care, for example. We assume that myside bias is measured for each of the opinions using any of the methods described in the first three chapters (evidence evaluation, argument generation, and so on). A myside bias score is indicated for each subject for each of the opinions. Following the results from the actual studies just reviewed, the degree of myside bias is highly correlated with the extremeness of the opinion.

Table 3.2.
Data Simulation of How Myside Bias Is Related to Strength of Prior Opinion

Subject	Ideology score	Opinion 1	Myside bias 1	Opinion 2	Myside bias 2	Thinking disposition
1	10	10	5	8	3	95
2	9	8	3	10	5	97
3	8	6	1	6	1	89
4	3	4	1	1	5	77
5	2	2	3	4	1	85
6	1	1	5	2	3	83

Correlations:

Ideology and opinion 1 = .97

Ideology and opinion 2 = .88

Opinion1 and opinion 2 = .82

Myside bias on opinion 1 and myside bias on opinion 2 = .00

Ideology and myside bias on opinion 1 = .00

Ideology and myside bias on opinion 2 = .11

Thinking disposition and ideology = .85

Thinking disposition and myside bias on opinion 1 = .36

Thinking disposition and myside bias on opinion 2 = .00

As you might suspect from looking at the numbers in the table, and as might actually occur in real life, political ideology is highly predictive of opinions on these two issues. For example, the issue of higher spending for public schools and the issue of single-payer governmental health care are issues closely associated with ideology. Thus, in table 3.2, ideology is correlated .97 with opinion 1 and .88 with opinion 2. Furthermore, and also as might be expected in real life, opinions on the two issues themselves are highly correlated ($r = .82$).

Nevertheless, even though ideology predicts both opinions, and even though the two opinions are highly correlated with each other, the degree of myside bias displayed on the two issues is totally *un*correlated. Furthermore, ideology predicts opinion valence, but it does not predict myside bias— exhibiting correlations of .00 and .11 with myside bias 1 and 2, respectively.

These results occur because the degree of myside bias is related to the *strength* of the opinion and not to its overall direction. An opinion level of 10 on one of these items is just as extreme as an opinion level of 1—it is just as strong a conviction in both cases and will lead to high levels of myside bias. An opinion level of 6 on one of these issues is similar to an opinion level of 4 in that, even though the two are in disagreement overall on the direction of their opinion, they are both weak and both will lead to weak levels of myside bias. Note that a thinking disposition correlated with ideology might not necessarily predict degree of myside bias. The last column of table 3.2 lists one such hypothetical thinking disposition, which correlates .85 with ideology, .78 with opinion 1, and .98 with opinion 2. In contrast, however, it only correlates .36 with myside bias on opinion 1 and is totally uncorrelated ($r = .00$) with myside bias on opinion 2.

Table 3.2 illustrates that it is much easier to predict opinions than it is to predict myside bias. For the levels of myside bias to be correlated, it is the *strength* of the opinion from issue to issue that must be correlated, not just the overall valence of the opinion. Of course, this is somewhat of a simplification. There may well be opinion direction effects that predict myside bias as well as just strength effects. As previously mentioned, Toner and colleagues (2013) found linear effects (direction effects) on four of their nine issues. Likewise, in our 2008 study (Stanovich and West 2008a), we found opinion direction effects for both the abortion and the drinking age issue. However, in both of these studies, the directional effect was substantially lower in magnitude than the strength effect. Further reinforcing our emphasis on strength of opinion is the finding of the Ditto and colleagues (2019a) meta-analysis that, overall, there were no differences in myside bias across the ideological spectrum. Thus political ideology—a major worldview driving myside thinking on many issues—is directionally balanced at the most macro level. This would not, however, prevent directional effects from appearing on specific micro issues. But even here, based on the results of the studies by Toner and colleagues (2013) and by Stanovich and West (2008a), we would expect any directional effect to be statistically swamped by the strength effect.

Thus the level of myside bias displayed on a particular issue in a particular paradigm is highly content dependent. This is because myside bias turns out to be an outlier bias. Most of the other biases, as previously noted, are negatively correlated with intelligence (those higher in intelligence are better at avoiding the bias). Myside bias is not—nor is it very highly predictable from any of the more-studied rational thinking dispositions. There are very few individual difference variables that can predict the degree of myside bias that a particular person will display. General political orientation also has limited ability to predict myside bias (Ditto et al. 2019a), unless very fine-grained information about the strength of belief across various micro issues is obtained (Toner et al. 2013). In short, myside bias is more tied to the content and strength of the specific belief than to broad psychological processes that can be measured as individual difference variables. In chapter 4, we will explore in greater detail the theoretical implications of this fact.

4 Where Do Our Convictions Come From? Implications for Understanding Myside Bias

In many different areas of psychology there is a theoretical dispute about the relative importance of psychological processes versus stored knowledge. In some areas, the dispute is never really resolved. For example, in the area of critical thinking, researchers still vacillate between emphasizing critical processing skills versus stressing that a rich knowledge base is necessary in order to think critically in a domain. In contrast, intelligence researchers appear to have reached a near-consensus on the Cattell-Horn-Carroll (CHC) theory of intelligence (Carroll 1993; Cattell 1963, 1998; Horn and Cattell 1967; see also Walrath et al. 2020), which emphasizes both fluid intelligence (process) and crystallized intelligence (stored knowledge).

Heuristics and biases research, long focused on miserly information processing (Dawes 1976; Kahneman 2011; Simon 1955, 1956; Taylor 1981; Tversky and Kahneman 1974) has seemed to place a much greater emphasis on processing issues than on stored knowledge. Recently, though, this has begun to change, with many theorists now emphasizing that an override of autonomous processes is not necessary if the correct response is overlearned, precompiled, and can be automatically triggered (De Neys 2018; De Neys and Pennycook 2019; Evans 2019; Pennycook, Fugelsang, and Koehler 2015; Stanovich 2018a). Richard West, Maggie Toplak, and I tried to capture this change of emphasis in our Comprehensive Assessment of Rational Thinking (CART: Stanovich, West, and Toplak 2016), which included several subtests that carefully assessed important knowledge bases that underlie rational thinking.

In chapter 3, we saw that opinion content accounts for more variance in myside bias than psychological process indicators do, although the default theoretical stance about myside bias tends to see it as process driven. The findings discussed there suggest that this default stance may need a reset. If myside bias is indeed process driven, then the processes determining it certainly seem to be unpredictable from the most-studied individual difference variables in psychology—intelligence and thinking dispositions such as actively open-minded thinking and need for cognition.

In this chapter, we will explore an alternative conceptualization, looking at myside bias as a content-based bias rather than an individual difference trait. Indeed, researchers in several areas of political and social psychology have recently been discovering that long-standing findings in their fields must often be reinterpreted or even overturned once the importance of the content of the stimulus materials is fully appreciated. What were largely thought to be domain-general relationships involving psychological characteristics turn out to be relationships that appear and disappear depending upon the content used in a particular experiment.

Overlooking Content Effects in Recent Psychological Science

A study by Jutta Proch, Julia Elad-Strenger, and Thomas Kessler (2019) demonstrates how researchers can too quickly jump to the conclusion that they are measuring a general psychological characteristic when they have not sampled content broadly enough. Their 2019 study challenges the longstanding view in the psychological literature that political conservatism is associated with resistance to change (Feldman and Huddy 2014; Jost et al. 2003; Kerlinger 1984). Proch, Elad-Strenger, and Kessler (2019) point out that a person's stance toward change may not be a function of change per se, but rather of how the person views the current status quo. People who approve of the status quo tend not to want to change it, whereas those who do not approve tend to favor change. Social, economic, technological, and cultural change was vastly slower in the 1960s, 1970s, 1980s, and even into the 1990s than it is now, and much of the status quo in those decades was not to the liking of liberals. Thus, when liberal respondents to a questionnaire indicated they wanted change, they were endorsing not just change per se, but change in directions they approved of.

But the situation is much different in modern industrialized societies, where many aspects of our current status quo have been engineered and built by those implementing a range of liberal social principles, from diversity in human resources departments, to pollution regulation of industry, to racial preferences in college admissions, to quotas of women on corporate boards. Thus it was not hard for Proch, Elad-Strenger, and Kessler (2019) to draw up a fairly long list of social and political policies that have produced a status quo approved of by liberals and to balance it with an equally long list of political and social policies that have produced a status quo approved of by conservatives.

Using these balanced sets of policies as stimuli, Proch, Elad-Strenger, and Kessler (2019) found no general tendency for conservative subjects to be more resistant to change than liberal subjects were. The results of their study pretty much confirm the commonsense conclusion that both political groups approve of the status quo when it matches their sociopolitical worldview and both disapprove of change when it moves the status quo away from that worldview.

The Proch, Elad-Strenger, and Kessler 2019 study shows how a biased selection of stimuli leads to the premature construction of theories that emphasize broad psychological traits rather than content-contingent responses to particular situations. Their findings converge with those of a thorough analysis Maggie Toplak and I performed using our actively open-minded thinking (AOT) scale (Stanovich and Toplak 2019; discussed in chapter 2). One key processing style measured by the AOT scale is subjects' willingness to revise beliefs based on evidence. Our early scales, first constructed decades ago, contained several items designed to measure this processing style. But what Maggie and I discovered was that subjects displayed no *generic* belief revision tendency. Belief revision needs to be measured with content—it is determined by the specific belief that subjects are revising: subjects are more or less willing to revise beliefs depending upon the content of the belief. Our 2019 findings are reminiscent of those from the myside bias studies reviewed in chapter 3, where subjects were more or less inclined to display myside bias depending upon the strength of their prior opinion on the *particular* issue in question. There was no general tendency toward myside bias independent of content and predictable from broad psychological traits.

Expanding the range of the stimuli used in research has been critical in the recent reconsideration of earlier social psychology research on prejudice, intolerance, and warmth of feelings toward various social groups (Crawford 2018), although concern about this earlier research goes back at least to the work of Philip Tetlock (1986; see also Ray 1983, 1989). It was long thought that out-group prejudice and intolerance were associated with conservative ideology, low intelligence, and low openness to experience. Proponents of the "ideological conflict hypothesis" (Brandt et al. 2014; Chambers, Schlenker, and Collisson 2013) questioned the generality of these earlier findings by pointing out that the target social groups in these studies (African Americans, LGBT people, Hispanics) were often groups who shared ideological affinity with liberals and whose values conflicted with those of conservatives. Thus the lower out-group warmth and tolerance shown by conservative subjects may well have been due to an ideological conflict with the target groups used in the earlier studies.

In a test of this hypothesis, John Chambers, Barry Schlenker, and Brian Collisson (2013) demonstrated how earlier studies of the relationship between conservatism and prejudice had confounded the target groups with ideology. The target groups in most of the classic experiments on prejudice were groups known to share liberal values, so when subjects had to indicate warmth toward a particular group or indicate that they would treat its members with tolerance, conservative subjects were faced with a conflict—the values of the group they had to evaluate were known to conflict with conservative values. Liberal subjects were faced with no such conflict—they were simply asked to indicate the degree of tolerance they would show target groups whose members believed exactly as they did.[1] When, however, Chambers, Schlenker, and Collisson (2013) measured the degree of tolerance and warmth liberal subjects displayed toward groups whose values conflicted with liberal values (businesspeople, Christian fundamentalists, the wealthy, the military), they found that liberal subjects displayed as much out-group dislike as conservative subjects did. Ideological similarity strongly predicted group liking, with correlations greater than .80.

Many empirical studies have put the ideological conflict hypothesis to the test. The results of these studies have converged on the conclusion that measures of out-group tolerance, prejudice, and warmth are more a function of the degree to which the values of subjects match or conflict with the values of the target groups than of the psychological characteristics of the subjects (Brandt and Crawford 2019; Chambers, Schlenker, and Collisson 2013; Crawford and Pilanski 2014; Wetherell Brandt, and Reyna 2013). Correlations of intolerance and lack of warmth with conservatism, low intelligence, or openness virtually disappear once social groups of a more diverse range are included in the rating tasks. It seems that liberal subjects can also display intolerance—but just toward groups who do not share their world-views or values (businesspeople, Christian fundamentalists, the wealthy, the military).

Riley Carney and Ryan Enos (2019) have demonstrated how specific content plays a role in determining responses on the much-used modern racism scales (Henry and Sears 2002). These scales are particularly prominent in attempts to link racism with conservative opinions. Typical are propositions like "Irish, Italian, Jewish, and many other minorities overcame prejudice and worked their way up; blacks should do the same without any special favors" or "It's really a matter of some people not trying hard enough; if blacks would only try harder, they could be just as well off as whites." Carney and Enos (2019) ran several experiments in which they inserted other groups in the slot for the usual target group, African Americans (often termed "blacks" in such scale items to focus subjects specifically on race). In different experimental conditions, they inserted as target groups Taiwanese, Hispanics, Jordanians, Albanians, Angolans, Uruguayans, and Maltese. Their startling conclusion was that, even though conservative subjects endorsed all of the propositions on the scale more strongly than liberal subjects did, they endorsed them *regardless* of the target group, whereas liberal subjects were less likely to endorse the propositions on the scale when the target group was African Americans (Carney and Enos 2019).

Carney and Enos (2019) further concluded that these modern racism scales captured not racial resentment specifically connected to conservatives, but instead racial sympathy specifically connected to liberals (see also al Gharbi 2018; Edsall 2018; Goldberg 2019; Uhlmann et al. 2009). For conservative subjects, the so-called modern racism scales served to measure not their racism but instead their belief in the relative fairness of current society in rewarding effort; and, as such, these scales have been mislabeled from their very inception. For liberal subjects, the scales did serve to measure something specifically directed at blacks, but that something, if anything, was liberal subjects' tendency to display a special affinity toward African Americans—or perhaps their awareness that African Americans were the target group with the highest payoff in terms of virtue signaling.[2]

More recent studies have shown that psychological relationships involving prejudice and tolerance are contingent, depending on the *congruency* between the values of the subjects and the values of the target groups in the stimuli used in the study (Brant and Crawford 2016, 2019; Brandt et al. 2014; Brandt and Van Tongeren 2017; Crawford and Brandt 2020; Crawford and Jussim 2018; Crawford and Pilanski 2014; Wetherell, Brandt, and Reyna 2013). In their nuanced discussion of recent developments in research on prejudice, Mark Brandt and Jarret Crawford (2019) show how many of the psychological traits thought to be generalized predictors (openness to experience, cognitive ability) are predictors of prejudice only in certain cases. They do not work as predictors for all target groups. Brandt and Crawford (2019) end up with a small list of just four consistent predictors of prejudice. But there is a clear reason that the list is too optimistic with regard to the goal of predicting prejudice from a subject's *purely psychological* characteristics. This is because the two most-established predictors in their list—worldview conflict and perceived threat—are not general psychological characteristics at all—that is, they are not individual difference variables solely contained within a subject but, rather, mismatch variables involving overlap between a distal belief and a target stimulus. Worldview conflict depends on the match between a subject's worldview and the social attitudes of the target stimulus. The same thing is true for perceived threat. They are variables reflecting the *fit* between a subject and the target stimulus. Neither of these variables are psychological characteristics of people. They are, instead, properties of the content of a subject's belief and how that content relates to a target stimulus.

In short, measures of a subject's personality traits and cognitive ability have often been found to be less predictive than the subject's specific belief. Myside bias seems to be an extreme case of this general observation. The studies reviewed in chapter 3 showed that myside bias is almost totally uncorrelated with cognitive ability and, at best, very weakly correlated with rational thinking dispositions. Indeed, myside bias is consistently associated only with the direction and strength of the focal belief itself. The tendency to display myside bias seems to be not an inherent characteristic of a person but, instead, more a function of the specific beliefs and opinions the person has acquired. We thus are in need of a perspective that emphasizes the *content* of belief (rather than processing tendencies) if we are to properly understand myside bias.

Beliefs as Possessions and Beliefs as Memes

One reason why myside bias might be content based rather than a psychological trait is suggested in the title of a paper written some years ago by

Robert Abelson (1986): "Beliefs Are like Possessions." Current critiques of overconsumption aside, most of us feel that we have acquired our material possessions for particular reasons, and that our possessions serve our ends in some way. We feel the same about our beliefs,[3] that beliefs are something we choose to acquire, just like the rest of our possessions. In short, we tend to assume: (1) that we exercised agency in acquiring our beliefs; and (2) that they serve our interests. Under these assumptions, it seems to make sense to have a blanket policy of defending our beliefs.

But there is another way to think about this—one that makes us a little more skeptical about our tendency to defend our beliefs, no matter what. As discussed in chapter 3, when intelligence increases or when thinking dispositions that are correlated with deeper thought increase, there is no corresponding decrease in myside bias. And the finding reviewed in chapter 3 that there is little domain generality in myside bias (e.g., Toplak and Stanovich 2003) suggests that it might not be people who are characterized by more or less myside bias but rather beliefs that differ in the degree of myside bias they engender. In short, beliefs may differ in how strongly they are structured to repel ideas that contradict them. This is precisely what a theoretical position in evolutionary epistemology has asserted, a position that allows us to explore the implications of a startling question: What if you don't own your beliefs, but instead, they own you?

Cultural replicator theory and the field of memetics have helped us to explore precisely this question. The term "cultural replicator" refers to an element of a culture that may be passed on by nongenetic means. An alternative term for a cultural replicator—"meme"—was introduced by Richard Dawkins in his famous 1976 book *The Selfish Gene*. The term meme[4] is also sometimes used generically to refer to what has been called a "memeplex"— coadapted memes that are copied together as a set of interlocking ideas (so, for example, the notion of democracy is a complex interconnected set of memes—a memeplex).

Memetics can help somewhat to dislodge the "beliefs as possessions" metaphor implied in phrases such as "my belief" and "my idea." Because the term "my meme" is less familiar, it does not signal ownership in the same way that "my belief" does. The meme concept can disrupt the defensive stance toward the distal belief that is the cause of most myside processing. And, by its analogy to the term gene, meme invites us to use the insights of universal Darwinism to understand belief acquisition and change (Aunger 2000, 2002; Blackmore 1999; Dennett 1995, 2017; Distin 2005; Sterelny 2006).

Organisms, Dawkins (1976) tells us, are built to advance the interests[5] of their genes (replication) rather than those of the organisms themselves. Although the interests of the genes and of the organisms in which they reside will most often coincide, this coincidence is not without exceptions. Extensive research in genetics and theoretical biology has shown that the genes—as subpersonal replicators—can increase their fecundity and lon- gevity in ways that do not always serve the instrumental goals of the organ- isms that contain them (Dawkins 1982; Skyrms 1996; Stanovich 2004). The selfish gene concept prompts the analogous insight that memes may occa- sionally replicate at the expense of the interests of their hosts, especially when they have been acquired unreflectively. Taking what Dennett (2017) calls the "meme's-eye point of view," we come to understand that memes (like genes) are replicators that act only in their own interests. In short, myside bias might be serving the interests of resident memes rather than those of the host. Perhaps that is why the psychological characteristics of people fail to predict the degree of myside bias displayed.

The fundamental insight triggered by the meme concept is that a belief may spread without necessarily being true or helping the person who holds the belief. Consider a chain letter with this message: "If you do not pass this message on to five people, you will experience misfortune." This is an example of a meme—an idea unit. It is the instruction for a behavior that can be copied and stored in brains. It has been a reasonably successful meme in that it replicates a lot. Yet there are two remarkable things about this successful meme: it is neither true nor helpful to the person carrying it. Yet the meme survives. It survives because of its own self-replicating proper- ties (the essential logic of this meme is that it does nothing more than say, "Copy me—or else"). All of the memes that currently exist have, through memetic evolution, displayed the highest fecundity, longevity, and copying fidelity—the defining characteristics of successful replicators.

Memetic theory has profound effects on our reasoning about beliefs because it inverts the way we think about them. Social and personality psychologists traditionally tend to ask what it is about particular individu- als that leads them to have certain beliefs. The causal model is one where a person determines what beliefs to have. Memetic theory asks instead, "What is it about certain memes that leads them to collect many 'hosts' for themselves?" Thus the question is not "How do people acquire beliefs?" but "How do beliefs acquire people?"

One commonsense view of why belief X spreads is the notion that belief X spreads simply "Because it is true." This notion, however, has trouble accounting for beliefs that are true but not popular, and for beliefs that are popular but not true. Memetic theory provides us with another reason why beliefs spread: Belief X spreads among people because it is a good replicator—it is good at acquiring hosts. Memetic theory focuses us on the properties of beliefs as replicators rather than the qualities of people acquiring the beliefs. This is the single distinctive function served by the meme concept, and it is a profound one.

Memes and memeplexes survive and proliferate for four reasons, thus leading to four successful meme strategies.[6] The historical spread of a meme might involve any combination of the four strategies:

1. Memes survive and spread because they are helpful to the people who host them.

2. Certain memes proliferate because they are a good fit to preexisting genetic predispositions or domain-specific evolutionary modules.

3. Certain memes spread because they facilitate the replication of genes that make organisms that are good hosts for those particular memes (religious beliefs that urge people to have more children would be in this category).

4. Memes survive and spread because of the self-perpetuating properties of the memes themselves.

No doubt most memes have survived for more than one reason. A meme might spread because it is useful to its host *and* because it fits genetic predispositions *and* because of its self-perpetuating properties (Richerson and Boyd 2005).

Strategy #4 is the problematic category because the replicative strategies used there do not serve the host. Various theorists have discussed some of the self-perpetuating strategies of these problematic memes. For example, there is "parasitic mindware" that mimics the structure of helpful ideas and deceives the host into thinking that the host will derive benefit from it. Advertisers are, of course, expert at constructing meme parasites— beliefs that ride on the backs of other beliefs and images (prompting unconscious associations like "If I buy this car, I will get this beautiful model"). Other self-preserving memetic strategies involve changing the cognitive environment. Many religions, for example, stoke people's fear of death in order to make their promise of an afterlife more enticing. More sinister are "adversative strategies," which alter the cultural environment in ways that make it more hostile for competing memes or that influence their hosts to attack the hosts of alternative beliefs. Many moderate religious believers refrain from criticizing extremist members of their communities out of fear of the memes other members may be harboring. Less sinister meme strategies simply prompt the host to avoid potentially conflicting information (Golman, Hagmann, and Loewenstein 2017).

Dennett's (2017) "meme's-eye point of view" leads us to see myside bias as a strategic mechanism that makes belief change difficult in order to preserve existing memes and to realize that we live in a "memosphere"[7] in which there is widespread hostility to examining beliefs. Educational theorists in critical thinking have bemoaned for decades the difficulty of inculcating the critical thinking skills of detachment, neutral evaluation of belief, perspective switching, decontextualizing, and skepticism toward current opinions. Critical thinking studies are virtually unanimous in showing how hard it is for people to examine evidence from standpoints not guaranteed to reinforce their existing beliefs. In short, the memes that currently reside in our brains seem singularly unenthusiastic about sharing precious brain space with other memes that might want to take up residence and potentially displace them.

That most of us share the trait of hostility to new memes does prompt some troubling thoughts. If most of our memes are serving us well, why wouldn't they want to submit themselves to selective tests that competitor memes, especially those which contradict them, would surely fail? One reason might be that memes in a mutually supportive relationship within a memeplex would be likely to form a structure that prevented memes that contradicted them from gaining brain space for some of the same reasons that genes in the genome are cooperative (Ridley 2000). Organisms tend to be genetically defective if any new mutant allele is not a cooperator, which is why the other genes in the genome demand cooperation. Likewise, resident memes are also selecting for cooperators—memes like them. Memes contradicting previously residing memes are not easily assimilated (Golman et al. 2016).

Such an account can explain our individual difference finding that a subject displaying high myside bias in one domain is not necessarily likely to display it in another and our more general finding that *domains* differ greatly in the amount of myside bias they provoke (Stanovich and West 2008a; Toplak and Stanovich 2003). This is because memes differ in how strongly they are structured to repel other memes that contradict them—and that might replace them. There is no general tendency for a *person* to have high or low myside bias. In contrast, however, certain memeplexes resist conflicting memes better than others.

Functionality and the Reflective Acquisition of Beliefs

In this section, we will touch on how the meme concept may help us overcome the tragedy of the communications commons that was discussed in chapter 2. Treating distal beliefs as possessions encourages the worst type of myside bias—projecting prior beliefs that are not based on evidence, but instead are extrapolations from untestable convictions. To avoid myside bias, we need to distance ourselves from our convictions, and, to do so, it may help to think of our beliefs as memes that may well have interests of their own.

Before discussing the distancing function of the meme's-eye view of beliefs, we should briefly review the unfortunate history of the meme concept, certain aspects of which have deterred researchers in psychology and other disciplines from appreciating the memetic approach. Dawkins (1993), although coining the term meme, helped the concept get off to a bad start when he famously, along with Blackmore (2000), claimed that most religions are essentially "copy-me" memeplexes, "backed up with threats, promises, and ways of preventing their claims from being tested" (Blackmore 2000, 35–36). Their arguments provoked a series of rebuttals in the psychology of religion literature (Atran and Henrich 2010; Barrett 2004; Bering 2006; Bloom 2004; Boyer 2001, 2018; Haidt 2012; Wilson 2002). Of course, the critics of the Dawkins–Blackmore position differ somewhat among themselves. Some believe that religion is an evolved adaptation. Others think it is a by-product of a series of cognitive mechanisms that evolved for other purposes (agent detection, theory of mind, and so on). Regardless of whether they take an adaptationist or a by-product stance toward religion, many theorists oppose the Dawkins–Blackmore position that religion is a meme virus—a "copy-me" instruction that is not functional for its human hosts.

The notoriety of the Dawkins–Blackmore position unfortunately fostered the misconception that the term meme refers only to ideas in category 4 listed in the previous section—that is, that the concept of a meme refs only to ideas that act to replicate themselves and that have no genetic functionality or functionality for the organism. As I stressed before, this is incorrect. Statistically, most memes have genetic or organismic functionality *in addition* to having their own self-replicating properties. The Dawkins–Blackmore position on religion prompted many people to believe that the concept of a meme referred exclusively to "virus beliefs"—those having no function other than replicating themselves. For example, Dan Sperber (2000, 163) uses the term meme not as a synonym for a cultural replicator in general, but as a cultural replicator "standing to be selected not because they benefit their human carriers, but because they benefit themselves." That is, he reserves the term for beliefs that reside solely in category 4. In contrast, my use of the meme concept (and the usage of most memetic theorists) is more generic, as a synonym for cultural replicator generally.

Aside from the definitional confusion, the Dawkins position[8] on religion as a meme virus had another deleterious side effect. In calling memes "viruses," Dawkins implied that they have two properties: (1) they are not acquired in a reflective manner; (2) they are not functional, and he also implied that these two properties always go together. From this there arose the assumption that if a meme *is* functional for the host, then it necessarily must have been acquired reflectively. This is an unfortunate assumption because it directs our attention away from a much more important and common situation: where a meme is *not* acquired in a reflective manner, yet is still functional in one way or another. The meme virus trope de-emphasizes an important point—that a meme can successfully replicate because of either strategy #1 or strategy #2 listed above and yet still not be acquired reflectively. In fact, most of the beliefs and ideas that animate and enable a successful life represent memes that were not acquired through conscious reflection but that are still functional for us.

Daniel Dennett (2017) sees this last insight as one of the great strengths of the meme concept.[9] It makes salient the fact that we may have built cultural artifacts through a series of unconscious decisions rather than from anything like what Dennett calls "conscious uptake": "The fact that changes in cultural features can spread without notice is hard to account for—and hence likely to be overlooked—when one adopts the traditional psychological perspective of ideas and beliefs" (Dennett 2017, 213). This is the cultural parallel to my argument that if a belief feels right to us or if it seems to be a functional tool in the achievement of our ends, it is a mistake to think that we must have consciously adopted the belief through the use of reflection and rational thought.

But how, then, do we acquire important beliefs (convictions) *without* reflection? Although the folk theory of the layperson ("My beliefs are things I have consciously thought through and made an intentional decision to believe") might find the answer to this question counterintuitive, it would not surprise a psychologist because there are plenty of examples in psychology where people acquire their declarative knowledge, behavioral proclivities, and decision-making styles from a combination of innate propensities and largely unconscious social learning. Thus, invoking just this model to explain moral beliefs and behavior, Jonathan Haidt (2012, 26) argues: "If morality doesn't come primarily from reasoning, then that leaves some combination of innateness and social learning as the most likely candidates. . . . I'll try to explain how morality can be innate (as a set of evolved intuitions) and learned (as children learn to apply those intuitions within a particular culture)."

The model that Haidt (2012) invokes to explain the development of morality is easily applied to the case of myside bias. Myside-causing convictions often come from political ideologies: sets of beliefs about the proper order of society and how it can be achieved. Increasingly, theorists are modeling the development of political ideologies using the same model of innate propensities and social learning that Haidt (2012) applied to the development of morality (see Van Bavel and Pereira 2018).

There is still much to be learned about the origins of our ideological inclinations, but only a broad conclusion is necessary for my current argument, namely, that there may be temperamental substrates that make a person into a conservative or a liberal, and these temperamental substrates increasingly look like they are biologically based. For example, measures of political ideology and values show considerable heritability (Alford and Hibbing, 2004; Bell, Schermer, and Vernon 2009; Funk et al. 2013; Hatemi and McDermott 2016; Hufer et al. 2020; Ludeke et al. 2013; Oskarsson et al. 2015; Twito and Knafo-Noam 2020). Also, liberals and conservatives differ on two of the "Big Five" personality traits (openness, conscientiousness, extraversion, agreeableness, and neuroticism) that are themselves substantially heritable (Bouchard and McGue 2003; Funk et al. 2013). Liberals tend to score higher than conservatives on openness and lower on conscientiousness (Carney et al. 2008; De Neve 2015; Fatke 2017; Hirsh et al. 2010; Iyer et al. 2012; McCrae 1996; Onraet et al. 2011; Sibley and Duckitt 2008).[10]

Not only are these personality differences heritable, but more direct studies have also linked genetic differences between liberals and conservatives to differences in neurotransmitter functioning (Hatemi et al. 2011; Hatemi and McDermott 2012, 2016). These findings have converged with a long-standing trend for psychological investigations to show that conservative subjects are more threat, negativity, and disgust sensitive than liberal subjects are (Carraro, Castelli, and Macchiella 2011; Hibbing, Smith, and Alford 2014a; Inbar, Pizarro, and Bloom 2009; Inbar et al. 2012; Jost et al. 2003; Oxley et al. 2008; Schaller and Park 2011). Other studies have linked sensation seeking (higher in liberal subjects) to political ideology (McCrae 1996). These differences in personality traits between liberals and conservatives seem to appear early in childhood, even among preschoolers (Block and Block 2006; De Neve 2015; Fraley et al. 2012; Wynn 2016). Finally, studies have correlated neurochemical and physiological differences in the brain with differences in ideology (Ahn et al. 2014; Dodd et al. 2012; Hatemi and McDermott 2016; Krummenacher et al. 2010; Van Bavel and Pereira 2018).

The conclusions from all of these studies on the temperamental and biological substrates of ideology will no doubt be challenged and refined by future research,[11] but how all the specific issues are resolved will not change the fact that those temperamental and biological substrates are not something any of us thought our way to. Nor are the memes that are good fits for those substrates something we thought our way to. Each of us was built a certain way, and when we encountered a certain memeplex, it felt right to us. Most of the mechanisms underlying how we came to our beliefs are System 1 mechanisms in dual-process theory (Evans and Stanovich 2013; Kahneman 2011), not processes of the reflective mind (the higher control functions of System 2 (see Pennycook, Fugelsang, and Koehler 2015; Stanovich 2011). Our innate propensities are beyond our control. As Jonathan Haidt (2012, 312) notes: "People whose genes gave them brains that get a special pleasure from novelty, variety, diversity, while simultaneously being less sensitive to signs of threat, are predisposed (but not predestined) to become liberal. . . . People whose genes give them brains with the opposite settings are predisposed, for the same reasons, to resonate with the grand narratives of the right."

Stressing that we didn't think our way to our ideological propensities is dealing with only half of Haidt's (2012) "innateness and social learning" formulation. For those of us who hold to the old folk psychology of belief ("I must have thought my way to my convictions because they mean so much to me"), the social learning part of Haidt's formulation provides little help. Values and worldviews develop throughout early childhood, and the beliefs to which we as children are exposed are significantly controlled by parents, neighbors, and friends, and by institutions like schools (Harris 1995; Iyengar, Konitzer, and Tedin 2018; Jennings, Stoker, and Bowers 2009).

Some of the memes to which a child is exposed are quickly acquired because they match the innate propensities already discussed. Others are acquired, perhaps more slowly, whether or not they match innate propensities, because they are repeated by cherished relatives and valued friends. They are often beliefs held by groups that the child values. That is, although the "side" in the term "myside bias" is indeed the side "my" conviction is on, that conviction often has more to do with group belonging than it does with personal reflection (see Haidt 2012 for a nuanced discussion; see also Clark and Winegard 2020; Tetlock 2002).

In short, children (and adults for that matter) have little direct control over their social world, the distribution of their social learning, or their innate propensities toward certain convictions. We didn't think our way to our innate propensities, and what we acquired through social learning was not the result of reflective thought either (see Hibbing, Smith, and Alford 2014b; Taber and Lodge 2016). That our ideological beliefs are largely acquired unreflectively is consistent with research showing that it is difficult to correct political misinformation by providing correct information (Flynn, Nyhan, and Reifler 2017; Nyhan and Reifler 2010). In contrast, Daniel Hopkins, John Sides, and Jack Citrin (2019) did find it possible to correct mistaken facts about the statistics of immigration in a group of subjects—but the correction had no effect at all on the subjects' higher-level political attitudes toward immigration. This led Hopkins, Sides, and Citrin (2019, 319) to conclude, consistent with Haidt's "innateness and social learning" formulation outlined here, that "attitudes toward immigration are grounded partly in stable predispositions, often established early in life and reinforced by later socialization, that render these attitudes resistant to information that challenges existing beliefs."

The general idea that distal beliefs are unreflective has been articulated by a wide range of scholars, from historians ("Most of our views are shaped by communal groupthink rather than individual rationality, and we hold onto these views due to group loyalty," Harari 2018, 223) to cognitive scientists ("Reasoning is generally motivated in the service of transmitting beliefs acquired from citizens' communities of belief. Cognition is largely a filter for attending to and sharing community norms," Sloman and Rabb (2019, 11). Despite the ubiquity of this view in a variety of behavioral disciplines, the layperson's notion of where convictions come from is still quite different. Most of us still prefer to think that we have thought our way to our deepest convictions.

The results of studies showing how the convictions that drive myside bias may have been acquired unreflectively converge nicely with those of studies (reviewed in chapter 3) showing that the avoidance of myside bias fails to correlate with intelligence. A sign that our convictions are acquired reflectively would be if a primary mechanism leading to well-calibrated opinions—the avoidance of myside bias—were strongly correlated with intelligence. The lack of such a correlation itself must raise serious questions about how reflective we are in acquiring our convictions.[12]

Recall from chapter 2 that the problematic kind of myside bias is the kind that results when a person projects a conviction as a prior probability rather than a testable belief that has resulted from the globally rational processing of evidence. Convictions such as ideological positions are quite often drivers of this problematic kind of myside bias. It is problematic because it leads to the tragedy of the communications commons (Kahan 2013; Kahan et al. 2017), discussed in chapter 2, which prevents society from reaching Bayesian convergence on matters of fact that are critical for optimal public policy decisions. Thus, it would help us to at least mitigate if not escape this commons dilemma by weakening our convictions just a little bit—making it at least a little less likely that we will use a conviction rather than an evidence-based, testable belief to formulate a prior probability.[13]

Thus, if each of us could become a bit more skeptical of our convictions (distal beliefs)—to avoid turning them into possessions—it might also help us to avoid projecting our convictions inappropriately. This section's approach to understanding where our convictions come from suggests that we need to talk in a more depersonalized manner about our beliefs. Memetics provides tools for doing just that.

Tools for Gaining Distance from Convictions

We need to change the folk psychology surrounding beliefs because in emphasizing conscious, personal agency, folk psychology tells us to look for individual psychological characteristics when trying to explain individual differences in myside bias. Folk psychology, as it is currently constituted,[14] encourages us to adopt a "beliefs as possessions" default. The fundamental memetic insight—that a belief may spread without having to be true or to help in any way the person who holds the belief—can help us loosen the grip of this default assumption.

The meme concept, combined with innateness and social learning forms a framework that helps to destroy the idea that we thought our way to everything we deem important. The combined framework essentially says to each of us, "You didn't think your way to that. You have a particular innate temperament and a memeplex latched onto it. You had a propensity to believe it, and that particular meme is structured to be particularly 'sticky' (or else it wouldn't have survived for so long)." In short, the memes that are your convictions may "fit" you—they may even be *functional* in your daily life (serving group identity functions, for example)—but this does not mean either that you reflected on them or that they are true.[15]

Memetic theory focuses us on the properties of ideas as replicators rather than the psychological qualities of the people acquiring the ideas. Consider, for example, a disarming strategy that indefensible memes use to ward off criticism: "We all have a right to our opinions." If taken literally, the claim is trivial. An opinion is merely an idea—a meme. We are not a totalitarian society. In free societies like ours, it is taken for granted that we're allowed to have whatever opinions—host whatever memes— we want as long as they do not lead us to harm others. No one has ever denied this "right to hold an opinion." So why is it that we so often hear people demanding this right, when in fact virtually no one wants to deprive them of their right to an opinion? By telling someone, "I have a right to my opinion," you are in fact demanding that someone stop asking you to defend your belief. Indeed, it is thought impolite for someone to persist in asking for justification once you've held up your "right to my opinion" shield. Thus a very useful inoculating strategy for a meme is to get itself labeled as an "opinion" and to have its host brandish the "right to my opinion" shield when its logic or empirical support is weak. Likewise, the use of the admonition "Never argue about politics or religion" is a fairly transparent attempt by current memes in those categories to inoculate their hosts against the proselytizing strategies (Golman et al. 2016) of memes that might attempt to replace those currently resident.

Many principles of instrumental rationality test memes for their consistency—for example, whether the sets of probabilities attached to beliefs are coherent and whether sets of desires hang together in logically consistent ways. Scientific inference is designed to test memes for their truth value—for example, whether they correspond to the way the world is. Memes that are true are good for us because accurately tracking the world helps us achieve our goals. But a meme might survive despite its not being true nor helping us to achieve our goals. Such memes are like the "junk DNA" in the body—DNA that does not code for a useful protein but is "just along for the ride," so to speak. Until the logic of replicators was made clear, this junk DNA was a puzzle. Once it was understood that DNA is there only to replicate itself and not necessarily to do anything good for us organisms, then there is no longer any puzzle about why there may be some junk DNA in the genome. If DNA can get replicated without helping to build a body, that is perfectly fine with it. Replicators care only about replicating.

And so it is with memes. If a meme can get preserved and passed on without helping its human host, it will do so (think of the chain letter example). Memetic theory leads us to a new type of question: How many of our beliefs are "junk beliefs"—serving to propagate themselves but not serving *us*? The principles of scientific inference and rational thought serve essentially as meme evaluation devices that help us determine which of our beliefs are true and therefore probably of use to us.

Scientific principles such as falsifiability are immensely useful in identifying possible "junk memes"—those which, in replicating, are really not serving our ends but merely serving their own. Think about it. You'll never find evidence that refutes an unfalsifiable meme. Thus you'll never have an evidence-based reason to give up such a belief. Yet an unfalsifiable meme really says nothing about the nature of the world (because it admits to no testable predictions) and thus may not be serving our ends by helping us track the world as it is. Such beliefs are quite possibly "junk memes"—unlikely to be shed even though they do little if anything for us who hold them. Memes that have not passed any reflective tests (falsifiability, consistency, and so on) are more likely to be memes that are serving their own interests only—that is, ideas that we believe only because they have properties that allow them to easily acquire us as hosts.

We also need to be more skeptical of the memes that we acquired in our early lives—those which were passed on by our parents, relatives, and our peers. The longevity of these early acquired memes is likely to be the result of their having avoided consciously selective tests of their usefulness. They were not subjected to selective tests because we acquired them during a time when we lacked the ability to reflect.

We are less likely to project our distal beliefs inappropriately as unjustified myside bias if we are a little more skeptical about them, a little more distanced from them. This distancing function is greatly aided by the language of memetic science, which suggests that our beliefs are not our chosen possessions, but rather entities separate from us and in need of constant evaluation. One way that the meme concept will aid our cognitive self-analysis is that, by emphasizing the epidemiology of beliefs, it will indirectly suggest to many of us the contingency of beliefs.

Summary and Conclusions

I opened this chapter by noting that researchers in several areas of political and social psychology have found content factors to be more potent predictors than individual difference variables. Myside bias might be another area of psychology where the properties of the beliefs themselves are more predictive than the individual psychological characteristics of the subjects (such as intelligence or open-mindedness) who hold those beliefs.

Studying myside bias is important because the tragedy of the communications commons arises when both sides in public policy debates that could be decided by evidence process new information with a myside bias. In some cases, as we saw in chapter 2, when people project prior beliefs that have been arrived at by properly accommodating *previous* evidence, then some degree of projecting the prior probability—a local myside bias— onto new evidence is normatively justified. When, however, we lack previous evidence on the issue in question, we should use the principle of indifference and set our prior probability at .50, where it will not influence our evaluation of the new evidence. Instead, what most of us tend to do in this situation is assess how the proposition in question relates to some distal belief of ours, such as our ideology, set $(H) > .50$, and then project this prior probability onto our evaluation of the new evidence. This is how our society ends up with political partisans on both sides of any issue seemingly unable to agree on the facts of that issue and never reaching Bayesian convergence.

In this chapter, I have suggested that we might at least mitigate if not remedy the tragedy of the communications commons by rethinking how we relate to our beliefs. First, it would help if we could realize that we have thought our way to our beliefs much less often than we may have imagined—that the distal beliefs we hold are largely a function of our social learning within the valued groups to which we belong and of our innate propensities to be attracted to certain types of ideas. Dual-inheritance theories of culture have stressed for some time that most people "feel in control of their culture and believe they came by most of it by choice. But the truth is, we often have much less choice than we think" (Richerson and Boyd 2005, 80).

We treat our beliefs as possessions when we think that we have thought our way to them and that they are serving us. The meme's-eye view leads us to question both that we have thought our way to these beliefs and that they are serving our personal ends. Our memes want to replicate whether they are good for us or not; and they don't care how they get into us—whether they get in through our conscious thoughts or are simply an unconscious fit to our innate psychological dispositions. The focus of memetics on the properties of beliefs[16] rather than the psychological characteristics of those who hold these beliefs also seems to be consistent with research showing that the degree of myside bias is better predicted by the former than by the latter.

We are often in situations where we have to calibrate the reasoning of others. This calibration often involves judging the degree of myside bias they are exhibiting, one of the trickiest judgments we have to make, for reasons discussed in chapter 3 and in this chapter. We have seen that subjects scoring higher on rational thinking dispositions scales and subjects of higher intelligence are better able to avoid most biases. This is not true in the case of myside bias, where it is the strength of the belief itself rather than the cognitive sophistication of the person holding the belief that predicts the level of myside bias. The direction of the belief sometimes makes a modest difference (Stanovich and West 2008a; Toner et al. 2013), but often it does not (Ditto et al. 2019a). This situation presents a particular obstacle for cognitive elites when it comes to evaluating myside bias. Their assumption that they are less biased than other people is actually correct for most biases in the heuristics and biases literature. That this assumption does not hold for myside bias, however, contributes to our currently vexing partisan political standoffs, which we will analyze in the more speculative final chapters of this book.

5   The Myside Blindness of Cognitive Elites

In chapter 3, we reviewed evidence indicating that myside bias was not attenuated by cognitive sophistication—not by high cognitive ability nor by well-developed rational thinking dispositions. In chapter 4, we examined a theory of why cognitive sophistication is not an inoculation against myside bias: because this particular bias is driven by the nature of acquired meme-plexes, not by personal psychological characteristics. In this chapter, we will explore how these two basic facts about myside bias interact to create a form of blindness toward a person's own myside bias that is particularly virulent among cognitive elites.

The Bias Blind Spot

The bias blind spot is an important meta-bias demonstrated in a paper by Pronin, Lin, and Ross (2002). They found that their subjects believed that various motivational biases were far more prevalent in others than in themselves, a much-replicated finding (Pronin 2007; Scopelliti et al. 2015). Bias turns out to be relatively easy to recognize in the thinking of others, but often difficult to detect in our own.

The bias blind spot itself appears to be a form of myside bias that may derive from a form of naive realism which causes us to believe that we perceive the world objectively (Keltner and Robinson 1996; Robinson et al. 1995; Skitka 2010). When other people's judgments differ from our own, we view the source of that difference as bias on their part rather than as their legitimate alternative interpretations of the evidence.

In two experiments, my research group (see West, Meserve, and Stanovich 2012) demonstrated that subjects had a bias blind spot regarding most of the classic cognitive biases (anchoring bias, outcome bias, base rate neglect, and so on), believing that most of these biases were more character-istic of others than of themselves. We found *positive* correlations between the subjects' having a bias blind spot and their cognitive sophistication—that is, more cognitively skilled subjects were more likely to have a bias blind spot. This makes sense, however, because as we saw in chapter 3, with the salient exception of myside bias, the display of most cognitive biases in the heuristics and biases literature is in fact *negatively* correlated with cogni-tive ability—that is, more intelligent people are less biased. Thus it would make sense for intelligent people to believe that they are less biased than others because, for most biases, they are.

But myside bias sets a trap for the cognitively sophisticated, who are used to thinking—rightly—that, in the case of most biases, they are less biased. The trap is that, though they may think that having intelligence and the cognitive sophistication that comes with higher education (which they have in abundance) inoculates them against biased thinking. Although this is true in some areas of reasoning, in the case of myside thinking it is not. Indeed, myside thinking may give rise to a particularly intense bias blind spot among cognitive elites.

If you are a person of high intelligence, if you are highly educated, and if you are strongly committed to an ideological viewpoint, you will be highly likely to think you have thought your way to your viewpoint. And you will be even less likely than the average person to realize that you have derived your beliefs from the social groups you belong to and because they fit with your temperament and your innate psychological propensities.

There is in fact a group of people who are highly intelligent, highly edu-cated, and strongly committed to an ideological viewpoint. That group happens to be the social scientists who study myside bias! They provide a case study of the effects of the tragedy of the communications commons.

The Perfect Storm for a Bias Blind Spot: Academics Studying Myside Bias

The university professoriate is overwhelmingly liberal, an ideological imbal-ance demonstrated in numerous studies conducted over the last two decades (Abrams 2016; Klein and Stern 2005; Langbert 2018; Langbert and Stevens 2020; Peters et al., 2020; Rothman, Lichter, and Nevitte 2005; Wright, Motz, and Nixon 2019). This imbalance is especially strong in university humanities departments, schools of education, and the social sciences; it is specifically strong in psychology and the related disciplines of sociology and political science, where much of the study of myside bias occurs (Buss and von Hippel 2018; Cardiff and Klein 2005; Clark and Winegard 2020; Duarte et al. 2015; Horowitz, Haynor, and Kickham 2018; Turner 2019).

Of course, there has never been an ideological balance in psychology faculties. Even thirty or forty years ago, there were more liberal psychology professors than there were conservative ones—more Democrats than there were Republicans. But much converging research has shown that this imbalance has become even more pronounced in the last twenty years (Duarte et al. 2015; Lukianoff and Haidt 2018)—so much so, that it would not be unfair to characterize the field of psychology as virtually an ideological monoculture. Studies of social science departments in universities have indicated that 58 to 66 percent of professors identify themselves as liberals and just 5 to 8 percent as conservatives (Duarte et al. 2015). The imbalance in psychology departments is even worse, with 84 percent of professors identifying themselves as liberals and just 8 percent as conservatives. This imbalance has grown far more pronounced in recent years. In 1990, the ratio was four liberals for every one conservative in psychology departments—a strong imbalance, but still, the 20 percent of faculty members who were conservatives at least provided some diversity. But, by the year 2000, the ratio had grown to six liberals for every one conservative (Duarte et al. 2015). And, by the year 2012, the ratio had risen to an astonishing 14 to 1. It is not unusual to find more than 90 percent of social psychology professors at a university identifying themselves as left of center and as voting Democratic in elections (Buss and von Hippel 2018; Ceci and Williams 2018). A survey of 500 arts and science faculty members at Harvard (Bikales and Goodman 2020) found that less than 2 percent identified themselves as conservative or very conservative, compared to more than 38 percent identifying themselves as very liberal and almost 80 percent as liberal or very liberal.

It is true that an ideological imbalance will not be a problem for many areas of psychology. Studies in physiological or perceptual psychology, for example, or in the very basic processes of human memory will not be affected by the political biases of the researchers. Indeed, I am not suggesting that even most areas of research in psychology have this problem, but only that it is a problem in many critical areas. People's distal political attitudes are intertwined with their prior beliefs on a wide range of issues, such as sexuality, morality, the psychological effects of poverty, family structures, crime, child care, productivity, marriage, incentives, discipline techniques, and educational practices. It is in these areas where we would be most concerned that the political ideology of the researchers might affect how they designed their studies or how they interpreted the results.

Science works as well as it does not because scientists themselves are never biased but because scientists are immersed in a system of checks and balances—where other scientists with differing biases are there to critique and correct. The bias of researcher A might not be shared by researcher B, who will then look at A's results with a skeptical eye. Likewise, when researcher B presents a result, researcher A will tend to be critical and look at it with a skeptical eye.

It should be obvious how this scientific process of error detection and cross-checking can be subverted when all the researchers share the same bias—and that bias bears directly on the research at hand. Unfortunately, this seems to be the case in the field of psychology, where the virtual homogeneity of political ideology among researchers means there can be no assurance that politically charged topics like those mentioned here will be approached with the necessary scientific objectivity.

It would be a mistake for psychologists to think that there are easy ways around the problem of this ideological monoculture which destroys the milieu of criticism and cross-checking that is essential to the pursuit of valid scientific research. However much they might think they could individually overcome the problem of myside bias by simply setting aside their ideological preferences while doing their science, study after study has shown that this is not possible. Indeed, such thinking would, in itself, indicate a bias blind spot.

Perhaps, though, there is an escape hatch for academic psychologists. It could be the case that academics actually have the "right" kind of ideology for studying myside bias. After all, for some years now, Democrats have argued that they are the "party of science" and that Republicans are the "party of science deniers" (more on this later). Perhaps the degree of myside bias that we have been observing in laboratory studies is all due to the Republicans in the sample and not due to the Democratic partisans at all. In such a case, the monoculture of Democrats in university social science research departments would not impede the study of any of the aforementioned topics. Alas, we know that this extreme hypothesis (we might call it the "immune Democrats hypothesis") is simply not true. Democrats do show myside bias in studies. Furthermore, we know that even a weaker form of this hypothesis—that Democrats are *less* disposed to myside bias than Republicans are—is also not true. The Peter Ditto and colleagues (2019a) meta-analysis mentioned in chapter 3 found that myside bias on social and political issues was equally strong on both ends of the ideological spectrum.

In short, there is no evidence that the particular *type* of ideological monoculture that characterizes the social sciences (liberal progressivism) is immune to myside bias. In fact, the findings of Ditto and colleagues (2019a) simply highlight the danger of academic cognitive elites thinking they can investigate controversial political topics about which they have strong opinions without compromising their research with myside bias. The particular ideologies of the academic cognitive elites are, in fact, no less driven by myside bias than the opposing ideologies of their study subjects are. But because of their cognitive sophistication and educational backgrounds, the cognitive elites of society will tend to think that their processing of evidence is less driven by myside bias than that of their fellow citizens.

A combustible brew of findings supports the existence of a massive myside bias blind spot among university faculty members, from studies showing that academics are largely of one ideological persuasion (e.g., Clark and Winegard 2020; Duarte et al. 2015) and from the Ditto and colleagues (2019a) meta-analysis showing that academics' particular ideological persuasion is as susceptible to myside bias as anyone else's. These same academics are cognitive elites in the sense that they have high cognitive ability as measured on intelligence tests and they have a high level of formal education. But, as we saw in chapter 3, high cognitive ability and a high level of education are no inoculation against myside bias. And, as we saw in chapter 4, few people—whether cognitive elites or not—have actually reasoned their way to their distal beliefs. Instead, both elite and nonelite thinkers have most often acquired their important distal beliefs unreflectively.

All of these findings point to the potential for cognitive elites having a particularly virulent bias blind spot. Universities are full of social scientists who believe they have *thought their way* to their viewpoints, whereas their ideological opponents have not—and this group of social scientists is not characterized by the kind of ideological diversity that would help its members ferret out myside bias in their research. But the myside bias blind spot in the academy is a recipe for disaster when it comes to studying the psychology of political opponents. Nowhere has this been more apparent than in the relentless attempts by academics to demonstrate that political opponents of liberal ideas are somehow cognitively deficient.

In Search of the Cognitive Deficiencies of Conservatives

The overwhelmingly left/liberal professoriate has been on a quest to find psychological deficiencies in their political opponents for quite some time, but the intensity of these efforts has increased markedly in the last two decades. The classic psychological work associating conservatism with authoritarian thinking (Adorno et al. 1950; Altemeyer 1981) was given new impetus by John Jost and colleagues' much-cited 2003 literature review reviving the "rigidity of the right" theme in modern social and political psychology. In the years since 2003, it has not been hard to find studies showing correlations between conservatism and intolerance, prejudice, low intelligence, close-minded thinking styles, and just about any other undesirable cognitive or personality characteristic.

The problem is that most of these relationships have not held up when subjected to critiques emanating from ideological framings different from most of the earlier research. These correlations were grossly attenuated or they disappeared entirely when important features of the research framing were changed (see Reyna 2018). For example, the 2013 study by John Chambers, Barry Schlenker, and Brian Collisson discussed in chapter 4 demonstrated that out-group tolerance, prejudice, and warmth are more a function of the degree to which the values of the target group match or conflict with the values of subjects than a function of the subjects' ideology. Liberal and conservative subjects alike were shown to display the same levels of intolerance and out-group rejection—they simply displayed these toward different groups.

In a follow-up study examining the responses of a representative sample of nearly 5,000 Americans, Mark Brandt (2017) showed that the perceived ideology of the target group was the main predictor of the relationship between ideology and prejudice. Liberal ideology was positively correlated with favorable attitudes toward LGBT people, atheists, immigrants, and women, but negatively correlated with attitudes toward Christians, rich people, men, and white people. Thus prejudice occurs on both sides of the ideological divide, but it tends to be directed toward different target groups (Brandt and Crawford 2019; Crawford and Brandt 2020). For example, Jarret Crawford (2014) found that the political intolerance directed at gun control advocates, pro-choice advocates, and gay marriage advocates by conservative subjects was matched in magnitude by the political intolerance directed at gun rights advocates, pro-life advocates, and anti–gay marriage advocates by liberal subjects. That is, both groups were equally likely to oppose the organizing, promoting, and information-disseminating efforts of the other side.

What all of these findings show is that neither liberals nor conservatives are intolerant or prejudiced *in general*. They are instead "culturist," to use Yuval Noah Harari's (2018) term—they support or oppose target groups depending upon whether they share cultural values with the groups in question (Goldberg 2018; Haidt 2016; Kaufmann 2019). Although overt racism is seldom openly articulated anymore in the United States, Americans will frequently display strong culturism. And, as Harari (2018) argues, it is not at all clear that culturism is a moral failing.

The "rigidity of the right" narrative has also been fueled by the misleading use of "feeling thermometers" in the relevant research (Regenwetter, Hsu, and Kuklinski 2019; see Brandt 2017; Correll et al. 2010), where groups are rated on a scale from 0 (cold/unfavorable) to 100 (warm/favorable) and the ratings are reverse-scored, with higher scores indicating degree of "prejudice." The potential for abuse here should be clear. When a finding deriving from these scales, such as "Psychological characteristic X is correlated with prejudice toward group Y," is reported, it does not at all mean that subjects low on characteristic X show any prejudice *at all* toward target group Y. It just means that subjects low on psychological characteristic X rate group Y lower than subjects who are high on psychological characteristic X. Both low and high scorers could be indicating highly favorable attitudes toward group Y and yet low scorers get labeled as "more prejudiced." Christina Reyna (2018) calls this "the high/low fallacy"—the tendency to split a sample in half, calling one group of subjects high and one group low, regardless of the absolute levels the two groups attain on the scale. This has allowed numerous researchers to label one group of subjects high in prejudice even though their absolute scores on the scale indicate very little antipathy. When the group labeled "high" also scores significantly higher on an index of ideological conservatism, the investigators then create the "clickbait" headline "Conservatives Higher in Racism."

This tactic is often used to label conservatives as "prejudiced." In chapter 4, we discussed the 2019 study by Riley Carney and Ryan Enos, who found that some observed correlations arose because liberal subjects showed more sympathy toward blacks than toward whites, whereas the conservative subjects in their study rated black and white target groups equally. Their results support Christina Reyna's (2018) point that many scales in the social psychology literature are measuring not prejudice or resentment or antipathy that conservative subjects display toward minorities but instead the special sympathy that liberal subjects display toward these minorities. They are not indications of the oppressive attitudes of conservatives, but are instead indicators of the hyperegalitarianism of liberals (al Gharbi 2018; Edsall 2018; Goldberg 2019; Uhlmann et al. 2009).

Research purporting to correlate conservatism with racism has also been given a boost by the use of racism scales that contain items that basically equate conservative social views with prejudice. Many of the different scales in use include items on policy issues such as affirmative action, crime prevention, busing to achieve school integration, or attitudes toward welfare reform. Subjects having legitimate policy differences with affirmative action or busing, or subjects indicating that they are concerned about crime, will almost always be scored in the "racist" direction on these scales (Reyna 2018; Snyderman and Tetlock 1986; Tetlock 1994). Even endorsing the view that hard work leads to success for many people in America will get subjects a higher score on a "symbolic racism" scale (Carney and Enos 2019; Reyna 2018). In such studies, the overt ideological bias of psychologists is blatantly obvious to any neutral observer. The clear purpose of such studies seems to be to label anyone who does not adhere to liberal orthodoxy as a "racist."

Jason Weeden and Robert Kurzban (2014) call this tendency to embed in a new scale items that assess the very concept that the researchers want to correlate with the new scale the "Direct Explanation Renaming Psychology (DERP) syndrome." The syndrome is ubiquitous in racism research. Psychologists want to investigate whether conservatism is associated with racism because, in actuality, they think that it *is*. First, they construct racism scale items that reflect conservative worldviews ("Anyone can get ahead in America if they work hard"; "Discrimination against African Americans in the United States is much less than it once was"; and so on). Then, they correlate this scale with a measure of self-reported liberalism or conservatism and, lo and behold, there is a correlation in the direction they expected. Basically, they have correlated a scale containing, in part, conservative beliefs, called the conservative beliefs "racist," and then reported as an empirical finding that conservatism correlates with racism—a perfect example of the DERP syndrome.

The tendency to use items that are biased toward liberal policy positions is not limited to research on prejudice and racism. José Duarte and colleagues (2015, 4) discuss a study that attempted to link the conservative worldview with "the denial of environmental realities." Subjects were presented with the following item: "If things continue on their present course, we will soon experience a major environmental catastrophe." If the subjects did not agree with this statement, they were scored as "denying environmental realities." But as Duarte and colleagues (2015) point out, "denying" implies that what is being denied is a descriptive fact. Without, however, a clear description of what "soon" or "major" or "catastrophe" means, the statement itself is not a fact—and so labeling one set of subjects as "science deniers" reflects little more than the ideological biases of the study's authors.

This tendency to conflate liberal responses with the "right" or ethical or fair or scientific or open-minded response is particularly pronounced in certain areas of social and personality psychology. It often takes the form of labeling any legitimate policy difference with liberalism as "dogmatism" or "authoritarianism" or "racism" or "prejudice" or "science denial." For more than two decades now, the items in so-called sexism scales have undergone such "concept creep" (Haslam 2016) in their attempt to label normal male behavior as psychologically damaging. There is now a form of sexism (called "benevolent sexism") that increases subjects' sexism scores if they endorse items affirming that women should be cherished and protected by men; that a man is not complete without a woman; that women should be rescued first in a disaster; that women are more refined than men; that women have a special moral sensibility; and that men should sacrifice in order to provide financially for the women in their lives (Glick and Fiske 1996). Someone would have to be entirely enveloped within the insular academic bubble not to see such studies as ideology masquerading as science. Indeed, the female subjects in these experiments disagree with the conceptual definitions of the authors of the studies. These experiments consistently find that women subjects do not view men who endorse these items as prejudiced against women (Gul and Kupfer 2019), and also that they view men who endorse such items as more "likable" and more "attractive."

In short, many of the research efforts to associate conservative attitudes with negative psychological characteristics, with labels such as "racist," "sexist," "science denier," "intolerant," or "prejudiced," fail to do so when the most standard and established scientific principles are invoked—principles such as convergent validity, testing of alternative explanations, accurate labeling of scale values, and operational definitions that do not guarantee what researchers set out to prove. There is, however, other research associating conservative ideology with negative psychological characteristics that is not so easy to dismiss.

There have been long-standing findings that conservatism displays a negative correlation with intelligence, although this correlation is quite modest. In a meta-analysis conducted by Emma Onraet and colleagues (2015), the correlation between conservatism and various measures of intelligence was −.13. However, there have been indications in the literature that social conservatism correlates negatively with intelligence, whereas, if anything, economic conservatism or libertarianism seems to correlate positively with cognitive ability (Federico and Malka 2018; Kemmelmeier 2008; Oskarsson et al. 2015). Noah Carl (2014b) found a −.26 correlation between a composite measure of social conservatism and intelligence but observed a +.21 correlation between a composite measure of economic conservatism and intelligence. This finding is consistent with other work showing that, although social conservatism shows a negative correlation with many desirable cognitive or personality traits, economic conservatism often displays a positive correlation with those same traits. Thus Noah Carl, Nathan Cofras, and Michael Woodley of Menie (2016) found that social conservatism was negatively correlated—but that economic conservatism was positively correlated—with scientific literacy and the tendency to rely on scientific evidence. Brian Caplan and Stephen Miller (2010) focused their study specifically on economic conservatism and found a positive correlation with intelligence.

Carl (2014a, 2014b) found, across several experiments and several measures of cognitive ability, that voters identifying themselves as Republicans had intelligence test scores 1 to 4 points higher than voters identifying themselves as Democrats. The differences were statistically significant because of the large sample size. When Yoav Ganzach (2016) reanalyzed the data reported by Carl (2014b) using race as an additional covariate and did the same with a new data set, he found virtually no difference between

Republican and Democratic subjects' IQs. Their studies actually converge in showing that differences in intelligence are essentially unrelated to party identification.[1]

Using the "feeling thermometers" method discussed earlier, Yoav Ganzach, Yaniv Hanoch, and Becky Choma (2019) studied the favorability ratings of the candidates in the 2012 and 2016 presidential elections as given by a large number of subjects in the ANES database. The correlations between favorability ratings and intelligence for Obama and Clinton were −.17 and −.03, respectively, and the correlations between the favorability ratings and intelligence for Romney and Trump were +.08 and −.08, respectively. Thus the favorability ratings of the Democratic candidates were no more correlated with intelligence than the favorability ratings of the Republican candidates were.

The large and growing literature on the relation between intelligence and ideology is at this point in time easy to summarize in the aggregate. There appears to be no evidence at all that Republicans are less intelligent than Democrats. When ideology is measured directly on self-report scales, the results are different for social conservatism and economic conservatism (Federico and Malka 2018). Social conservatism tends to show negative correlations with intelligence and economic conservatism tends to show positive correlations. Studies that do not differentiate between social and economic conservatism and liberalism will end up with measures of both ideologies that are unknown amalgams of social and economic concerns (Feldman and Johnston 2014). Omnibus, confounded measures of conservatism have shown negative correlations between it and intelligence, but these correlations are minuscule.[2] Thus academic researchers hoping to prove that their political opponents are less intelligent than their political allies have failed in their quest to find the cognitive deficiencies they clearly assumed were there.

On the other hand, it may be that whatever psychological deficiencies conservatives may have lie not in cognitive ability but rather in behavioral/thinking dispositions. In chapter 4, we discussed research showing that, when tested on the Big Five personality traits, liberal subjects tend to score higher than conservative subjects on openness and lower on conscientiousness. These findings may be comforting to liberals because most would rather be thought open-minded than conscientious if they had to choose between the two. But it is important to understand where thinking dispositions fit in a full model of rational thinking (see Stanovich, West, and Toplak 2016 for an extended discussion). Because thinking dispositions such as openness, flexible thinking, conscientiousness, and so on are the psychological mechanisms that *underlie* rational thought, maximizing these dispositions is not the criterion of rational thought itself. Rationality involves instead the maximization of goal achievement through judicious decision making and through optimizing the fit of belief to evidence. The thinking dispositions of the reflective mind are a means to these ends.

Certainly, high levels of commonly studied thinking dispositions such as actively open-minded thinking, belief flexibility, need for cognition, deliberativeness, and conscientiousness are needed for rational thought and action. But "high levels" does not necessarily mean that a maximum level is the optimal level for all people. Thus maximizing the thinking dis-position of deliberativeness, for example, might result in getting lost in interminable pondering and never making a decision. And maximizing the thinking disposition of belief flexibility might result in a pathologically unstable personality. Although it is clear that subjects scoring higher on tests of intelligence are cognitively superior, it is not at all clear that subjects scoring higher on tests of thinking dispositions such as openness or consci-entiousness are more likely to have a more optimal psychological makeup.

Another problem when interpreting a finding such as the correlation between liberalism and a trait like openness is that this finding reflects the DERP syndrome, at least to some degree (Weeden and Kurzban 2014). Evan Charney (2015) has pointed out how some items testing the thinking dis-position openness to experience on the much-used Revised NEO Personal-ity Inventory (NEO PI-R; Costa and McCrae 1992) require subjects to have liberal political affinities in order to score highly. The purpose of the item "I believe that we should look to our religious authorities for decisions on moral issues" is clearly to probe whether the individual is inclined to rely on authorities to determine moral beliefs. But the specific authority that subjects have to ignore in order to score highly is a religious authority. There is no corresponding item testing whether subjects are equally reli-ant on secular authorities. Is it more close-minded to rely on a theologian for moral guidance than to rely on a university "bio-ethicist"? To liberal subjects, the answer would be yes, but to other subjects, this item might seem to indicate the DERP syndrome. Charney (2015) notes that another item—"I believe that the different ideas of right and wrong that people in other societies have may be right for them"—seems to require that full-blown moral relativism be endorsed in order to receive a high openness score. But such strong moral relativism exists almost exclusively on the political left. Thus the item builds in a correlation between openness and liberalism.

One thinking disposition that has most consistently been correlated with ideology is the actively open-minded thinking (AOT) disposition, originally conceptualized by Jonathan Baron (1985, 1988) and subsequently operationalized in largely overlapping ways by several research groups (Baron, 2019; Haran, Ritov, and Mellers 2013; Sá, West, and Stanovich 1999; Stanovich and Toplak 2019; Stanovich and West 1997, 2007). A particular type of item, called a "belief revision item," tends to magnify correlations between the AOT scale and religiousness because it requires more cognitive decoupling (belief revision) from subjects who are religious-minded than it does from subjects who are not (see Stanovich and Toplak 2019). To a lesser extent, belief revision items disadvantage conservative-minded subjects as well. Nevertheless, even AOT scales containing none of the problematic belief revision items show significant correlations between liberalism and actively open-minded thinking in the range of .20 to .30 (Stanovich and Toplak 2019).

These results would seem to have established that liberals are superior on a crucial thinking disposition, one that should be directly related to myside thinking. The conceptual and operational definition of actively open-minded thinking is displaying tendencies to seek and process information that disconfirms prior beliefs; act for good reasons; tolerate ambiguity; and show a willingness to postpone closure in order to gather more information (Stanovich and Toplak 2019; Stanovich and West 2007). All of these tendencies would seem to be the ideal cognitive proclivities to have in order to avoid myside bias.

The problem is that the findings of empirical studies simply do not support this "Actively open-minded thinking reduces myside bias" narrative. Instead, Robyn Macpherson and I (Macpherson and Stanovich 2007) found that actively open-minded thinking failed to correlate with myside bias in both an argument generation and an evidence evaluation task. Richard West and I (Stanovich and West 2007) investigated four naturalistic myside bias effects: smokers were less likely to acknowledge the negative health effects of secondhand smoke; the more alcohol a respondent consumed, the less likely they were to acknowledge the health risks of alcohol consumption;

people who were more highly religious were more likely to think that religiosity led to honesty than were the less religious; and women were more likely to think that females were paid unfairly. However, we found that actively open-minded thinking interacted significantly with only one of these effects despite the large sample size (more than 1,000 subjects) and that it explained less than 1 percent of the variance.

Dan Kahan and Jonathan Corbin (2016) found an interaction between AOT scores and myside thinking, but the interaction was in the opposite direction from the one they had expected. Conservative and liberal subjects who scored high in actively open-minded thinking had more diverging opinions on climate change than conservative and liberal subjects who scored low did. Neil Stenhouse and colleagues (2018) found no significant interaction between actively open-minded thinking and ideological differences in climate change attitudes. Although not replicating the interaction observed by Dan Kahan and Jonathan Corbin (2016), the Stenhouse and colleagues (2018) results converged with both the Kahan and Corbin (2016) and the Macpherson, West, and Stanovich results (Macpherson and Stanovich 2007; Stanovich and West 2007) in finding no evidence that higher AOT scores attenuate tendencies toward myside thinking.

In a follow-up study, April Eichmeier and Neil Stenhouse (2019) found a significant correlation between actively open-minded thinking scores and party identification, but when they used an argument evaluation paradigm, they found no correlation between AOT scores and the myside bias observed in the argument strength ratings. Thus the findings from the Stenhouse lab (Eichmeier and Stenhouse 2019; Stenhouse et al. 2018) exactly parallel those from the Stanovich lab (Macpherson and Stanovich 2007; Stanovich and Toplak 2019; Stanovich and West 2007). Both labs found that AOT scores correlate in the .20 to .30 range with ideology or partisanship, but neither lab found an indication that actively open-minded thinking itself actually predicts the avoidance of myside bias.

When one steps back and looks at the last two decades worth of studies attempting to find links between conservative ideology and negative cognitive/personality psychological traits, one is struck by the low yield of these attempts, given the effort expended in terms of the sheer number of studies. There are a plethora of studies finding significant correlations between conservatism and measures of prejudice, but most of this literature is impeached because it does not control for the value conflict between the subjects and the target stimuli (Brandt and Crawford 2019; Chambers, Schlenker, and Collisson 2013; Crawford and Brandt 2020).

Some of the psychological characteristics that have been correlated with ideology are difficult to interpret because they have inverted U-shaped relationships with optimality. Personality characteristics such as openness and conscientiousness are traits of this type. When unbiased scales are used, studies find consistent negative correlations in the range of −.20 to −.30 between actively open-minded thinking scores and conservativism. Nevertheless, although conservatives score lower on AOT scales, they do not display larger myside bias effects than liberals.

A widespread tendency among psychology researchers is to build conservatism into the measurement of negative traits such as dogmatism and authoritarianism and then present the correlations between conservatism and these negative traits as if they were new, independent findings (Conway et al. 2016; Conway et al. 2018; Snyderman and Tetlock 1986; Ray 1983, 1988; Reyna 2018). Indeed, Lucian Gideon Conway and colleagues (Conway et al. 2016; Conway et al. 2018) have shown that it is possible, by using commonly used scales and building liberalism into the measurement of negative traits, to arrive at findings in the *opposite* direction— positive correlations between liberalism and authoritarianism, for example.

Conway and colleagues (2018) designed an authoritarianism scale on which liberal subjects score higher than conservative subjects. They simply took old items that had disadvantaged conservatives and substituted content terms that disadvantaged liberals. For example, the old item "Our country will be great if we honor the ways of our forefathers, do what the authorities tell us to do, and get rid of the 'rotten apples' who are ruining everything" was changed to "Our country will be great if we honor the ways of progressive thinking, do what the best liberal authorities tell us to do, and get rid of the religious and conservative 'rotten apples' who are ruining everything"; and similarly for other items in the scale. With these new items in place, liberal subjects scored higher on the new authoritarian scale for the same reason that conservative subjects had on the old scales— the content of the new scale specifically targeted the liberal subjects' views. Conway and colleagues (2016) had shown that exactly the same thing could be done with dogmatism scales.

It is embarrassing that the field of psychology took decades to acknowledge the necessity for such obvious controls as those employed by Conway and colleagues. Philip Tetlock (1986, 825) urged these controls on the field over thirty years ago: "Systematic study of such Ideology×Issue interactions should be a major goal of future laboratory and archival studies on this topic." That it took so long could itself be viewed as an indicator of the ideological monoculture in psychology that is now much discussed (e.g., Clark and Winegard 2020; Duarte et al. 2015). Indeed, I share in this embarrassment. It took me more than twenty years to realize that the belief revision items in my early actively open-minded thinking scales might be biased against religious subjects (see Stanovich and Toplak 2019). Even after all that time, I did not spontaneously have that idea. I was provoked into thinking that something was wrong when I observed the gigantic .70 correlations in the literature caused by items that had been invented in my own lab two decades before.

The Great White Whale of the Cognitive Elites: Finding Deficiencies in Trump Voters

Despite the low yield of the psychological research attempting to link conservatism with negative psychological traits, the impetus to find such associations became magnified by the surprising US presidential election results of 2016. Trump's victory increased the myside bias blind spot among cognitive elites because it seemed to make them even more sure that their political opponents were cognitively deficient.

In September 2016, in collaboration with my colleagues Richard West and Maggie Toplak, I published *The Rationality Quotient* (Stanovich, West, and Toplak 2016), which described our attempt to create the first comprehensive test of rational thinking. Because the book is very much an academic volume, we had expected our academic peers to engage with its statistics and technical details, and they began to do just that soon after it was published.

But then the November 8, 2016, United States presidential election intervened.

The tone of the emails I was receiving suddenly changed to gallows humor or outright sarcasm, like "Wow, you'll sure have a lot to study *now*" or "We sure need your test *now*, don't we?" Many of these emails implied that I now had the perfect group to study—Trump voters—who were obviously irrational in the eyes of my email correspondents.

After the election, I also received many invitations to speak, several with the subtle (or sometimes not-so-subtle) implication that I surely would want to comment—after first giving my technical talk, of course—on the flawed rational thinking of the voters who had done this terrible thing to the nation. One European conference that solicited my participation had as its theme trying to understand the obviously deficient thinking not only of Trump voters, but of Brexit voters as well. The wordy conference prospectus clearly presumed that every educated person would view any opposition to increased globalization as obviously irrational. As the author of a rational thinking test, I was seen as the ideal candidate to give the imprimatur of science to this conclusion. No less insistent have been friends and relatives who assume that I am the perfect person to affirm their view that a substantial number of people who cast ballots for Trump were irrational in their thinking.

My correspondents certainly reflected the prevailing opinion among cognitive elites in both Europe and America—that psychologically deficient and uninformed voters had endorsed disastrous outcomes that just happened to conflict with the views of the hypereducated (Fuller 2019). Certainly, subsequent to the 2016 election in the United States, high-caliber publications, from the *Atlantic* (Serwer 2017) to the *New Republic* (Heer 2016) to the *Wall Street Journal* (Stephens 2016), were nearly uniform in their relentless portrayal of Trump voters as "racist," "sexist," and "xenophobic." Writing in *Foreign Policy* magazine, Jason Brennan (2016) informed us that "Trump owes his victory to the uninformed" and that his victory was due to "the dance of the dunces." The agenda was sometimes baldly displayed, as in James Traub's 2016 essay "It's Time for the Elites to Rise Up against the Ignorant Masses." In the United Kingdom, the portrayal of Brexit voters in the elite media was largely similar (see Fuller 2019).

Despite the virtually unanimous feelings among cognitive elites, the results discussed in the previous section would seem to give us little reason to think that the average Trump voter was more irrational than the average Clinton voter. Rational thinking dispositions and intelligence are underlying cognitive processes that facilitate rational thinking. However, we have just seen that there are very small or nonexistent correlations between basic intelligence, personality, and thinking dispositions, on the one hand, and ideology or partisanship, on the other. This makes it unlikely that there would be differences in rationality between Trump and Clinton voters. In fact, as we shall see, from the standpoint of theory and other empirical data in cognitive science, it is actually very hard to argue that there are rationality differences between voters in any election, including the 2016 election.

When we talk about the Trump voters, the first thing to understand is that the vast majority of them were Romney voters in the previous election and McCain voters in the election before that. Statistically, most Trump voters were standard-issue Republicans. Some analyses, such as that of Ganzach, Hanoch, and Choma (2019), attempt to analyze whether there were characteristics over and above party affiliation that were different among the Trump voters, but it is important to realize that analyses such as these are isolating a tiny sliver of voters on the margins (al Gharbi 2018). The sliver of voters who may have tipped the election in favor of Trump in the Electoral College are not the same as the much, much larger slice of "Trump voters."[3] So when the charge is (as it was from my email correspondents) that the Trump voters are "irrational" (or that they are "racist" or "deplorable"), the "irrational" charge would have to apply to the Romney and the McCain voters, too. Thus when we analyze the upcoming evidence on rationality, I will use research that looks at partisan affiliation and ideology as well, because it has a 90 percent overlap with comparisons based strictly on Trump versus Clinton voters in 2016. The second caveat is that our focus will be on the *comparison* between voters of different types (Clinton voters versus Trump voters)—not the more global question of the *absolute level* of rationality among voters, which is a much larger and more difficult issue.[4]

We will take up issues of instrumental rationality (what to do) first and then move on to issues of epistemic rationality (what is true). The model of instrumental rationality used by cognitive scientists is one where a person chooses which of the available options has the largest expected utility. But "utility" is a slippery term, however. As used both by cognitive scientists and by decision theorists, utility does not refer to its common dictionary definition, "usefulness." Instead, in decision theory—and, specifically, in rational choice theory— utility refers to the good that accrues when a person achieves a goal. More important for our discussion of voter rationality, however, is that, in rational choice theory, utility is more closely related to the notion of worth or desirability than it is to that of pleasure or monetary value. For instance, people can gain utility from holding and expressing specific beliefs and values. Failing to realize this is the source of much misunderstanding about voting behavior.

When a person acts, the person's wants and desires are expressed as preferences. Decision theory is actually neutral on what a want or desire can be. It is the public that tends to emphasize money or material wealth, not decision theorists. Decision and rational choice theorists are perfectly happy to call the nonmaterial goal of seeking social prestige a desire with a utility value. Nor does every goal need to reflect strict self-interest in a narrow sense to have utility value. Thus we can have as *our* goal that other people achieve *their* goals, and that goal can have utility value for *us*. Many goals that motivate people are neither self-interested nor material, such as preserving the environment for posterity.

Oversimplified views of rational choice theory are behind many of the claims that the Trump voters were irrational. A common complaint about them among Democratic critics is that they were voting against their own interests. A decade ago, this was the theme of Thomas Frank's popular 2004 book *What's the Matter with Kansas?*, and it has recurred frequently since then. The idea is that lower-income people who vote Republican are voting against their interests because they would receive more government benefits if they voted Democratic. Many of these critiques contain the presumption that, to be rational, preferences must be self-interested and that people's primary desires are monetary. But, as previously noted, rational choice theory contains no such presumption, so, on that basis alone, the claim that those who vote against their monetary interests are irrational is unfounded.

Liberals making this critique of working-class Republican voters never seem to realize not only how misplaced but also how insulting it is. Their failure to see the insult illustrates precisely what they get wrong in evaluating the rationality of the Trump voters. Consider that these "*What's the Matter with Kansas?*" critiques are written by highly educated pundits, professors, and advocates. Perhaps we should ask some of them whether their own votes are purely self-interested and for their own monetary benefit. They will say no, of course—and they will deny as well that their votes are irrational. They will say that they often vote against their own monetary interests in order to do good for *other* people. Or they will say that their vote reflects their values and worldviews—that they are concerned about the larger issues (abortion rights or combating climate change or gun restrictions) that are encompassed by their worldviews. It never seems to occur to them that Republican voters may be just as attached to *their own* values and worldviews. The stance of the educated liberal making the "*What's the*

Matter with Kansas?" argument seems to be this: "No other voters should vote against their monetary interests, but it is not irrational for *me* to do so, because I am enlightened."

The implicit insult in the *"Kansas"* argument, which often goes unrecognized, represents a form of myside bias. For example, liberals who work for nonprofit organizations are often choosing their values over monetary reward. Likewise, conservatives joining the military are often also choosing their values over monetary reward. The *"What's the Matter with Kansas?"* argument seems to ignore or deny this symmetry. Many Republican voters with modest incomes cast a vote to help others rather than to serve their own monetary interests—precisely as do the liberal Democrats who find such Republican behavior puzzling. So no, neither the Kansas voters in Frank's book, nor the Trump voters are voting against their interests as these are broadly—and correctly—defined. Even if part of the *"Kansas"* critique is correct (they are voting against their purely monetary interests), that they may be sacrificing monetary gain in order to express their values or worldview does not make them irrational.

But what about temperament, character, and fitness for office? Surely it was irrational to vote for Trump if temperament, character, and fitness for office are important, Democrats might say. But this argument is not a slam dunk from the standpoint of rationality. It is simply not self-evident how people should trade off temperament, character, and fitness for office versus worldview in their voting choices. This is especially true in the 2016 presidential election, where the candidates were unusually far apart in their worldviews. In her speeches and comments, Clinton signaled to the electorate that she represented global concerns (supporting global climate change agreements, greater intake of refugees, and rights and protections for noncitizens) and the interests of the identity groups favored by most Democrats (LGBT people, African Americans, Hispanics)—or what I will call the "global and groups" worldview. In his speeches and comments, Trump signaled to the electorate that he represented the country ("Make America great again") and citizens with nation-level interests rather than group interests (opposing trade deals that disadvantaged American workers; securing the country's borders)—or what I will call the "country and citizen" worldview.[5]

Clinton and Trump differed more sharply in their worldviews than any other pair of candidates in 2016. Bernie Sanders would have watered down the global and groups worldview by opposing some trade deals, which made him less of a globalist than Clinton,[6] and by placing less emphasis on appealing to the Democratic identity groups. Similarly, Jeb Bush or Marco Rubio as a Republican candidate would have watered down the country and citizen worldview by being sympathetic to global trade deals and by appealing to certain identity groups favored by Democrats (Hispanic voters in particular). Clinton and Trump represented the global and groups and the country and citizen worldviews in much purer form. The issue for a Republican voter or an independent voter with a country and citizen worldview was thus how to weight the temperament, character, and fitness for office issue against worldview. Because there is no way to ascertain what weighting of these factors (temperament, character, fitness for office versus worldview) is optimal for a given voter, it cannot be said that a voter who chooses worldview over temperament, character, and fitness for office is irrational.

For my Democratic friends who demurred from my conclusion here, I posed a thought experiment in an essay I wrote for *Quillette* in 2017. I proposed that we imagine a scenario in which the candidates for a presidential election were Ted Cruz on the Republican side and Al Sharpton on the Democratic side. In this thought experiment, it is now the candidate with the global and groups worldview who has the character and fitness-for-office issues. Who would you vote for?

When I am successful in forcing Democrats to give a response to this imaginary election, a substantial number admit that they would vote for Sharpton.[7] They justify their choice by citing things that are very rational, given their worldview: they worry about appointments to the Supreme Court, abortion, and gun control legislation. The Democrats justify their choice in much the same way that the Trump voters did when they refused to disqualify him on the basis of temperament, character, and fitness for office. The Trump voters worried about open borders and encouraging cities to defy federal immigration law, and so on—they worried about threats to their country and citizen worldview in the same manner that the hypothetical Sharpton voters worry about threats to their global and groups worldview. The calculus of rational choice theory is not precise enough to dictate a particular weighting of temperament, character, and fitness for office versus worldview in something as abstract and multidimensional as a presidential voting choice. After choosing Al Sharpton over Ted Cruz, few

Democrats would consider themselves irrational. But, in the same manner, when those with the opposite worldview voted for Trump over Clinton, they were being no less rational.

If you are particularly ill disposed toward Trump voters, at this point, you may still be feeling that, deep down, there is something else wrong with them that was not covered in my discussion of instrumental rationality. You may feel that something in the domain of knowledge is wrong with the Trump voters: they don't know enough, or they seem to be misinformed, or they don't seem to listen to evidence. You would be right that there is something else that is worth assessing—another aspect of rationality that covers these additional concerns: epistemic rationality.

Concern with Trump voters in the epistemic domain is, however, not unique because Democrats have charged Republicans with epistemic irrationality for some time now. Liberal Democrats have become accustomed, as we all have, to media presentations that are critical of conservative Republicans who do not accept the conclusions of climate science, or those of evolutionary biology. These media presentations are correct, of course. The role of human activities in climate change is established science, and evolution is a biological fact. Thus it would be very tempting to say: "Well, the Democrats get climate science right, and Republicans get it wrong; the Democrats get evolution right, and conservative Republicans get it wrong; so therefore we liberal Democrats are getting everything factually right about all of the other charged topics that figure in political disputes—crime, immigration, poverty, parenting, sexuality, and so on." Such an argument is essentially the claim that Democrats are epistemically more rational than Republicans.

Some years ago, this type of thinking prompted the Democratic Party to declare itself the "party of science" and to label the Republican Party as the "party of science deniers." That stance spawned a series of books with titles like Chris Mooney's *The Republican War on Science* (2005). As a political strategy, this "party of science" labeling might be effective, but epistemic superiority cannot simply be declared on the basis of a few examples. In fact, any trained social scientist would be quick to point out the obvious selection effects that are operating. The issues in question (climate science and creationism versus evolution) are cherry-picked for reasons of politics and media interest. To correctly call one party the "party of science" and the other the "party of science deniers" would of course require a representative sampling of scientific issues to see whether members of one party are more likely than the other to accept scientific consensus (Lupia 2016).

In fact, it is not hard to find scientific issues on which it is liberal Democrats who fail to accept the scientific consensus. There are enough examples to produce a book parallel to Mooney's *The Republican War on Science*—one titled *Science Left Behind: Feel-Good Fallacies and the Rise of the Anti-Scientific Left* (Berezow and Campbell 2012). To mention an example from my own field of psychology: liberals tend to deny the overwhelming consensus in psychological science that intelligence is moderately heritable and that there is no strong evidence that intelligence tests are biased against minority groups (Deary 2013; Haier 2016; Plomin et al. 2016; Rindermann, Becker, and Coyle 2020; Warne, Astle, and Hill 2018). Liberals become the "science deniers" in this case.

Intelligence is not the only area of liberal science denial, though. In the area of economics, liberals are very reluctant to accept the consensus view that, when proper controls for occupational choice and work history are made, women do not make 23 percent less than men for doing the same work (Bertrand, Goldin, and Katz 2010; Black et al. 2008; CONSAD Research Corporation 2009; Kolesnikova and Liu 2011; O'Neill and O'Neill 2012; Solberg and Laughlin 1995). Just as conservatives tend to deny or obfuscate the research indicating the role of human activities in global warming, so liberals tend to deny or obfuscate the research indicating the greater incidence of behavioral problems among children in single-parent households (Chetty et al. 2014; McLanahan, Tach, and Schneider 2013; Murray 2012). Overwhelmingly, liberal university schools of education deny the strong scientific consensus that phonics-based reading instruction helps most readers, especially those who are struggling the most (Seidenberg 2017; Stanovich 2000). Many liberals find it hard to believe that the scientific consensus is that there is no strong evidence of bias in the hiring, promotion, and evaluation of women in STEM and other disciplines in universities (Jussim 2017a; Madison and Fahlman 2020; Williams and Ceci 2015). Liberal gender feminists routinely deny biological facts about sex differences (Baron-Cohen 2003; Buss and Schmitt 2011; Pinker 2002, 2008). In largely Democratic cities and university towns, people find it hard to believe that there is a strong consensus among economists that rent control causes housing shortages and a diminution in the quality of housing (Klein and Buturovic 2011).

I will stop here because the point is made. There is plenty of science denial on the Democratic side to balance the science denial of Republicans with regard to climate change and evolutionary theory. Neither political party is the "party of science" or the "party of science deniers." Each side of the ideological divide finds it hard to accept scientific evidence that runs counter to its own ideological beliefs and policies. This is consistent with the Peter Ditto and colleagues (2019a) meta-analysis finding of equal partisan myside bias.

But what about knowledge per se? Possessing the requisite knowledge relevant to social and political issues is also part of epistemic rationality (see Stanovich, West, and Toplak 2016). Perhaps the Trump/Republican voters have a deficit here, compared to the Clinton/Democratic voters. Most studies, however, have indicated that there are few differences in factual knowledge between Republicans and Democrats. The Pew Research Center (2015) News IQ surveys of 2015 reported results that are typical. Respondents in the survey sample answered twelve questions about current events (identifying the route of the Keystone XL pipeline, knowledge of how many Supreme Court justices are women, and so on). The results indicated that Republicans outperformed the Democrats on seven of the twelve items; Democrats outperformed the Republicans on the other five. On average, the Republicans in the sample answered 8.3 items correctly, the Democrats answered 7.9 items correctly, and the independents answered 8.0 items correctly (the 2013 survey produced similar results; Pew Research Center 2013).

Similar findings are obtained in specific areas of knowledge related to voting such as economics. Presenting an online seventeen-item questionnaire on economics to more than 2,000 respondents, Daniel Klein and Zeljka Buturovic (2011) found that respondents identifying themselves as "libertarian" or "very conservative" scored higher than those identifying themselves as "liberal" or "progressive." Rather than concluding that conservative respondents actually knew more about economics than liberals did, however, Klein and Buturovic stressed how such surveys can be skewed by the selection of questions (see Lupia 2016 for an extensive discussion).[8] For example, the item "Rent control laws lead to housing shortages" (correct answer: true) is more difficult for liberals to accept as true because it challenges their ideology; whereas the item "A dollar means more to a poor person than it does to a rich person" (correct answer: true) is more difficult for conservatives to accept as true because it challenges their ideology.

Measures of "knowledge" in such a domain are easily skewed in a partisan manner by selection effects. This is a version of the "party of science" problem already discussed. Whether the Democrats or the Republicans are the "party of science" depends entirely on how the issue in question is selected. The seventeen-item questionnaire used by Klein and Buturovic (2011) was relatively balanced in its selections (eight items biased against liberals and nine items biased against conservatives).

Similar sampling problems plague studies of conspiracy beliefs. These are important to study because the problem with the Trump voters may be not that they have acquired too little knowledge but that they have acquired too much *misinformation*. The early research literature on the relation between ideology and conspiracy belief seemed to suggest that conspiratorial thinking was, in fact, more strongly associated with the political right. But more recent research has suggested that this finding was simply a function of the distribution of specific conspiracy beliefs that were studied. Research using more balanced items has suggested that conspiracy beliefs are equally prevalent on both the political right and the political left (Enders 2019; Oliver and Wood 2014). We have confirmed this latter trend in the research literature in our own studies of our rational thinking measure, the Comprehensive Assessment of Rational Thinking (CART), which contains a subtest measuring the tendency to believe in conspiracy theories (Stanovich, West, and Toplak 2016).

Our subtest covered a wide range of conspiratorial beliefs (Dagnall et al. 2015; Goertzel 1994; Majima 2015; Oliver and Wood 2014; Swami et al. 2011). Most important, however, our measure included both right-wing and left-wing conspiracy items as well as a good number of conspiracy items that straddled the political divide. Unlike some previous measures, it was not just a proxy for right-wing political attitudes. Some of the commonly studied conspiracies that we assessed were about the assassination of President John F. Kennedy, the 9/11 attacks, fluoridation, the moon landing, the pharmaceutical industry, the spread of AIDS, the oil industry, and the Federal Reserve. The results from our study were consistent with more recent work on this issue. There was no significant correlation between political ideology and the score on the CART conspiracy beliefs subtest.

Although there is no strong evidence that there are differences in the knowledge acquired by liberal and conservative voters, it might be that the problem with conservatives (and Trump voters) is in the *way* they acquired that knowledge (in belief-*forming* mechanisms). There are right and wrong ways to acquire knowledge. A person can acquire a true fact in the wrong manner. A person acquiring a true political fact by searching exclusively for things that support the person's political position may well be acquiring knowledge in the technical sense, but the knowledge base will be skewed and selective. It will have been acquired in the wrong way. The degree of myside bias is a direct measure of this general tendency. But, as we saw in chapter 1, myside bias is ubiquitous, so the strong hypothesis that Republicans are characterized by myside bias and that Democrats are not was falsified years ago. Furthermore, the recent meta-analysis of Ditto and colleagues (2019a) addressed a weaker form of the hypothesis. They meta-analyzed forty-one experimental studies of partisan differences in myside bias that involved more than 12,000 subjects. After amalgamating all of these studies and comparing an overall metric of myside bias, Ditto and colleagues concluded that the degree of partisan bias in these studies was quite similar for liberals and for conservatives. Thus the lack of partisan differences found in actual acquired knowledge discussed here is mirrored by a lack of partisan differences in the biasing process of myside thinking.

In summary, both in terms of what knowledge is acquired and how that knowledge is acquired, there is no strong evidence that the Trump voters were more epistemically irrational than the Clinton voters were. In terms of both components of rationality—instrumental and epistemic—there is no strong support in the empirical literature for attributing a unique problem of rationality to Trump voters. But those who do not find this conclusion palatable might object that the analysis so far seems somehow too narrow. They would be correct: there are indeed broader aspects of rationality that I have not yet addressed.

We have discussed the idea that to think rationally, a person needs to take appropriate action given the person's goals and beliefs (instrumental rationality), and to hold beliefs that are congruent with the available evidence (epistemic rationality). It would be natural to think that what is being left out of this analysis is a person's tendency to adopt *appropriate* goals. But taking into account this third consideration moves us, critically, from a narrow to a broad conception of rationality (Elster 1983; Nozick 1993; Stanovich 2004, 2013). Traditional views of instrumental rationality are narrow theories because a person's goals and beliefs are accepted as they are, and evaluation centers only on whether a person is optimally satisfying the person's desires given those goals and beliefs. The content of a person's desires is not evaluated.

It might seem that a narrow conception of rationality that fails to evaluate desires allows a great deal of bad thinking to escape evaluation. But most work in cognitive science disproportionately addresses this narrow form of rationality—for good reason. Broad theories implicate some of the most difficult and vexing issues in philosophy, such as "When is it rational to be (narrowly) rational?" and "What goals are rational to pursue?" Our earlier discussion in fact strayed into the territory of broad rationality with my Ted Cruz versus Al Sharpton thought experiment. With that example, I was trying to illustrate the difficulty of evaluating goals. From the standpoint of a voter with the global and groups worldview, the choice was between a candidate who shared the voter's worldview but whose temperament was poorly suited to the presidency (Sharpton) and a candidate whose worldview was unpalatable to the voter but whose temperament was much better suited to the presidency (Cruz). The point was not to show that one or the other choice was correct for this voter, but simply to illustrate the difficulty of this type of trade-off and to provoke some associated recognition of the fact that the voter with a citizen and country worldview was presented with a similarly difficult trade-off when faced with a Trump versus Clinton choice. It was to highlight the potential myside bias involved in such judgments: a Democrat feeling the attraction of Sharpton over Cruz should similarly understand the attraction of Trump over Clinton for Republicans.

Of course, the thought experiment does not depend on a one-to-one feature analogy between Trump versus Clinton and Cruz versus Sharpton, only a gross similarity in the feature trade-off (worldview versus fitness for office). It is also revealing of the myside bias operating when we attempt to evaluate goals. Democrats who choose Sharpton in the thought experiment and who think that the Trump voters were irrational are showing a strong myside bias. They are signaling that they think they can do what philosophers cannot—discern which goals are irrational to have. Similarly, Republicans who voted for Trump and who think that the Democrats who pick Sharpton in the thought experiment are irrational are also showing a strong myside bias.

Evaluations of the expressive rationality (discussed in chapter 2) of our partisan opponents are invariably saturated with myside bias. Why our own side would choose to signal a value at a utility cost seems perfectly obvious—yet when our political opponents do it, it seems utterly irrational. Republicans can clearly see the irrationality of Democratic city councils divesting themselves of investments in corporations disliked by the left often at a substantial cost in real return on city-invested dollars. Democrats likewise can clearly see the irrationality of the Republicans not caring whether their "Just say no" to drugs campaigns actually work. Such judgments are overwhelmingly determined by myside bias. The other side is judged deeply irrational when it abandons cost-benefit analysis to signal a value choice, but when our own side sacrifices utility, money, or outcome goals in order to signal a value, that is okay because our values are right, seems to be the reasoning.

A similar myside bias occurs in the domain of beliefs. Climate change is the clear example of an issue that has become highly politicized and symbolic (Kahan 2015, 2016). When conservatives respond to a questionnaire item indicating that they doubt the evidence on anthropogenic climate change, their liberal opponents point in glee at their science denial. But in many cases the conservatives are responding in this manner simply to signal opposition to their political opponents, liberals, on an issue they know liberals hold dear (Bullock et al. 2015; Bullock and Lenz 2019). What the conservatives are really saying is that they will not accept the way that liberals will use the data from climate science (e.g., to argue for greater government control of the economy). The conservatives are concerned with expressing a value, not with epistemic accuracy.

The politics are reversed when it comes to data on the existence of sex differences or the heritability of intelligence. These are politicized areas, just as climate change is. When liberals respond to questionnaire items indicating that they doubt the evidence on sex differences or the evidence that intelligence is heritable, their conservative opponents point in glee at their science denial. But, in many cases, the liberals are responding in this manner simply to signal opposition to their political opponents, conservatives. What the liberals are really saying is that they do not trust the way conservatives will use the data from intelligence research or sex differences research. In short, each side accuses the other of epistemic irrationality when the opposing side switches from purely epistemic to expressive modes of reasoning. Even if we were to stipulate that expressive modes are less rational, there simply is no strong evidence that they are more prevalent among Trump voters than they are among Clinton voters.

In summary, the "great white whale" search for the deficient cognitive characteristics of the Trump voters has backfired on liberal psychologists,[9] who are just going to have to reconcile themselves to the conclusion that the cognitive science of rationality does not support their judgment in this case. You can say whatever you want about the rationality or irrationality of Trump *himself*, but cognitive science does not support the claim that his voters were irrational—or, more precisely, that they were any less rational than the Clinton voters were. Indeed, the judgment that these voters were irrational was driven by convictions of just the type that engender intense myside bias. Our judgments in the domain of politics are uniquely susceptible to myside bias.

6 What Should We Do about Myside Bias?

As the most curious of the cognitive biases, myside bias fits poorly within the list of biases previously identified in the heuristics and biases literature. It is not related to traditional measures of cognitive sophistication such as intelligence or education, nor to the thinking dispositions that underlie rational thought. The other biases in the literature tend to be less problematic for subjects scoring higher on these measures. It is also unusually hard to show that most myside processing is normatively inappropriate. Thinking in ways that bolster one's own group or social connections seems, even in the modern day, to have many instrumental advantages. Even when we choose to focus strictly on epistemic rationality, it appears that much of our myside processing is warranted. Jonathan Koehler's (1993) proof B positively sanctions our using a prior belief to evaluate new evidence in many situations, as long as the prior belief is a testable belief based on the rational accumulation of previous evidence. Only when the prior belief being projected onto new evidence is a distal belief (that is, a conviction) and not based on evidence relevant to the issue at hand can the projection of a prior belief onto new evidence be justifiably criticized. Even here, there may be little lost for the individual as long as the conviction is serving their instrumental ends of group solidarity.

There are, however, severe costs associated with myside bias at the societal level. In the United States (and in many other Western nations), political parties and ideologies have become the equivalent of modern tribes (Clark and Winegard 2020; Greene 2013; Haidt 2012; Iyengar et al. 2019; Mason 2018b; Westwood et al. 2018). Regrettably, we have let these tribes run roughshod over the nation's cognitive life—putting nonintellectual strategies designed to "score points" for the tribe ahead of objective debate about specific public policy issues. The myside thinking fueled by these tribal politics has rendered any consideration of evidence virtually moot in public policy disputes.

Dan Kahan and colleagues (Kahan 2016; Kahan et al. 2017) have written eloquently on how we need to decontaminate the discussion of public policies from the poisonous effects of conviction-based myside reasoning. They have argued that we need strong institutions that form a barrier between evidence evaluation and the projection of convictions. But, sadly, those institutions—in particular, the media and universities—have failed us in the early twenty-first century. Far from serving as an antidote to partisan-based myside processing (Golman et al. 2016; Iyengar et al. 2019), media entities such as Fox News, MSNBC, Breitbart, Vox, the *Washington Times*, and the *Washington Post* have turned tribalism and partisanship into workable business models. For their part, the universities have totally abdicated their responsibility to be neutral, unbiased arbiters of evidence on controversial issues. Instead, they have turned themselves into intellectual monocultures that police expression through political correctness in precisely the areas where we need open discussion the most: crime, immigration, poverty, abortion, affirmative action, drug addiction, race relations, and distributional fairness.

What is to be done? How can we counteract the most toxic kinds of conviction-based myside bias? In this chapter, we will explore some ideas at both the individual and institutional levels that might be helpful.

Avoid the Bias Blind Spot of the Cognitive Elites

If you have made it to this point in the book, you are definitely one of the cognitive elites discussed in chapter 5. Likewise, the many email correspondents upset with the 2016 election results who contacted me after the publication of *The Rationality Quotient* (Stanovich, West, and Toplak 2016) are also cognitive elites. Those correspondents thought (wrongly, as we saw in chapter 5) that any study of human reasoning would provide ample support for their view that the deciding voters in both the United States (the presidential election) and Great Britain (Brexit) in that same year were irrational. My correspondents seemed to think that political disputes are entirely issues of rationality or knowledge acquisition—and that greater general (or specific) knowledge will inevitably lead to their own political beliefs.

In short, my correspondents seemed to be engaging in what political scientist Arthur Lupia (2016, 116) calls the "error of transforming value differences into ignorance"—that is, mistaking a dispute about legitimate differences in the weighting of the values relevant to an issue for one in which your opponents "just don't know the facts." Years ago, in an elegant essay, Dan Kahan (2003) argued that this was exactly what had happened in the debate over gun control, which had been characterized by the "tyranny of econometrics"—arguments centered on "what studies show" in terms of lives saved by the use of weapons in self-defense, deterrence of crime, and the risk factor of having a gun in the home. Kahan (2003) further argued that the central issue would never be resolved nor would compromises ever be reached by mutual agreement on what the facts were because at the center of the debate was culture: what kind of society Americans wanted to have. Gun control proponents were swayed by the value they put on nonaggression and mutual safety enforced by the government. Gun control opponents were swayed by the value they put on individual self-sufficiency and the individual right of self-defense. These values tracked urban versus rural demographics (among others), and the weighting of these values by a particular individual in either of the opposing groups was not going to be much affected by evidence, if at all. Kahan (2003) recommended instead a more open and unconstrained discussion of cultural differences. He advocated for a more expressive debate in which people would feel free to articulate their values and cultural differences. But, after noting that "the hope that the gun control debate can be made less contentious by confining it to empirical arguments is in fact an idle one," Kahan (2003, 10) warned that "the unwillingness of most academics, politicians, and ordinary citizens to engage in a frank airing of their cultural differences ultimately deepens the acrimonious quality of the gun debate."

I think that a combination of strategic advantage and myside bias leads cognitive elites to resist the expressive debates about culture that Kahan (2003) recommended. With a view that clearly reveals their myside bias, they believe that if a dispute can be resolved by reasoning about facts, then they will always win because they are the experts on facts and reasoning. These cognitive elites believe that that their opponents disagree because they are ignorant and that appealing to the facts will expose their ignorance. As we saw in earlier chapters, however, cognitive elites are no more likely than nonelites to avoid projecting untestable distal beliefs onto evidence.

When it comes to political disputes, cognitive elites tend to overestimate how much these disputes are about which side has a better grasp of the facts and to underestimate how much of partisan disagreement is actually about a clash of honestly held values. We have undergone decades of progress (Pinker 2011, 2018) in which we have greatly mitigated most societal problems that have solely empirically based, non-zero-sum solutions (where some people in society can gain from a policy solution without other people losing). The contentious societal problems we are left with are those which are particularly refractory to solution through the use of the knowledge—facts—we already have. If a societal problem is squarely and contentiously in the domain of politics, it is probably *not* "just a matter of facts."

Two years ago, I participated in a special issue of the *Journal of Intelligence* (Sternberg 2018) on the role of intelligence and other thinking skills in solving contemporary world problems such as climate change, poverty, pollution, violence, terrorism, a divided society, and income inequality (among others). I argued that the many problems on this list may be in very different categories. Some of them, like poverty and violence, may be solvable by more rational policies. And, indeed, these problems actually *have* been greatly mitigated over time (Pinker 2011, 2018).

But other problems on this list—such as climate change, pollution, terrorism, income inequality, and a divided society—are of an altogether different kind from poverty and violence. For some of these, we may be looking not at problems we would expect to solve with greater intelligence, rationality, or knowledge, but rather at problems that arise from conflicting values in a society with diverse worldviews. For example, reducing pollution and curbing global warming often require measures that entail, as a side effect, restraining economic growth. The taxes and regulatory controls necessary to markedly reduce pollution and global warming often fall disproportionately on the poor. For example, raising the cost of operating an automobile through the use of congestion zones and increased vehicle and gas taxes impedes the mobility of poorer people far more than it does that of the affluent. Likewise, there is no way to minimize global warming and maximize economic output (hence jobs and prosperity) at the same time.

People differ on their "parameter settings" for trading off environmental protection against economic growth, but they do so not because some of them lack knowledge and others don't. Instead they differ because they hold different worldviews.

Because problems like climate change and pollution control involve trade-offs, it is not surprising that the differing values people hold may result in compromises that please *neither* side. It is the height of myside bias to think that if only those who oppose us were more intelligent, or more rational, or wiser, then they would set their trade-offs exactly where we set ours. There is in fact empirical evidence showing that more knowledge or intelligence or reflectiveness does not resolve zero-sum value disagreements such as these (Henry and Napier 2017; Kahan 2013; Kahan, Jenkins-Smith, and Braman 2011; Kahan et al. 2017; Kahan, Peters, et al. 2012).

The case of income inequality provides another illustration of the trade-offs involved in solving some societal problems. Political disputes about income inequality are conflicts between those who have differing values— not between those who are knowledgeable and those who are not. There is no *optimal* level of income inequality.

Take, for example, the fact that, even though income inequality has been increasing in the past few decades in most industrialized, first-world countries, *worldwide* indices of income inequality have been *decreasing* during the same period (Roser 2013). These two trends may well be related— through the effects of trade and immigration (Borjas 2016). The very same mechanisms that are supporting decreases in *world* income inequality may well be supporting increases in income inequality *within* the United States (Krugman 2015). Which of the two income inequality measures (world or United States) we want to focus on is, of course, a value judgment.

Likewise, consider the following facts about income inequality in the United States in the last thirty years: the top 10 percent of the population in income and wealth has pulled away from the middle of the population more than the middle has pulled away from the poor (OECD 2011). So, when trying to reduce overall income inequality—in the manner that would affect an omnibus statistic like the Gini index—we need to make a value judgment about which of these gaps we want to concentrate on more. The obvious answer here for any advocate for greater income equality— that we want to work on *both* gaps—simply will not do. Some of the policies focused on closing one of these gaps may well work to open up the other gap (Reeves 2017). When we say we are against income inequality, we really have to make a value judgment about which of these gaps means more to us.

In short, the "problem" of income inequality does not have a unique solution. Disagreements about income inequality arise from differences in values—not because one segment of the population has knowledge that the other lacks. Another societal problem on the list—a divided society—is a quintessential illustration of the kind of "problem" that is going to be most intractable to solution by appealing to intelligence, rationality, knowledge, or wisdom. Political divisiveness in society is largely the result of conflicts between values. Thinking that political divisiveness can be resolved by increasing any cognitive capacity would seem to be the epitome of a myside bias blind spot. To put it in plainer terms, for a conservative to think that if all of us were highly intelligent, highly rational, extremely knowledgeable, and very wise, all divisiveness would disappear because we would then all be Republicans would seem to be the height of myside thinking, just as it would be for a liberal to think that if all of us were highly intelligent, highly rational, extremely knowledgeable, and very wise, all divisiveness would disappear because we would then all be Democrats.

As cognitive elites, we can tame our myside bias by realizing that, in many cases, our thinking that certain facts (which, thanks to cherry-picking, we just happen to know) are shockingly unknown to our political opponents is really just a self-serving argument about knowledge that masks the fact that the political dispute we are talking about is a conflict of values. We focus on the "ignorance" of our opponents simply to deflect attention from our conviction that our *own* value weightings should prevail.[1]

Recognize That, within *Yourself*, You Have Conflicting Values

When liberals see conservatives opposing green initiatives, they accuse conservatives of not understanding the implications of global warming for the future. But when conservatives see liberals supporting expensive green initiatives, they accuse liberals of not understanding the facts about how declines in economic growth translate into more poverty and greater economic hardship for the most vulnerable members of our society. Both liberals and conservatives are mistaken in their characterizations. Most conservatives do care about the state of the environment and about the implications of global warming. Most liberals do understand that economic growth reduces poverty as well as hardship. Often both groups do know the facts— they just give different weightings to the value trade-offs: concern about the effects of future global warming and the maintenance of maximum economic growth. The more we realize that, for any given issue in contention, there are value trade-offs to consider, the less mysided our thinking will be.

Our myside bias can sometimes be tamed at the individual level by recognizing that such a clash of values is occurring not just *between* groups of partisans but also *within ourselves*, as suggested by the Philip Tetlock 1986 study discussed in chapter 3. The object of Tetlock's study, a differentiation complexity measure, was really an inverse measure of myside bias—one that operationalizes the processes that enable us to *avoid* myside bias. The subjects in his study reasoned about the kind of highly valenced issues— environmental protection, crime control, health care—that tend to generate a high level of myside processing. Tetlock (1986) found considerable domain specificity: individual difference variables were poor predictors of the differentiation complexity displayed by particular subjects on a specific issue. Instead, the differentiation complexity displayed on a specific issue was more strongly predicted by the degree of value conflict the subjects experienced in contemplating that particular issue. For example, when reasoning about their views on government surveillance, Tetlock's subjects reasoned with less myside bias when they valued both privacy *and* national security.

The way to get liberals to reason with less myside bias about the priority given to climate change initiatives is to remind them that they also care about the poor people who will be the first victims of any slowing in economic growth. Likewise, the way to get conservatives to reason with less myside bias about the priority given to climate change is to remind them that they also care about having a livable world for their children and grandchildren.

Samara Klar (2013), for example, found that Democratic voters, normally very supportive of reduced sentences for criminals, including sex offenders; of decreased spending on antiterrorism; and of increased spending on social services became less supportive of all three positions when reminded of the values they attached to their roles as parents. Awareness of their deeply felt need to protect their children and the future world their children would inhabit had the effect of making these Democratic voters less sympathetic to criminals and more concerned both with future terrorism and with budget deficits. Reminding them of their parental roles made them aware that conflicts in their values entailed trade-offs in their positions on these issues.

Unfortunately, politics as normally practiced operates under conditions totally unlike those set up in Klar's 2013 study. Politicians and political partisans present issues to us as if they entailed no value trade-offs. They imply that only one value is at stake and if we hold onto that value and take the most partisan position, then nothing is lost on other issues that we might care about. Because this is a fallacy embraced by both sides in our ideologically divided electorate, we could encourage less mysided political discussion by recognizing and exposing it as a cognitive trick that is being played on all of us.

Recognize That, in the Realm of Ideas, Myside Bias Causes an Obesity Epidemic of the Mind

Anything that makes us more skeptical about our beliefs will tend to decrease the myside bias that we display (by preventing beliefs from turning into convictions). Understanding that our beliefs are memeplexes with their own replicative interests can help us cultivate skepticism about them (see chapter 4). The memeplexes resident in our brains will tend not to take on ideas that are hostile to themselves because those hostile ideas might displace the current beliefs.

As we saw in chapter 4, organisms tend to be genetically defective if any new mutant allele is not a cooperator. The logic of memes is slightly different but parallel. Memes in a mutually supportive relationship within a memeplex would be likely to form a structure that prevented contradictory memes from gaining brain space. Memes that are easily assimilated and that reinforce previously resident memeplexes are taken on with great ease. Both social and traditional media have exploited this logic, with profound implications. We are now bombarded with information delivered up by algorithms specifically constructed to present congenial memes that are easily assimilated (Lanier 2018; Levy 2020; Pariser 2011). All of the congenial memes we collect then cohere into ideologies that tend to turn simple testable beliefs into convictions.

In *The Robot's Rebellion* (Stanovich 2004), I described the parallel logic of how free markets come to serve the unreflective first-order desires of both genes and memes. Genetic mechanisms designed for survival in prehistoric times can be maladaptive in the modern day (Li, van Vugt, and Colarelli 2018). Thus our genetic mechanisms for storing and using fat, for example, evolved in times when doing this was essential for our survival. But these mechanisms no longer serve our survival needs in a modern technological society, where there's a McDonald's on almost every corner. The logic of markets will guarantee that exercising a preference for fat-laden fast food will invariably be convenient because such preferences are universal and cheap to satisfy. Markets accentuate the convenience of satisfying uncritiqued first-order preferences.

Markets will do exactly the same thing with our preferences for memes consistent with beliefs that we already have—markets will make them cheap and easily attainable. For example, the business model of Fox News (targeting a niche meme market) has spread to other media outlets on both the right and the left, such as CNN, Breitbart, the *Huffington Post*, the *Daily Caller*, the *New York Times*, and the *Washington Examiner*. This trend has accelerated since the 2016 presidential election in the United States. The *New York Times* describes voters on the losing side of the election as flocking to media outlets that reinforce their beliefs (Grynbaum and Koblin 2017). One voter describes being increasingly drawn to MSNBC because "it's reinforcing to watch. It's the same reason I marched in the women's march. It's because I believe in it, and I want to be surrounded by other people who believe in it, too" (Grynbaum and Koblin 2017). Activist and writer Gloria Steinem wrote in an email: "I watch MSNBC for Joy Reid, Chris Hayes, Rachel Maddow and Lawrence O'Donnell because I trust them as journalists. . . . A journalist's job is not to be balanced; it's to be accurate" (Grynbaum and Koblin 2017).

In short, just as we are gorging on fat-laden food that is not good for us because our bodies were built by genes with a selfish replicator survival logic, so we are gorging on memes that fit our resident beliefs because cultural replicators have a similar survival logic. And just as our overconsumption of fat-laden fast foods has led to an obesity epidemic in this country, so our overconsumption of congenial memes has made us memetically obese as well. One set of replicators has led us to a medical crisis. The other set has led us to a crisis of the communication commons whereby we cannot converge on the truth (Kahan 2013, 2016; Kahan et al. 2017) because we have too many convictions that drive myside bias. And we have too many mysided convictions because self-replicating memeplexes rejecting memes unlike themselves have brought too much coherence to our belief networks.

The antidote to this obesity epidemic of the mind is to recognize that beliefs have their own interests, and for each of us to use this insight to put a little distance between our self and our beliefs. That distance might turn some of our convictions into testable beliefs, and the fewer of our beliefs that are convictions, the less myside bias we're likely to display.

Treat Your Beliefs Less Like Possessions by Realizing "You Didn't Think Your Way to That"

The title of this section is a play on a much-discussed political riff by President Obama on the campaign trail in July of 2012—the famous "You didn't build that" riff, where he said, "Look, if you've been successful, you didn't get there on your own. . . . I'm always struck by people who think, well, it must be because I was just so smart. . . . If you were successful, somebody along the line gave you some help. There was a great teacher somewhere in your life. Somebody invested in roads and bridges. If you've got a business—you didn't build that. Somebody else made that happen. The Internet didn't get invented on its own. Government research created the Internet so that all the companies could make money off the Internet" (Kiely 2012). The president's statement caused a controversy in our partisan age, but of course it should not have. The point here is pretty clear and actually well established in the literature of social psychology. Psychologists have studied what is known as the "fundamental attribution error" (Ross 1977), which occurs when people underemphasize the situational determinants of their own behavior.

My version of President Obama's riff extends to our strongest beliefs (convictions), and it goes even deeper than his examples do. Our resident beliefs are the result of interacting with the ideas of others. They are the products of our lifetime of experience. But decades of research in cognitive science have taught us that much of our information processing occurs beyond our awareness. This is particularly true when new information melds well with preexisting biological substrates in our brains. We tend to overestimate how much we have consciously thought our way to our beliefs. Like successful businesspeople who overestimate how much of their wealth was due to their own unique creativity and efforts, most of us tend to overestimate how much conscious thought we have used to arrive at our strongest opinions and convictions.

Fully processing this insight might make it easier for us to heed the admonition to project only testable beliefs onto new evidence rather than convictions that have a partisan origin. When you treat your convictions less like possessions, you are less likely to project them onto new evidence inappropriately. And you will feel less like your convictions are your possessions when you realize that you did not consciously reason your way to them. It is important, though, to understand what does not follow from this point. First of all, to say that you have not thought your way to your convictions does not mean that your convictions are meaningless. To the contrary, you value your beliefs for good reasons. Indeed, your beliefs may reflect the biological substrate that makes up your behavioral and psychological temperament. Your beliefs may also reflect your life experiences, including experiences within your family, your employment, and your romantic experiences, all of which carry great meaning and are a part of you. But it is important to understand that none of this reflects *thinking* on your part. For even though your current beliefs are a valued part of your life, you should not value them because you think they are things you *consciously* chose.[2]

Be Aware That Myside Bias Flourishes in Environments of Ambiguity and Complexity

In a study we touched on in chapter 1, Kyle Kopko and colleagues (2011) found that rulings on the adequacy of challenged ballots in elections were infected by partisan bias. Examining performance based on whether the rules for classifying the ballots were specific or ambiguous, Kopko and colleagues also found that the more ambiguous the rules, the more myside bias was displayed. Although this may not seem to be a surprising result, it is an important one nonetheless—one that highlights a kind of meta-awareness we can all use in taming our own myside bias. For when it comes to controlling our own myside reasoning, ambiguity is not our friend.

It is not encouraging to know that ambiguous situations spawn myside bias. Complexity magnifies ambiguity, and the ever-proliferating, internet-fueled universe of information we are experiencing is increasing the complexity of the world. Thus the more evidence there is, of all types—good and bad, on this side and on that—the easier it is to select from it with a myside bias. Both the increasing complexity and the increasing quantity of social exchange that occurs over the Internet make verifying what is actually going on in the world much more difficult. Now we want to know what proportion of Twitter accounts are really Russian bots, and how many millions of people saw how many thousands of fake political advertisements on Facebook and where the advertisements came from. We want to know whether social media harassment of a certain type is growing or declining, and where the harassment is coming from, and who are the sources of the harassment. We want to know the answers to questions like this, but we are also asking these questions in a context that includes facts like (1) as many as 15 percent of Twitter accounts (47 million) may actually be bots (Varol et al. 2017); and (2) the number of people logging on to Facebook in the same day recently reached one billion (Levy 2020).

In such a context, these are not questions that even the most accomplished scientists can address on their own. In fact, questions about social media and Internet-related topics can only be answered by those with big data resources and infrastructure. Jeff Horwitz (2020) describes the difficulties that researchers face when they attempt to study the nature and extent of fake news on social media. In the year 2018, Facebook announced that it would cooperate with a group of researchers in a project called "Social Science One," in which Facebook would provide access to a billion gigabytes of information so that academic researchers could study how information is shared on the platform and examine patterns in the spread of fake news. The researchers expected that they would have a functioning data set within about two months after initiating the project. Instead, it took them two *years* to have a functional data set, with most of that time spent negotiating with Facebook. Very few academic researchers can afford to spend that much downtime on a politically charged project that might fall through in the end because, ultimately, a private company controls the data set.

Questions about communication patterns over the Internet and social media are unprecedented in their high levels of complexity and thus also in their ambiguity. As such, they will almost certainly become areas for the display of high levels of myside bias. In early editions of my supplemental research text (Stanovich 2019), I talked about replication in psychology as an open process in the sense that any researcher could embark on a replication of virtually any study in psychology with a minimal set of resources.

This is unfortunately no longer true: big data resources are now necessary to answer more and more questions about behavior on the Internet. And these questions are unapproachable by most researchers both because of the logistics of dealing with gigantic data sets and because the nature of the activity is made opaque by the proprietary algorithms of major corporations (Levy 2020; Pariser 2011). When Facebook, for example, began its investigation into Russian interference in the 2016 election through politically based ads on its platform, its researchers had to start searching through the activity of five million advertisers at the time who were creating millions of different ads every single day (Levy 2020).

The sheer magnitude of Internet communication makes answering questions that involve algorithmic targeting (questions like "Exactly who saw exactly what, sent by exactly whom?") extremely hard, if not impossible, to answer. In 2018, the cloud software company Domo reported that humans were generating more than 2.5 quintillion (2.5×10^{30}) bytes of data daily (Domo 2018). The resulting exponential growth in data on the Internet has combined with technological complexity to greatly increase the number of ambiguous environments that we then "clarify" for ourselves by projecting our own myside bias. Given that Facebook has already removed at least one billion fake accounts (Facebook, n.d.), our concerns about conspiracy theories and fake news will not be going away anytime soon. Several years ago, the term "infodemic" (a play on the term "epidemic") was coined to mark certain situations of modern life (Zimmer 2020) where we have such an overabundance of information, both accurate and inaccurate, that it is almost impossibly hard for people to come to accurate conclusions. Whether "cyberattacks" or "hate campaigns" have occurred on the Internet or whether particular claims of such attacks are themselves hoaxes (Neuding 2020) is almost impossible for the average citizen to ascertain. As a result, average citizens are entirely reliant on media "experts" to help them decide on what is actually true. The selection of which experts to listen to, however, will be an entirely mysided affair.

Issues do not have to be partisan to become entangled with misinformation on the Internet. The pseudoscientific theory that autism is connected to the early vaccination of children against measles, mumps, and rubella was, and is, kept alive by "paranoia peer groups," to use Jaron Lanier's (2018) phrase. This theory is false, disproved by voluminous findings to the contrary (Grant 2011; Nyhan et al. 2014; Offit 2011), but it is impossible to quell the misinformed conversations about it that circulate in the uncontainable memosphere of the Internet.

Ambiguity also arises when people try to argue about small segments of a much larger set of events. So, for example, arguments about whether particular weather events are due to climate change are likely to be highly saturated with myside bias because the causal history of a *particular* event in a much larger aggregation is often quite ambiguous. In contrast, because large aggregations of particular weather events are much less causally ambiguous, discussion of global warming itself, as an *aggregate* pattern extending over many years, should be much less mysided. And arguments about the trend of the economy *right now* are apt to be subject to a great deal of myside bias because such a short-term trend is highly ambiguous, whereas, over longer periods of time, aggregate economic trends are much less ambiguous, and arguments about them are therefore apt to be much less mysided.

Avoid Activating Convictions by Resisting Unprincipled Bundling

Myside bias is driven by our convictions, but many of those convictions are themselves driven by partisanship (Leeper and Slothuus 2014). In this section, we will explore a few of the curious properties of partisanship as a generator of myside bias. We will see that some of the mysided behavior generated by partisanship is, in a certain sense, unnecessary. That is, we would not have the conviction driving our mysided behavior on many issues had we not known the position taken by our partisan group. Hyperpartisanship turns testable prior beliefs that we might have held with modest confidence into protected distal beliefs that we cling to with the strength of convictions. Often, we would never have arrived at a partisan conviction by independent thought.

Research has shown that most people are not very ideological (Kinder and Kalmoe 2017; Mason 2018b; Weeden and Kurzban 2016). They do not think much about general political principles, and they hold positions on particular issues only when the issues tend to affect them personally. Their positions from issue to issue tend to be inconsistent and are not held together by a coherent political worldview that they can consciously articulate. Studies tend to find that positions on issues consistently cohere in a way that looks like an ideology only for people who are deeply involved in politics or highly educated and immersed continuously in high-level media sources. In contrast to this ideological-minded minority, Jason Weeden and Robert Kurzban (2016) classified 80 percent of the sample they studied as only "nominally ideological": although they used ideological labels like "liberal" and "conservative" in a meaningful manner and classified themselves as such, they displayed very little ideological alignment in their stances on issues across a variety of domains. Thus, if they were "liberal" in the religious domain, they had little tendency to also be "liberal" in the economic domain (correlations in the range of .02 to .05); if they had "liberal" positions on issues in the social domain, they were only moderately likely to have "liberal" positions on issues in the economic domain (correlations in the range of .35 to .45); and they also showed very little ideological consistency when taking positions in both religious and social domains (correlations in the range of .05 to .10).

In contrast, the 20 percent of the sample subjects who appeared to be genuinely ideological showed ideological consistency correlations of .20 to .30 across the religious and economic domains; correlations of .20 to .35 across the religious and social domains; and correlations of .55 to .60 across the social and economic domains. More important, with their high levels of education and high scores on tests of knowledge and cognitive ability, these subjects were, in short, cognitive elites. And only among these cognitive elites was there ideological alignment. For example, across the three time periods examined in the Weeden and Kurzban 2016 study, party preference was moderately to strongly predicted by the positions taken on the issues for the genuinely ideological 20 percent of the sample (multiple R squares of .258, .360, and .476, respectively). But for the remaining 80 percent of the sample subjects in those same three time periods, party preference was much less strongly predicted by the positions taken on the issues (multiple R squares of .083, .126, and .194, respectively).

Weeden and Kurzban (2016) found that ideological consistency increased over time for the 20 percent in their sample who were cognitive elites, but that this trend did not hold for the remaining 80 percent of the sample. Other studies have converged with their findings in showing that the vast majority of the population is only nominally ideological, and their stances on issues lack principled alignment (Kinder and Kalmoe 2017; Mason 2018a, 2018b). These findings present a puzzle in terms of understanding the increasing partisan animus and polarization that most people observe in United States politics (Westwood et al. 2018). If most of us are not ideological, why are we politically polarized as a society?

That most people lack ideological consistency does seem genuinely at odds with the fact that our nation has become increasingly characterized by angry partisanship. Political scientists have for many years been measuring the phenomenon of affective polarization between partisans. There are many different questionnaires and indicators used to measure affective polarization, and all have shown a striking increase in partisan animosity over the last few decades, particularly in the last decade (Iyengar et al. 2019; Pew Research Center 2019). Studies using the "feeling thermometers" discussed in chapter 5 found that, whereas the affective polarization was roughly 23 degrees in 1978, it had almost doubled to roughly 41 degrees in 2016 (Iyengar et al. 2019). Most of the increase in polarization, it is important to note, came from an increase in "negative partisanship"— from subjects increasing their negative feelings toward the opposing party rather than from increasing their positive feelings toward their own party (Abramowitz and Webster 2016, 2018; Groenendyk 2018; Pew Research Center 2019). Social distance measures have supported a similar conclusion. In 1960, fewer than 5 percent of Americans reported that they would be upset if their child married someone from the other political party. By 2008–2010, that proportion had grown to between 25 and 50 percent (Iyengar, Sood, and Lelkes 2012; Iyengar et al. 2019). Americans were eight times as likely in 2008 as they were in 1960 to think that members of the opposing party were less intelligent and more than twice as likely in 2008 as they were in 1960 to think that members of the opposing party were more selfish than members of their own party (Iyengar, Sood, and Lelkes 2012).

Thus our nation has become increasingly divided politically, even though studies show that, as voters, most of us are neither increasingly extreme nor increasingly consistent in our ideologies. What is behind this seeming paradox? The key insight here is that this is really not a paradox at all. First, increasing partisanship is not driven by the increasing extremity of people's ideologies nor by the increasing consistency of their ideologies. Instead, it has been driven by parties and party ideologies taking on the roles and characteristics of tribes (Clark and Winegard 2020). In chapter 2, we touched on a study by Lilliana Mason (2018a) that found the degree of affective polarization between groups of political partisans to be driven much more by "identity-based" than by "issue-based" ideology. Finding partisan identification to be statistically a much stronger predictor than actual differences on specific issues, Mason (2018a, 885) concluded: "The power behind the labels 'liberal' and 'conservative' to predict strong preferences for the ideological in-group is based largely in the social identification with those groups, not in the organization of attitudes associated with the labels," and she titled her paper "Ideologues without Issues" (see Cohen 2003 and Iyengar, Sood, and Lelkes 2012 for converging findings).

Noting the well-replicated finding that most Americans hold what political scientists call "unconstrained attitudes" on issues (attitudes that do not hang together in any ideologically coherent way), Mason (2018a) argued that a partisan stance can be a way not just of reflecting a subject's policy attitudes but also of marking both the subject's identity and the "otherness" of those in the opposing party. She suggested that party as identity may simply mark a sense of inclusion and exclusion—a sense of us versus them (see also Greene 2013; Haidt 2012). Our sense of partisanship, Mason (2018a) concluded, is more about our sense of connection to like-minded others than about our stances on specific issues; her conclusion converges with that of other studies finding that partisanship is a matter more of identity-based expression than of issue-based instrumental calculation (Huddy, Mason, and Aaroe 2015; Johnston, Lavine, and Federico 2017).

Mason's (2018a, 2018b) findings converge with those of Weeden and Kurzban (2016) discussed earlier and buttress the larger conclusion that our nation is being led into affective polarization by cognitive elites. Four-fifths of the subjects in the Weeden and Kurzban (2016) sample showed very little cross-domain ideological consistency, and their degree of consistency did not seem to increase over time. In contrast, the cross-domain consistency among the cognitive elite 20 percent in their sample was much higher and, more important, it did increase over time. This suggests a model where a relatively unideological population, through identification with parties controlled by cognitive elites, is being led to support positions on issues they would not otherwise have held.

Understanding the implications of the results of Weeden and Kurzban (2016) can help us avoid myside bias on specific issues. They remind us that when we move from one issue to another, our political opponents are *not the same people*. The modest correlations across domains ensure that, statistically, our political opponents on issue A are a very different subset of people than our opponents on issue B. You may feel less tribal and less inclined to engage in mysided reasoning if you take this to heart.

Based on the findings of a wide range of studies, most American voters can't articulate a principle behind their stance on a particular issue and often don't know their stance on many issues until they hear the stance supported by their own partisan group. A study by Geoffrey Cohen (2003) is relevant here. Using attitudes toward welfare policies as the focal issue, he found that party recommendation of a policy was a more potent predictor of subjects' approval than the actual content of the policy. It was as if the subjects did not know their position on the issue until they were told which party was supporting it. Reporting longitudinal survey evidence that increasing ideological consistency is not driving affective polarization, Yphtach Lelkes (2018) pointed out that many partisans dislike one another even when they do not disagree very much about most issues.

The issue-by-issue inconsistency of most people suggests a way we might alleviate myside bias fueled by partisan polarization. My recommendation would be to follow the lead of the *non*elites. Go ahead and be "inconsistent" from your party's point of view. Stop trying to be consistent because many of the issues that are bundled together to define our political parties are simply *not linked by any consistent principle*. They have instead been bundled for political expediency by partisan elites on both sides.[3] As Christopher Federico and Ariel Malka (2018, 34–35) note: "Political elites strategically bundle substantively distinct political preferences and attempt to 'sell' these bundles as ideologies to the general public. . . . Such menu-dependent and expressive motivation can sometimes lead one to adopt an issue position . . . that is opposite of the position one might have 'organically' preferred."

If major political issues really *should not* cohere very strongly with one another, then maybe those of us who wish to tame our own tribe-based myside bias (Clark and Winegard 2020) should be skeptical about taking a position on an issue we know nothing about just because that's the position our party takes. Understanding the arbitrariness[4] and expediency behind position bundling by both parties should help us all to avoid letting our partisanship turn our testable beliefs into distal ones.

It is important to realize that, by being a partisan, you will often end up supporting positions that you would not otherwise have taken were it not for the fact that these positions have been bundled by the political operatives of your party for reasons of electoral advantage. At worst, by being a partisan, you will end up supporting positions you do not actually believe in. In his philosophical analysis of this problem, which he frames as an epistemic challenge for modern partisanship, Hrishikresh Joshi (2020) lists a whole set of issues through which we channel our partisan-based affective polarization: gun control, policing, abortion, regulating corporations, the minimum wage, taxing carbon emissions, illegal immigration, gay marriage, race-based college admissions. He begins by pointing out that positions on many of these issues are as likely to be orthogonal as they are to be correlated. Joshi argues that, ironically, the epistemic challenge is largest for the partisan cognitive elites because it is they who show the highest partisan correlations across issues (Lelkes 2018; Mason 2018a; Weeden and Kurzban 2016). Because of their high alignment with the positions of their respective parties, partisan cognitive elites on both sides support a variety of positions that do not in fact cohere—indeed, actually conflict—with one another

In light of the research we reviewed in chapter 5, which indicated that partisans on both sides of the political divide exhibit very few differences in knowledge, reasoning ability, or epistemic tendencies, it is extremely unlikely that partisans on either side are "right about everything," to borrow a phrase from the title to Joshi's 2020 paper. That being the case, it follows from Joshi's analysis that those with high issue correlations on both sides should feel the maximum rational or reflective pressure to moderate their beliefs.

Thus it is the readers of this book and its author who should feel the most pressure to moderate our partisanship. We, and indeed all cognitive elites, are the ones who have high levels of issue alignment with party, not those with less cognitive capital (Weeden and Kurzban 2016). In fact, it is relatively easy to see the fissures in the modern position bundles, or "menus," as Federico and Malka (2018) call them. Actually, some of the juxtapositions seem downright incoherent. Consider, for example, that conservative Republicans say they are for traditional values, stable families, cohesive communities, and free-market capitalism. The problem is that the last of these four simply does not cohere with the first three, for there is no greater disruptive force in the world than unrestricted capitalism. The business pages of our newspapers and electronic media constantly tell us that capitalism's "creative destruction" (leaving behind old ways of production in order to promote the more efficient new ways) is what generates our impressive material wealth, and this may well be true. But among the most notable things that are "creatively destroyed" by capitalism are traditional values, stable social structures, families, and cohesive communities. Things like the rise in temporary employment and just-in-time manufacturing make the time and place of day-to-day employment unstable in ways that disrupt family life. Big-box stores and e-commerce have destroyed the commercial districts in small towns. The traditional values that conservative Republicans have historically espoused are at war with the societal disruption spawned by the global capitalism also espoused by their party (Lind 2020).

Similarly, the liberalism of the Democratic Party is characterized by issue positions at war with one another. Liberal Democrats, for example, have taken the lead in pushing legislation aimed at combating future global warming. In many liberal cities, the local legislation takes the form of encouraging people onto bikes and mass transit by making commuting by automobile more difficult and more expensive. But the push toward green initiatives at the city level clashes badly with the liberal Democrats' claim to always be on the side of the poor, for the very first people most harmed by making driving more expensive will be poor Americans forced out of their cars and onto mass transit, and out of jobs that require a vehicle. The affluent will simply pay the increased DMV charges, vehicle taxes, congestion charges, and transportation levies and keep on driving. Thus the Democratic Party's concerns about climate change and its advocacy for the poor are at war with each other, just as the Republican Party's support for global capitalism and the party's championing of family values are.

In fact, each side in our partisan debates often argues—convincingly— how positions on the *other* side are inconsistent and aligned in a seemingly incoherent manner, and such arguments are often quite effective. In the abortion debate, it is common for pro-choice advocates to point out the inconsistency of the pro-life advocates who want to preserve the life of the unborn but not the life of someone on death row. This argument is often effective and compelling, but so is the counterargument by pro-life advocates, who point out the inconsistency of their pro-choice opponents in opposing the death penalty but supporting abortion—in seeming to find the deaths of criminals—but *not* the deaths of the unborn—unacceptable. When pro-choice advocates argue that many innocent people have been executed, the pro-life advocates counter that *all* of the unborn are innocent. Thus, when it comes to inconsistency on the part of their opponents, both pro-choice and pro-life advocates seem to have compelling arguments. The normative recommendation here, following Joshi (2020), would be that each side moderate its opinion on at least one, if not both, of these issues. These two issues are much more independent of each other than you might expect from the tight bundling encouraged by partisan thought leaders.

Michael Huemer (2015) discusses several cases of seemingly strange position bundling in our current politics. Supporters of animal rights wish to extend the umbrella of moral concern to beings less sentient and less biologically complex than humans. It would seem, then, Huemer (2015) argues, that animal rights activists should be pro-life proponents as well. The human fetus, a being less sentient and biologically complex than a born human, would seem to be in the forefront of beings in need of the extended moral protection at the heart of the animal rights position. Yet the results of empirical studies of political attitudes consistently find that the correlation goes, somewhat shockingly, in the opposite direction: people who support protections for animals that are much less complex and sentient than humans are *more* likely to support aborting human fetuses. Some vegans, for example, who will not eat honey because of the damage it might do to the bees, turn out to be vociferous supporters of unrestricted access to abortion.

We could argue about whether the correlation between these issues should be negative, but it is hard to think of one coherent moral principle that links these two issues in a *positive* direction. To be clear, I am not arguing that *either* of the positions on these *particular* issues is wrong or irrational, only that the juxtaposition of these two clashing moral judgments seems more likely to have resulted from people accepting the partisan bundling of these positions than it does from independent thought about each.

Other bundlings of issue positions are equally strange. It is not clear why forgiving student loan debt is a position of the Democratic Party—the party that deplores wealth inequality—when forgiving student loan debt favors the more affluent (Looney 2019). The expansion of charter schools is opposed by the Democratic Party and a majority of its white voters (Barnum 2019). However, a bundling conflict arises around this issue position because the party purports to be the advocate of minorities—but in fact a much greater percentage of African Americans and Hispanics than of white Democrats support the expansion of charter schools. Of course, the electoral calculus here is no secret. The Democratic Party wants to placate the teacher unions who are part of its coalition. But that is just my point. This bundling is done for political, not principled, reasons.

That the bundling of issue positions is done for reasons of political expediency is strongly suggested by the speed and magnitude of changes in the policy positions of the two parties. It took only a few years for the Republican Party to go from opposition to budget deficits when President Obama was in office, to support for massive budget deficits under the Trump administration (Alberta 2019). It took not much longer for the Democratic Party to go from opposing illegal immigration because it depressed the wages of low-skilled workers to being the party that supports sanctuary cities and that advocates for almost all undocumented persons (Borjas 2016; Lind 2020). Realizing that these shifts are caused by changes in electoral strategy, not by adherence to political principles can help us to tamp down our own myside bias.

Understand that your political party is functioning more like a social identity group than like an abstract ideology (Voelkel and Brandt 2019), and it is bundling issues to serve its own interests, not yours. Thus I recommend that, when you encounter a relatively new issue, you should treat it as you would a testable belief with at most a modest nonuniform prior probability, not as a distal belief projected with the confidence of a high prior probability. It is from extrapolating partisan convictions to new issues—issues that really should be empirically decided based on the likelihood ratio, not on a strong prior belief—that we get the bad kind of myside bias discussed in chapter 2. You should not, for example, hold a particular conviction about Health Savings Accounts or the efficacy of charter schools just because your party holds that position on these issues.

To head off any misunderstanding, I wish to stress that there is nothing wrong with being a committed member of a political party. Your belonging to your party may be a conviction for you. As discussed in chapter 4, that conviction most likely reflects your genetic background and your experience. But understand that, even though your party allegiance may be a conviction for you, if you are uninformed about the technical details of an otherwise testable issue, you should not be projecting a confident prior belief about this issue just because it is part of your party's "menu" of issue positions (Federico and Malka 2018).

Be Aware That Partisan Tribalism Is Making You More Mysided Than Political Issues Are

When arguing about a political issue, your opponents may be closer to you than you think because, in many cases, the issue isn't the issue—the tribe is. What I mean by this is that the divisiveness in our modern society is driven by party affiliation more than by people becoming more extreme or more consistent in their actual positions. It is important to understand the statistical logic by which this can happen. It may make us more sympathetic toward our fellow citizens if we know that the sources of affective alienation from them derive more from business strategies of the media and electoral strategies of parties rather than from people drifting farther apart in their basic beliefs about American society.

Much has been written about the "Big Sort" (see Bishop 2008) that has been occurring in our society, whereby we have been geographically sorting ourselves into communities of like-minded people for several decades. We increasingly live and socialize with people who are like us not only in their demographics but also in their personal habits, recreational choices, lifestyles, and politics. The Big Sort results in interesting clustering patterns of political and lifestyle choices. For example, in the 2012 election, Barack Obama won 77 percent of the counties in America that had a Whole Foods grocery store, but he won only 29 percent of the counties in America that had a Cracker Barrel restaurant (Wasserman 2014, 2020). Thus we are increasingly living near people who share our views politically (Golman et al. 2016). Bill Bishop (2008), for example, calculated how many Americans lived in "landslide counties"—counties where, in a presidential election, one candidate won by 20 percent or more. He found that in the 1976 presidential election, 26.8 percent of Americans lived in landslide counties, whereas, by the 2008 presidential election, 47.6 percent—almost half—of all Americans lived in counties that tilted strongly toward one political party over the other.

In another kind of sorting that is taking place, people are more consistently clustering into political parties based on certain issues. Although this sorting does make each party differ more from its rival, it is important to understand what does *not* follow from this phenomenon, that people are getting more *extreme* on the issues in question. Partisan sorting by issues can occur without any change in the distribution of attitudes. Also, merely sorting on the basis of party does not necessarily increase the alignment of beliefs within a person.

Because there are several fairly interactive concepts in play here, it might help to illustrate them using a small-scale statistical simulation. Table 6.1 displays a hypothetical sixteen-subject data set indicating each subject's original party identification (party A versus party B); group membership (group X versus group Y) according to some common demographic variable (socioeconomic status, gender, race, and so on); and attitude on each of two issues (issue 1 and issue 2) on a 1 to 10 scale, where 10 indicates maximum support for the policy exemplified by the issue statement and 1 equals maximum opposition to it.

Table 6.1.
Data Simulation Showing Effects of Party Sorting

Subject	Original party identification	Group membership	Issue 1	Issue 2	Party identification after changes
1	A	X	5	8	B
2	A	X	4	3	B
3	A	X	9	6	A
4	A	X	8	5	A
5	A	Y	6	5	A
6	A	Y	8	9	A
7	A	Y	10	6	A
8	A	Y	7	8	A
9	B	X	6	4	B
10	B	X	7	8	B
11	B	X	3	2	B
12	B	X	2	5	B
13	B	Y	8	6	A
14	B	Y	7	4	B
15	B	Y	2	5	B
16	B	Y	8	6	A

Correlations:

Party (original) and opinion 1 = .37

Party (original) and opinion 2 = .33

Party (original) and group membership = .00

Opinion 1 and opinion 2 = .45

Party (after changes) and opinion 1 = .76

Party (after changes) and opinion 2 = .40

Party (after changes) and group membership = .50

In table 6.1, although the original party identification is uncorrelated with group membership, being in party A *is* correlated .37 with the position on issue 1 and .33 with the position on issue 2. Positions on issue 1 and issue 2 are correlated, although the correlation is modest (.45). In short, party is only a mild differentiator in this simulation set. It is only moderately correlated with positions on these two issues (.37 and .33), and it is totally uncorrelated (.00) with demographics (our one indicator of group membership). Furthermore, most subjects in this simulation set are not all that extreme on either issue (only 4 out of 16 score 1 to 2 or 9 to 10 on issue 1 and only 2 out of 16 score 1 to 2 or 9 to 10 on issue 2).

Now imagine that a small subset of these subjects sort themselves—they change parties. The final column of table 6.1, which reflects the state of party membership if just 4 of the 16 subjects were to switch parties, indicates that subjects 1 and 2 have switched from party A to party B. This is understandable because being in party A is correlated with *high* scores on issue 1 and these two subjects display rather low support (4 and 5, respectively) for this issue. Also indicated in the last column is the fact that subjects 13 and 16 have switched from party B to party A. This is understandable because being in party A is correlated with high scores on issue 1 and these two subjects display rather high support for this issue (both support it at level 8).

Four out of sixteen subjects is a fairly small number to switch parties, but note that they have had a profound effect on the sorted characteristics of the parties in this simulated data set. Now the correlations between party and the issues are higher. The correlation between issue 1 and party A has become markedly stronger (moving upward from .37 to .76); the correlation between issue 2 and party A has become modestly stronger (moving upward from .33 to .40). But what is even more significant, party is now moderately correlated with group membership (.50) when it was totally uncorrelated (.00) with group membership before. Six of the eight members of group X are now in party B, and six of the eight members of group Y are now in party A. Being in a party now encompasses not only a stronger connection to these two issues, but also a connection to a subject's demographic group. To whatever extent this group membership represented an identity for the subject, that identity is now more strongly tied up with party membership.

The important point to take from the simulation in table 6.1 is that we can intensify partisanship without at all changing people's positions on the issues themselves—that is, *issue partisanship* and *issue alignment* are not the same thing (Baldassarri and Gelman 2008; Westfall et al. 2015). Specifically, in the simulation, subjects are no more extreme on issue 1 than they were before (12 of the 16 subjects have moderate views on it, ranging from 3 to 8), and they are no more extreme on issue 2 than they were before the sort (14 of the 16 subjects have moderate views on it, ranging from 3 to 8). Moreover, the correlation between issue 1 and issue 2 is exactly what it was before (.45). Positions on the two issues are, as they were before, only modestly correlated—even though both are now more correlated with party membership.

The simulation in table 6.1 illustrates what has *actually* been going on in our electorate (Baldassarri and Gelman 2008; Groenendyk 2018; Johnston, Lavine, and Federico 2017; Mason 2015). Parties are becoming much more associated with issue positions and demographics. Because party affiliation more highly correlates with demographics, many studies have shown an increase in affective polarization over the past couple of decades (e.g., Iyengar, Sood, and Lelkes 2012; Iyengar et al. 2019; Pew Research Center 2019). For example, Lilliana Mason (2018a) found that partisan identification was a much stronger predictor of affective polarization than actual differences on specific issues. In a study previously mentioned, Yphtach Lelkes (2018) found that partisan animus can stoke negative feelings on opposing sides of an issue even when the opposing partisans actually disagree very little on the issue in question.

Table 6.1 shows, statistically, why we have come to this "ideologues-without-issues" moment in our politics, to use Mason's (2018a) phrase, where political opponents tend to viciously disagree with each other even on issues where there is little disagreement among members of the general public. Once partisan sorting has occurred, demographic and lifestyle differences with our opponents become more salient, and we may feel more estranged from them despite modest policy differences. This ends up turning an abstract philosophical position on an issue into a viscerally felt social identity (Mason 2015). We end up disagreeing more rancorously over an issue even though the actual scope of our disagreement on the issue has not changed at all.

What partisan sorting is doing is disrupting "crosscutting identities" across the political parties (Bougher 2017; Iyengar et al. 2019; Johnston, Lavine, and Federico 2017; Lelkes 2018; Mason 2018b). Decades ago, the Democratic Party in the United States encompassed a substantial minority of pro-life proponents, but this is much less true now (when a pro-life Democratic candidate for national office is virtually unthinkable). The significant presence of these crosscutting identities used to keep partisan animus in check. Instead, currently, what Lilliana Mason (2015) finds, in practice, is that partisan anger increases with alignment, independent of any change in the distribution of the issue positions, just as the simulation in table 6.1 illustrates in theory. As Mason (2015) notes, a party identity aligned with a demographic identity aligned with an issue position is a much stronger identity than a nonaligned one. Hence the tribal nature of our politics, where we end up with "an electorate whose members are more biased and angry than their issue positions alone can explain" (Mason 2015, 140).

Thus it is important not to let the *social* elements of polarization intrude into our reasoning about specific policy positions. When our social and tribal allegiances come into play, we tend to act more "groupish," to use Jonathan Haidt's (2012) term, and an aspect of that "groupishness" is that we tend to start projecting convictions—we tend to show more nonnormative myside bias. To use Mason's (2015) simile, we begin to behave more like sports fans than like bankers choosing an investment (see Johnston, Lavine, and Federico 2017). There is good news here from the standpoint of giving us tools to reason better—that is, with less myside bias about specific issues. The moral here, regarding specific issues, is that we are closer to our fellow citizens than it seems from the social level of our tribe-based allegiances and lifestyles.

These, then, are the implications of the demographic Big Sort originally described by Bishop (2008), as it has increasingly spilled into the political domain. What the political parties seem to have done (to use an analogy we all understand) is collect every type of kid you hated from your high school and gather them together. Those kids you hated have grown up now and, not surprisingly, they look totally different than you do, their lifestyles are different from yours, and they have teamed up with other people whose lifestyles you don't like—and they have *all* joined the *other* political party!

But, despite this, what the research shows is that, on the specific issue at hand, whatever it happens to be (tax deductions for minor children, expanding charter schools, minimum wage, and so on), the chances are that our fellow citizens do not feel all that different than we do. If we mildly support the issue proposition in question, the chances are that even if they oppose it, others oppose it only mildly. We are not that far apart from our fellow citizens on the other side as long as we focus on a *specific issue* and *not* on overall lifestyle. And, of course, focusing on the issue and resisting the temptation to project our convictions is exactly what we should be doing to avoid myside bias in a political argument.

Oppose Identity Politics Because It Magnifies Myside Bias

If myside bias is the fire that has set ablaze the public communications commons in our society, then identity politics is the gasoline that will turn a containable fire into an epic conflagration. Jonathan Rauch (2017) defines identity politics as "political mobilization organized around group characteristics such as race, gender, and sexuality, as opposed to party, ideology, or pecuniary interest." For the purposes of understanding the role that identity politics plays in fostering myside bias, however, Rauch's definition is too broad and anodyne to be useful to us. If we are to understand the toxic role that identity politics plays in cultural and political discourse, we need to focus on the version of it that specifically poisons intellectual debate—the version that has turned university campuses from lively forums of contending ideas into encampments of groupthink.

Greg Lukianoff and Jonathan Haidt (2018) do us a service by clearly differentiating two kinds of identity politics: the "common-humanity" kind and the "common-enemy" kind. Common-humanity identity politics, the kind practiced by Martin Luther King Jr., emphasizes a universalistic common ground we all should aspire to, but points out that certain groups are being denied the dignity and rights that all of us should have under a universalistic conception of society.

Common-humanity identity politics presents no problem for reasoned debate in the university communications commons. We would not have a crisis in academia if this were the version of identity politics that had gained currency there. Indeed, we would have no need for organizations like the Heterodox Academy and the Foundation for Individual Rights in Education (FIRE) if the common-humanity type of identity politics was being practiced on university campuses. There would be no heckling of speakers, deplatforming, and "bias response team" intimidation chronicled in the annual reports of organizations like FIRE (Campbell and Manning 2018; Kronman 2019; Lukianoff and Haidt 2018; Mac Donald 2018). Professors would not have to pay a sometimes steep professional price for discussing findings and theories that did not support politically correct conclusions on large and important cultural and socio-behavioral topics such as immigration, gender differences, educational achievement gaps, abortion, family structure, poverty, parenting, sexual orientation, and crime rates (see Clark and Winegard 2020; Crawford and Jussim 2018; Jussim 2018, 2019a, 2019b, 2019c; Kronman 2019; Murray 2019; Reilly 2020). They would be able to write op-eds on any of these or other such topics without being denounced by their colleagues (unlike Amy Wax; see Lukianoff and Haidt 2018; Mac Donald 2018). They would be able to argue against faculty members being forced to write politically correct "diversity statements" without other professors rejecting their arguments as "dangerous" and urging students not to attend their classes (see Thompson 2019). In short, the rampant myside bias that seeks to stifle intellectual debate on university campuses would not be fueled by an identity politics of the kind promoted by Martin Luther King Jr.

It *is*, however, fueled by the *common-enemy* identity politics that Greg Lukianoff and Jonathan Haidt (2018) describe in their nuanced discussion, which I will only briefly review here. In our universities, identity ideas have been jumbled together with various strains of Marxism and a heavy dose of "repressive tolerance" from the writings of Herbert Marcuse (see Wolff, Moore, and Marcuse 1969, 95–137) and the modern academic fads of "intersectionality" and critical theory (Pluckrose and Lindsay 2020). The resulting doctrinal stew is virtually the antithesis of the common-humanity identity politics of Martin Luther King Jr.

Common-enemy identity politics views society as composed of massive social forces working on very large demographic categories of people. These forces are largely power relations that make people "privileged" (defined as "having the power to dominate") or "oppressed," depending upon the conjunction of their demographic characteristics (race, gender, sexual orientation, and so on). Completely unlike common-humanity group politics, where no one has to lose if common rights are granted to a group previously left out, the common-enemy power politics is strictly zero sum, specifically intended to reduce the power of the privileged and redistribute it to designated "victim groups." Certain demographic categories and combinations of such categories are deemed to include greater victims than others (the result has been characterized by many different authors as the "oppression Olympics"; see Chua 2018; Lilla 2017). The members of these victim groups are all oppressed, to varying degrees, depending upon their demographic status profile, by the same common enemy (the white, heterosexual male).

Instead of seeking social and cultural integration for particular victim groups, common-enemy identity politics wants to give *priority* to certain groups, especially in the contexts of politics and argumentation. Our focus will be on argumentation because the nonuniversality of common-enemy identity politics has the effect of magnifying myside bias and shutting down intellectual discussion. The concepts of "inclusion"[5] and "respect for diversity" as played out on current college campuses have the effect of encouraging students to think that intellectual discourse should never make them feel uncomfortable (a trend well discussed in Kronman 2019 and in Lukianoff and Haidt 2018). This is especially true for the designated victim groups in the common-enemy identity politics hierarchy,[6] who have been led to believe that expressing their distress should either end the discussion, or force their interlocutors to show deference to their opinions.

Common-enemy identity politics thus inflates myside bias in two ways. By encouraging people to view every issue through an identity lens, it creates the tendency to turn simple beliefs about testable propositions into full-blown convictions (distal beliefs) that are then projected onto new evidence. Although our identity is central to our narrative about ourselves, and many of our convictions will be centered around our identities, that doesn't mean that every issue we encounter is relevant to our identities. Most of us know the difference and do not always treat a simple testable proposition as if it were a conviction. But identity politics (from now on, it will be clear that I am talking about the common-enemy version) encourages its adherents to see power relationships operating *everywhere*, and thus to enlarge the class of opinions that are treated as convictions. Then it deems the convictions of those from designated victim groups as something they can win an actual intellectual argument with by asserting their "official" victim status when disagreement comes their way.

Students thus get used to framing all arguments from the standpoint of their respective identity groups (or combinations of groups). In universities, professors always know what is coming when they hear "Speaking as an X"[7]—the framing of the argument as it looks from a particular demographic category. This stratagem, from the professor's standpoint, sets a classroom discussion back a mile—immediately subverting the cognitive styles that the professor has been trying to develop all term (of reliance on logic and empirical evidence; use of operationalized terms; use of triangulated perspectives).

Common-enemy identity politics has a particular method of valuing and devaluing arguments. That method is not at all based on the logical or empirical content of the argument; rather, it is based on the position of the source of the argument in the oppression hierarchy. This is actually an old idea in postmodern academic thought—the "epistemic privilege of the oppressed" (a phrase I first heard in the early 1990s, at a conference on the teaching of reading, no less). By this reasoning, your arguments count for more if you have earned a higher medal in the victim Olympics. The next step is to find a way to deal with situations where those who are not oppressed continue to speak and press their views. This is where Marcuse's concept of "repressive tolerance"—that tolerance requires intolerance—comes in (see Wolff, Moore, and Marcuse 1969, 95–137) and accounts for the depressing frequency of heckling and "deplatforming" of speakers on campuses over the past decade (see Ceci and Williams 2018; Jussim 2019c; Lukianoff and Haidt 2018; Mac Donald 2018). The critical feature of common-enemy identity politics that makes it strikingly different from the common-humanity identity politics of Martin Luther King Jr. is its mission: it intends not to restore equality, but to *invert* power relations. Or, as Lukianoff and Haidt (2018, 66) explain: "The end or goal of a Marcusean revolution is not equality but a reversal of power."

Of course, all of this should be antithetical to what professors are trying to teach in a university, and I will say more about that in the next section. Our focus here is on how identity politics turns testable propositions into convictions by making virtually everything of sociocultural substance about an adherent's identity. Because, if it is about your identity, it is always going to be a conviction, and this will magnify the myside bias you display in just about anything you talk about. Philip Tetlock's 1986 work (discussed in the "Recognize That, within Yourself, You Have Conflicting Values" section of this chapter) is relevant here. Tetlock found that subjects could most easily avoid myside bias in their thinking about an issue when they became aware that they had values in conflict. Indeed, he warned about "monistic ideologies," where all values come from a single perspective and, tending not to conflict with one another, lead to strong myside reasoning (Tetlock 1986, 820). Like other "monistic ideologies," identity politics urges its adherents to develop their values from the single perspective of their identity group and thus is likely to make the mysided reasoning in society much worse.

A telling example of how playing identity politics can bring normal social discourse to a standoff occurred in a much-talked-about 2018 podcast. Writers and podcasters Sam Harris and Ezra Klein (Harris 2018).were discussing Sam's interview with Charles Murray on the subject of intelligence and intelligence differences. The key part of the exchange goes as follows:

Ezra Klein: You have that bewildering experience because you don't realize when you keep saying that everybody else is thinking tribally, but you're not, that that is our disagreement.

Sam Harris: Well, no, because I know I'm not thinking tribally—

Ezra Klein: Well, that is our disagreement. . . . Right at the beginning of all this with Murray you said you look at Murray and you see what happens to you. You were completely straightforward about that, that you look at what happens to him and you see what happens to you.

Sam Harris: It's not tribalism. This is an experience of talking about ideas in public.

Ezra Klein: We all have a lot of different identities we're part of all times. I do, too. I have all kinds of identities that you can call forward. All of them can bias me simultaneously, and the questions, of course, are which dominate and how am I able to counterbalance them through my process of information gathering and adjudication of that information. I think that your core identity in this is as someone who feels you get treated unfairly by politically correct mobs.

Here, in this standoff, we can see the alternative universes of the tribalist (Klein) and the antitribalist (Harris) created by common-enemy identity politics. Klein wants to play identity politics—he wants to get Harris to admit that he is part of a tribe, too. Harris does not want to play the game of identity politics—he wants Klein to agree to approach social issues from a standpoint that is independent of identity, where everyone is on an equal footing. He wants Klein to at least try to argue from a neutral perspective— from something that is akin to what philosopher Thomas Nagel (1986) calls "the view from nowhere." Klein denies that such a stance exists and thinks this is just a way for Harris to avoid revealing the biased identity from which he speaks—his tribal perspective.

It is clear why Harris is recalcitrant here. He knows that Klein wants to assign him an identity—such as affluent white heterosexual man—and then, using the usual calculus of identity politics, devalue Harris's opinion by considering it impeached on the topic at hand: individual differences in intelligence. Although Klein is a white man, too, Harris knows that, acting as an ally and representative of the victim identity politics groups, Klein is going to invoke "Speaking as an X"—the most toxic stratagem of identity politics from the standpoint of rational argument.

In his discussion of this ploy, Mark Lilla (2017, 90) reminds us, "This is not an anodyne phrase. It tells the listener that I am speaking from a privileged position on this matter. . . . And it turns the encounter into a power relation: the winner of the argument will be whoever has invoked the morally superior identity and expressed the most outrage at being questioned." This stratagem treats identity as a weight in the argument, when in fact what students should be learning at the university is how to decouple arguments from irrelevant contexts and irrelevant personal characteristics. A good university education teaches students to make these decoupled stances a natural habit. Instead, identity politics turns back the clock some 100 years on our notion of the purpose of a university education and specifically encourages students to take stances that assign unchangeable demographic characteristics additional weight in the intellectual fray.

Anthony Kronman (2019) argues that any person who thinks that a person's feelings and emotions should have actual weight in an argument shuts down the conversation. "The students who invoke this idea," Kronman (2019, 115) notes, "didn't invent it themselves. They are following the lead of the faculty, who ought to know better—who turned Socrates on his head by inviting their students to defer to the power of private experience rather than working to judge it in a disinterested light." The justificatory value of an emotion cannot be assessed by others because it is something that is entirely internal, and, as such, will tend to be immune from criticism. Kronman (2019) points out what all professors should know—that they need to teach their students to support arguments with intellectual propositions that everyone can evaluate on a shared basis. Indeed, the only "Speaking as an X" a university that is true to its proper ethos should allow is "Speaking as a rational human being"—an ethos that many university faculty members have shamefully abandoned.

In the podcast, Sam Harris knows only too well where all of this is going, and that explains his stonewalling of Ezra Klein's request to acknowledge his identity group.[8] "Speaking as an X," Lilla (2017) tells us, is really a claim of privileged position in the debate because the "winner" is the one who invokes the morally superior identity. The specter of the argument descending to such premodern levels was probably what made Harris so recalcitrant in the exchange with Klein. No doubt Harris was pressing (rightly, in my view) for an argument where no one claims special privilege. Harris wants both parties to take the stance "Speaking as a rational human being," so that their arguments can be evaluated on their merits without invoking special scoring points for demographic characteristics over which neither party has control.

When I started teaching critical and scientific thinking in a psychology department in the late 1970s, it was every professor's ideal to teach students to think as Harris wants Klein to think. Best practice was to teach students the counterintuitive superiority of "the view from nowhere" implicit in the scientific worldview and to point out the pitfalls of relying on what is now often termed "lived experience" to adjudicate knowledge claims. My students and I discussed how, in science, the truth of a knowledge claim is not determined by the strength of belief of the individual putting forth the claim, nor by intuition, authority, or "personal experience," as we called it then. The problem with all nonempirically based systems of belief is that they have no mechanism for deciding among conflicting claims. When all disputants in an argument base their claims on lived experience, but the claims conflict, how do we decide whose lived experience actually reflects the truth? Sadly, history has shown that such conflicts usually result in power struggles.

Rather than relying on personal experience, science makes its knowledge claims public so that conflicting ideas can be tested in a way that is acceptable to all disputants. True scientific claims are made in the public realm, where they can be criticized, tested, improved, or perhaps rejected. This allows a selection among theories to take place by peaceful mechanisms that all disputants agree on in advance, which is why science has been a major humanizing force in human history.

As a voluble new instructor back in the 1970s trying to direct my students' attention to the importance of the material, I'm sure that, at some point, I must have exclaimed, "Science doesn't care about your personal experiences! It doesn't care about your feelings!" It got the students' attention. If I were to declare that in a classroom now, I'm sure the students would think I was denying the meaning of their "lived experience." And it would probably lead to a visit from the "bias response team" and to my writing memos back to the dean explaining myself.

Ironically, in the 1970s, it was seen as politically *progressive* to move students from personal worldviews to scientific worldviews—to move students from egocentric perspectives ("Speaking as an X") to "the view from nowhere." The larger assumption was that revealing the objective truth about the human condition would aid in—not impede—constructing a just society. This mindset has been lost in the modern university.

A robust defense of the scientific adjudication of truth claims is no longer the accepted norm on university campuses, at least not according to the official policies coming from university administrations. And it is certainly not the norm in the politically correct atmosphere in which professors in the social sciences and humanities must now work (making it vital that there be organizations like Heterodox Academy and the Foundation for Individual Rights in Education). The new normal is what Sam Harris experienced with Ezra Klein. Universities are now more likely to side with Klein. The extensive "diversity" and "inclusion" administrative infrastructure no longer assumes that the role of the university is to help students construct a unique model of themselves as they incorporate the best thoughts that the world's cultures have preserved. Instead, the diversity infrastructure assumes that social forces have already given the student a preordained identity and that the role of the university is to affirm the student's attachment to that identity.

Indulgence in political correctness and identity politics is why the university has lost the public's confidence as a neutral arbiter of evidence. If we are to remedy the poor state of the public communications commons, we must restore the university to its rightful place as a truth-seeking institution. Anyone is free to play identity politics in the political domain. It is fair to say, as a *political* argument, "You have had power for quite a while, it's time to give it to me" and hope that that argument is morally compelling and persuasive to your opponents.[9] Alternatively, it is fine to say, as a *political* argument, "My minority groups, combined, are larger than your groups, so give power to me and my groups." In contexts such as this, identity is put forth in the service of power politics. That at least puts identity politics in an appropriate place. But when we reason, the focus should be on rational argument and justified belief. Identity as argument has no place in a university devoted to reasoning and true belief.

Rebuilding the University as a Corrective to Myside Bias

The last section was focused on the problem of how identity politics impedes students' ability to develop the cognitive decoupling skills that are necessary to avoid myside bias. In this section, we will examine the role of the university[10] in teaching students those skills. I will argue that recent developments within the university are making it harder to teach students the decoupling and decontextualizing skills that are necessary for avoiding myside bias.

What is cognitive decoupling, and why is it central to avoiding myside bias? Two critical functions are enabled by decoupling: inhibition and sustained simulation. The first function—suppression of the automatic response—is akin to the inhibitory processes studied in the executive functioning literature (Kovacs and Conway 2016; Miyake and Friedman 2012; Nigg 2017). The second critical function served by decoupling is to enable hypothetical reasoning (Evans 2007, 2010; Evans and Stanovich 2013; Oaksford and Chater 2012; Stanovich and Toplak 2012). When we reason hypothetically, we create temporary models of the world and test out actions in that simulated world. Aristotle was referring to hypothetical thinking in a quotation attributed to him: "It is the mark of an educated mind to be able to entertain a thought without accepting it."

In order to reason hypothetically, however, we must be able to prevent our representations of the real world from becoming confused with our representations of imaginary situations. Decoupling our representations from the world enables us to do just this. Dealing with these "secondary representations"—keeping them decoupled—is costly in terms of cognitive capacity. However, the *tendency* to initiate such decoupling for the purposes of simulation is a dispositional variable, separable from cognitive capacity (Stanovich, 2011). This tendency can be developed through experience and training—training not just in logic and reasoning, but also in the informal types of decontextualized thinking that are part of many disciplines in the university.

Many different theorists have emphasized the importance of decontextualizing in the development of higher-level thought. Thus Jean Piaget's (1972) conceptualization of formal operational thought places the mechanisms of decontextualizing in positions of paramount importance, and many scholars in the critical thinking literature (e.g., Neimark 1987; Paul 1984, 1987; Siegel 1988) have emphasized the decontextualizing modes of decentering, detaching, and depersonalizing as the foundational skills of rational thought. Looming large in that literature is the ability to adopt perspectives other than one's own. The avoidance of myside bias is dependent on these perspective-switching abilities and tendencies.

But our ability to switch perspectives will be limited by the fact that our human brains are cognitive misers—their basic tendency is to default to processing mechanisms of low computational expense. This is a well-established theme throughout the past fifty years of research in psychology and cognitive science (Dawes 1976; Kahneman 2011; Simon 1955, 1956; Shah and Oppenheimer 2008; Stanovich 2018a; Taylor 1981; Tversky and Kahneman 1974). Miserly cognitive processing arose for sound evolutionary reasons of computational efficiency, but that same efficiency will guarantee that perspective switching (to avoid myside bias) will not be the default processing action because, as we have known for some time, it is cognitively demanding to process information from the perspective of another person (Gilbert, Pelham, and Krull 1988; Taber and Lodge 2006). Thus we must practice the perspective switching needed to avoid myside bias until it becomes habitual. But identity politics prevents this from happening by locking in an automatized group perspective, by contextualizing based on preapproved group stances, and by viewing perspective switching through decoupling as a sellout to the hegemonic patriarchy.

True perspective switching—the kind of reframing that allows us to conceptualize the world in new ways—requires a kind of alienation from the self. It requires that we sometimes avoid framing things from the easiest perspective to model—inevitably our own and that of our most important affinity groups. It is not that our default framing is always wrong, as we saw in chapter 2. However, university undergraduates are in precisely the stage of life as young adults where they need to learn *other* framing strategies.

When teaching my cognitive psychology course, I use the example of broccoli and ice cream. Some cognitive processes are demanding but necessary. They are the broccoli. Other thinking tendencies come naturally to us and they are not cognitively demanding processes. They are the ice cream. In lectures, I point out to my students that broccoli needs a cheerleader, but ice cream does not. This is why education rightly emphasizes the broccoli side of thinking. These processes need cheerleaders in order to help them overcome the natural tendency to default to "ice cream thinking."

Perspective switching is a type of cognitive broccoli. Taking students out of the comfort zone of their identities or those of their tribes was once seen as one of the key purposes of a university education. But when the university simply affirms students in identities they have assumed even before they arrived on campus, then it is hard to see the value added by the university anymore. In stressing identity politics, the university is simply cheerleading for ice cream. Instead, students need to be taught that the benefits of leaving the comfort and safety of perspectives they have long held are worth the risks—that, in the long run, myside processing will never lead them to deep understanding of the world in which they live.

In the arena of the public communications commons, Kahan (2016, 19) recommends that, to foster decoupling, we need to "dissolve the attachment between policy-relevant facts and the antagonistic social meanings that transform them into badges of membership in and loyalty to competing groups." And the institution designed to do just this is the university. As discussed in the Sam Harris–Ezra Klein exchange in the previous section, as an institution, the university used to take the Harris position. The unique epistemic role of the university in our culture was to set up conditions where students could learn how to bring arguments and evidence to a question, and to teach them not to project convictions derived from tribal loyalties onto the evaluation of evidence on testable questions. The rise of identity politics should have been recognized by university faculties as a threat to their ability to teach decoupled argumentation and evidence evaluation. As a monistic ideology (Tetlock 1986), where all values come from a single perspective, identity politics entangles many testable propositions with identity-based convictions. It fosters myside bias by reversing Kahan's (2016) prescription—by transforming positions on policy-relevant facts into badges of group-based convictions. One of the most depressing social trends of the last few decades has been universities becoming *proponents* of identity politics—a doctrine that attacks the heart of their intellectual mission.

Predictably, the myside bias displayed in parts of the modern university is undermining trust in them as institutions, as captured in a Twitter comment by Bret Weinstein (2019): "The spread of oppression studies is an abdication of scientific responsibility. As universities promote ideology over inquiry, science skepticism is the inevitable result."[11]

If we are ever to remedy the "tragedy of the science communications commons" (Kahan 2013; Kahan et al. 2017)—if we are ever to have a society that can converge on the truth about important social and public policy issues—we must have institutions that foster decoupling by discouraging the projection of convictions onto evidence. Although they once served that purpose, universities are now the primary incubators and purveyors of intellectually deadening identity politics, whose thinking styles have in recent years spread widely into the corporate world. The James Damore incident at Google is a primary case in point—an employee was fired for circulating an essay that contained fair comments based on largely accurate social science findings on sex differences (Damore 2017; Jussim 2017b).

That the university is failing to be a fair adjudicator of evidence in public policy disputes was strongly suggested by the widespread incidents of inappropriately partisan stances by university administrators and faculty members in the wake of the 2016 presidential election in the United States (see Campbell and Manning 2018 for a long list of examples). Many instructors across the country cancelled classes and others openly decried the election results in their classrooms. The president of the University of Michigan, Mark Schlissel, attended a "somber vigil" in the wake of the election to "comfort" the students upset with the results, and fueled their feelings of disappointment and anger by attacking the president-elect (Fournier 2016). This is totally inappropriate behavior on the part of a public institution, to say nothing of the irony of it occurring in a state (Michigan) where a majority of people voted against the political stance that Schlissel was taking as a representative of a state institution.

The examples of inappropriate institutional behavior chronicled by Campbell and Manning (2018) suggest that universities have reached the tipping point described by James Hankins (2020, 12), whereby "if all your colleagues in a nonpolitical institution are progressive (or political radicals of any stripe), the temptation to politicize the institution, to use its power to achieve political goals unrelated to its formal purpose, becomes irresistible." The result of succumbing to this irresistible temptation is that we have arrived at the point Weinstein warned us about: "As universities promote ideology over inquiry, science skepticism is the inevitable result."

When the universities make it professionally difficult for academics to publish politically incorrect conclusions in one politically charged area, the public will come to suspect that the atmosphere in universities is skewing the evidence in *other* politically charged areas as well. When the public sees university faculty members urge sanctions against a colleague who writes an essay arguing that the promotion of bourgeois values could help poor people (the Amy Wax incident; see Lukianoff and Haidt 2018, 107), then we shouldn't be surprised when the same public becomes skeptical of research on poverty and income inequality conducted by university professors. When a professor compares the concepts of transracialism and transgenderism in an academic journal and dozens of colleagues sign an open letter demanding that the article be retracted (the Rebecca Tuvel incident; see Lukianoff and Haidt 2018, 104–105), the public can hardly be blamed for being skeptical about university research on charged topics such as child rearing, marriage, and adoption. When university faculty members contribute to the Internet mobbing of someone who discusses the evidence on differing interest profiles between the sexes (the James Damore incident; see Jussim 2018), then we shouldn't be surprised that the public is skeptical about research that comes out of universities regarding climate change. In short, we shouldn't be surprised that only Democrats thoroughly trust university research anymore, and that both Republicans and independents are much more skeptical (Blank and Shaw 2015; Cofnas, Carl, and Woodley of Menie 2018; Funk et al. 2019; Gauchat 2012; Pew Research Center 2017).

In short, members of the identity-politics left have succeeded in making certain research conclusions within the university verboten and in making it very hard for any university professor (particularly the junior and untenured ones) to publish and publicly promote any conclusions that they dislike. Faculty now self-censor on a range of topics (Clark and Winegard 2020;

Honeycutt and Jussim 2020; Peters et al., 2020; Zigerell 2018). The identity politics ideologues have won the on-campus battle to suppress views that they do not like. But what the same politicized faculty members and students (and, increasingly, university administrators) cannot seem to see is that one cost of their victory is that they have made the public rightly skeptical about *any* conclusions that now come out of universities on charged topics—even conclusions that are congenial to the political positions that the ideologues advocate.

University research on all of the charged topics where identity politics has predetermined the conclusions—and there are many (immigration, racial profiling, gay marriage, income inequality, college admissions biases, sex differences, intelligence differences, and the list goes on)—is simply not believable anymore. Whether some cultures promote human flourishing more than others; whether men and women have different interests and proclivities; whether culture affects poverty rates; whether intelligence is partially heritable; whether the gender wage gap is largely due to factors other than discrimination; whether race-based admissions policies have some unintended consequences; whether traditional masculinity is useful to society; whether crime rates vary between the races—these are all topics on which the modern university has dictated the conclusions before the results of any investigation are in (Campbell and Manning 2018; Ceci and Williams 2018; Jussim 2018, 2019c; Lukianoff and Haidt 2018; MacDonald 2018; Murray 2019; Pluckrose & Lindsay 2020). Or, as Kronman (2019, 179) observes, outside academia, many people are prepared to engage in lively debate about such topics, "but inside its walls doing so is a recipe for isolation and disgrace."

The more the public comes to know that the universities have approved positions on certain topics, the more it quite rationally loses confidence in research that comes out of universities. As we all know from our college training in Popperian thinking, for research evidence to scientifically support a proposition, that proposition must itself be "falsifiable"—capable of being proven false. However, the public is increasingly aware that, in universities, for many issues related to identity politics, preferred conclusions are now dictated in advance and falsifying them in open inquiry is no longer allowed. We now have entire departments within the university (the "grievance studies" departments, see Heying 2018; Pluckrose, Lindsay, and Boghossian 2018) that are devoted to advocacy rather than inquiry. Anyone who entered those departments with a "falsifiability mindset" would be run out on a rail—which of course is why conclusions on specific propositions from such academic entities are scientifically worthless. University scholars serve to devalue data supporting conclusion A if they create a repressive atmosphere in which faculty members are discouraged from arguing not-A, or pay too heavy a reputational price for presenting data in favor of proposition not-A.[12]

Identity politics has rendered public policy evidence that comes out of academia unreliable.[13] This loss of confidence in university-based evidence as a way to adjudicate public policy questions is exacerbated by increasing awareness of the unscientific practices that have been allowed to spread within the administrative structure of academia itself. Many university policies have in recent years employed terms such as "microaggression," "hate speech," "rape culture," "social justice," and "white privilege" to drive their policy actions even though none of these terms has met the most fundamental criterion of science—having a minimally agreed-upon operational definition in terms of common measurement procedures. Thus "hate speech" has no minimally agreed-upon definition (Ceci and Williams 2018; Chemerinsky and Gillman 2017; Fish 2019). And "microaggression," one of the targets of the Orwellian "bias response teams" on campuses, is a conceptually confused term with no consistent operational definition either (Lukianoff and Haidt 2018). Scott Lilienfeld (2017, 2019) has thoroughly explained what it would take to properly ground the concept of microaggression—to change it from its present status as a mere political weapon into a behavioral science concept—but virtually no effort has been made to do this.

Indeed, the term "diversity," the dominant moral principle and policy concept in universities now, remains vague, ill defined, and used for political rather than educational purposes, likely because of its odd origin as a university concept in Justice Lewis Powell's tie-breaking opinion in *Regents of the University of California v. Bakke* in 1978 (see Kronman 2019 for a thorough discussion). And, as used within universities, the concept of diversity has been so grotesquely twisted that it became the basis for Harvard, in *Students for Fair Admissions v. Harvard* (Hartocollis 2020), to argue in effect (though not in words) that it is in the name of the moral concept of diversity that Harvard discriminates *against* Asian Americans in its admissions processes. Harvard was reduced to arguing that its use of race in its admissions policies "can only help, not hurt" a student's chances of admission (Hartocollis 2018; Ponnuru 2019). Of course, we would expect even a high school student to recognize that this argument, in a zero-sum admissions context, is laughable. In the end, we are left with a prestigious university using an illogical argument to defend a term they will not operationally define. It is hard to criticize the public when it fails to credit research on pressing issues that comes out of institutions that routinely engage in such self-serving myside bias themselves.

This massive failure of intellectual responsibility on the part of universities is exactly the opposite of what we would have expected or hoped for. Our hope would be that universities will teach their students about the intellectual strategies that fuel myside bias and create an environment to help them avoid using these strategies. All too often, the opposite occurs, as the university fails its communications commons responsibilities again and again.

Take, for example, the case of the "disparity fallacy" (Clark and Winegard 2020; Hughes 2018; Sowell 2019), the notion that any difference in an outcome variable viewed as unfavorable to one of the victim groups of identity politics must be due to discrimination. The fallacy is commonly advanced in the general media (indeed, in recent years, the *New York Times* has seemed to be one of its keenest promoters) and in political discussions. Because, in our current information-rich environment, it is quite easy to find a disparity that makes your group look like a victim, the disparity fallacy has become a major source of myside bias. Universities could help reduce the number of mysided arguments that are fueled by this fallacy. In their psychology, sociology, political science, and economics departments, they have all the tools (regression analysis, causal analysis, detection of confounds) they need to test whether disparities can be explained by variables other than discrimination. But instead of aggressively deploying these tools to curtail the spread of the fallacy, universities all too often become its *purveyors*. This, of course, is especially true in the proliferating "grievance studies" departments, but it is also true even in legitimate departments, such as psychology and sociology, which should know better.

For example, we are not surprised when political campaigns proclaim the bogus idea that women make 77 cents (or 79 cents, or 81 cents—the figure varies) on the dollar for doing the same work as men. But it is absolutely egregious that many university students finish their college degrees thinking that the 77-cent figure is actually one of the insightful things they learned at university. In our society, being aware of the "gender pay gap" is even taken to be a sign of cultural sophistication. It is something young people can flash at a bar to show that they have been to college.

Of course, the 77-cent factoid is an example of the disparity fallacy. The 77-cent figure is simply arrived at by dividing the average income of all working women by the average income of all working men. The fact that the figure is lower for women does not, by itself, indicate that women are paid less for doing the same work. It is simply gross income, averaged across a variety of occupations, for two different populations that have very different work profiles. In order for the figure to be consistent at all with the hypothesis that discrimination is involved, it would have to be corrected (using the aforementioned regression techniques, which are common in all social science departments) for a wide variety of factors such as occupational choice, work history, exact hours worked, qualifications, overtime pay, willingness to forgo nonwage benefits, willingness to work on short notice, and many others. When those controls are applied statistically, the so-called gender wage gap largely disappears. There is no strong evidence that the 77 cents on the dollar is due to gender discrimination in wage rates, as is so often claimed in political contexts (Bertrand, Goldin, and Katz 2010; Black et al. 2008; CONSAD Research Corporation 2009; Kolesnikova and Liu 2011; O'Neill and O'Neill 2012; Phelan 2018; Solberg and Laughlin 1995). University faculty members, so (rightly) eager to correct public misinformation about climate change, are much less aggressive in their attempts to correct this piece of misinformation, which appears regularly in the traditional media and in political campaigns.

The disparity fallacy appears again in the claim that African Americans are disproportionately killed by the police. This claim has proven very politically useful, but it again derives from using statistics uncorrected for things like overall crime rates and encounters with the police. When calculated using the appropriate base rates, the data reveal that the probability of the fatal shooting of African Americans by the police is actually not higher than that for whites (Fryer 2019; Johnson et al. 2019; Lott and Moody 2016; Miller et al. 2017). But again, because it is politically useful to use the disparity as a direct indicator of discrimination, the disparity argument continues to be used in the media, and again, most distressingly, in the very university departments one would expect would be teaching the analytic tools necessary to expose the fallacy and correct the inferences that are drawn from it.

The disparity fallacy is one of the primary tools now used in partisan debates to create mysided arguments. That it exists within the university itself, in precisely the environment that should be providing tools to fight myside bias, represents another way that the university has been failing to cleanse a public communications commons filled with myside bias. For example, you would think that most university faculty members would agree that it is a bad idea to institutionalize departments, institutes, and centers that serve advocacy rather than investigative roles. And, of course, the advocacy trap is not limited to the identity politics of grievance studies centers. For researchers who fall prey to it, it is easy to slip from studying a religion into advocating for it, and from studying an economic system into advocating for it. But in all these cases, when the research mission drifts into an advocacy one, then the university needs to withdraw support, and to both reaffirm and reinforce the university's mission as a place of open inquiry where conclusions are not drawn before investigations begin.

Of those who decry the intellectual monoculture within universities, almost no one wants to see a quota system of mandatory hiring of equal percentages across the ideological spectrum. Indeed, to most of these critics, ideological quotas are anathema as much as racial ones are. But there are now formal mechanisms of ideological conformity within universities that are such egregious engines of myside bias that one would think there would be universal agreement that they constitute grave institutional mistakes. The diversity, equity, and inclusion statements that are now required of applicants for faculty positions at the entry level as well as for promotions to higher levels are a case in point.

When current or potential faculty members are asked to write diversity statements, they certainly know not to interpret "diversity" as meaning *intellectual* diversity.[14] Arguing that these statements represent a kind of de facto political discrimination in the name of social justice, Lee Jussim (2019a) asks us to imagine a diversity statement he might submit, highlighting his discussions of free speech and censorship in his classes, his membership in the Heterodox Academy, his speech to the Foundation for Individual Rights in Education, his essays criticizing academic intolerance in the *Wall Street Journal*, *Quillette*, and *Areo*, and his research on political intolerance among academics. Everyone knows that such a statement would immediately disqualify him as a candidate for a new position or promotion on the faculty of a modern-day university, and thus that universities are now, as Jussim, 2019a) puts it, "essentially requiring a professed commitment to social justice activism."

Faculty members also know not to interpret "diversity" in the classic, older sense of fostering diversity in academia: that is, a Martin Luther King Jr. common-humanity version of identity politics whereby faculty members strive to include all kinds of students and all kinds of viewpoints in their classes in an ecumenical, evenhanded way. A faculty applicant who wrote a diversity statement from within this classic framework would rate very poorly on the scoring rubric used for such statements by the University of California system (University of California 2018). On their scoring rubric, a letter containing the statement "I always invite and welcome students from all backgrounds to participate in my research lab, and in fact have mentored several women" is placed in the *lowest* scoring category. Likewise, "Diversity is important for science" receives the lowest category rating; whereas the highest rating is reserved for "Interest in dimensions of diversity that result from different identities, such as ethnic, socioeconomic, racial, gender, sexual orientation. . . . This understanding can result from *personal experiences*" (italics added). Abigail Thompson (2019) argues that the scoring rubric penalizes those who adhere to the classical liberal tenet of treating people as individuals and not as representatives of groups, noting that instead, "candidates must subscribe to a particular political ideology, one based on treating people not as unique individuals but as representatives of their gender and ethnic identities."

Scoring rubrics such as this make it clear that diversity statements are meant to reveal whether the current or prospective faculty member accepts the basic axiom of common-enemy identity politics that large demographic groups are oppressed by other groups in the United States and whether the faculty member's political beliefs match those of critical race theory (Pluckrose and Lindsay 2020). By forcing faculty members to endorse one particular social theory over many others that should be in play in an institution dedicated to open inquiry, these diversity statements represent an attempt to close off inquiry rather than to open it up. Because the faculty member is forced to pledge allegiance to one particular social theory in the face of many competing alternatives, these statements are more prescriptive than even the loyalty oaths of the 1950s.

Open inquiry, rather than inculcating specific beliefs, used to be the sine qua non of the university. With the advent of diversity statements, the goal seems now to be tribal: requiring allegiance to specific political content on the part of faculty and students. If the state universities will not refrain from requiring diversity statements, state legislatures should withhold funds from them until they do. Although administrators and faculty organizations may view my recommendation as an attack on the institution as a whole, it is not. Rather, compelling state universities to do away with these statements—and, one hopes, persuading private universities to follow their example when they do—would represent a valid attempt by the public to steer all universities back to their true mission. Only then will the universities be able to staunch the myside bias that is ruining our public communications commons.

Notes

Chapter 1

1. Although Kahan, Hoffman, and colleagues (2012) actually measured political attitudes more complex and multidimensional than simple conservative and liberal social attitudes, I am simplifying their study for the purposes of this description.

2. Much of what researchers ended up examining in the early studies of confirmation bias were its nonmotivated components—Evans's (1989) positivity effects or Klayman and Ha's (1987) positive test strategy, for example—not a myside bias in the sense of processing information in order to advantage a *favored* hypothesis. There are still many problems with the term confirmation bias, despite or perhaps because of its growing use among the general public. Sometimes confirmation bias is used as a synonym for what I call myside bias—processing information in a manner that is advantageous to a favored hypothesis. The main problem here is that confirmation bias does not necessarily connote myside bias (Eil and Rao 2011; Mercier 2017). A reasoner testing a *focal* hypothesis is not necessarily processing information in a way that advantages the reasoner's *favored* hypothesis.

3. Note that what normative means in cognitive science is performance that is optimal according to a model of perfect rationality, *not* the response that is most common, in the sense of a "norm."

4. The key reasoning principle captured by Bayes's theorem is that evaluation of the diagnosticity of the evidence (the likelihood ratio) should be conducted independently of the assessment of the prior odds favoring the focal hypothesis (e.g., De Finetti 1989; Earman 1992; Fischhoff and Beyth-Marom 1983; Howson and Urbach 1993).

5. See Hahn and Harris (2014) on the complexities surrounding the term "bias" in psychology.

6. Matthew Fisher and Frank Keil (2014) found that subjects were not well calibrated when judging their ability to justify their beliefs through argumentation. Most relevant

to the study of myside bias was Fisher and Keil's finding that the closer subjects' beliefs were to convictions, the more poorly calibrated subjects were in their judgments—almost always believing that they could provide good arguments for their convictions when, in fact, they could not.

7. Although myside bias and wishful thinking are both subclasses of effects within the general literature on motivated reasoning, they differ in several respects. Wishful thinking involves thinking that a future or unknown outcome will be consistent with our own *preferences*—that what is going to happen is exactly what we *want* to happen. Myside bias involves interpreting evidence in a manner that makes it consistent with our strongly held *beliefs* or convictions. Wishful thinking is about something we want to *happen* (a pragmatic concern), whereas myside bias is about beliefs that we want to be *true* (an epistemic concern).

8. The abstract version of Peter Wason's (1966) four-card selection task shows the subject four rectangles, each representing a card lying on a table. The subject is told that each one of the cards has a letter on one side and a number on the other side and is given the rule: "If a card has a vowel on its letter side, then it has an even number on its number side" Two of the cards are letter-side up, and two of the cards are number-side up. The subject's task is to decide which card or cards must be turned over in order to find out whether the rule is true or false The four cards confronting the subject have the stimuli K, A, 8, and 5 showing. The correct answer is A and 5 (the only two cards that could show the rule to be false), but most subjects answer, incorrectly, "A and 8" (showing a "matching bias"; see Evans 1989, 2010). In some studies, rules with content are used ("Whenever the menu has fish on one side, wine is on the other") and in others rules that govern which actions are required, forbidden, or permitted are used ("Any sale over $30 must be approved by the section manager").

9. I use the phrase "at first glance" because, as we will see in chapter 2, the normative issues here are more complex than they first appear (see Hahn and Harris 2014).

10. Independent of empirical evidence, a thought experiment might suggest why this is. Imagine the four quadrants of the scatterplot of risk and benefit. Of the four cells, one of them—that for activities of high risk and low benefit—will likely be vastly underpopulated in a natural environment. Activities of this type are usually not adopted, and they are often proscribed by authorities. Such activities have so low a benefit to risk ratio that they will likely be selected out in most environments. If the high-risk, low-benefit quadrant is underpopulated, then the joint distribution of risk and benefit in the actual world must be positively correlated (see Finucane et al. 2000).

11. Although it is irrelevant for my argument here, the *Times* seems to have been incorrect in claiming that the criminal conviction rate for undocumented immigrants in the United States was actually lower than that for native born citizens (see Martinelli 2017).

12. We will see in chapter 2 that it is myside bias driven by a distal rather than testable belief that is problematic. Where Mercier and Sperber (2016, 2017) say we are good at evaluating evidence without myside bias (in the domain of a testable belief) is precisely where myside bias is less of a problem; and where they say we are poor at suppressing myside bias (in the case of a distal belief) is precisely where myside bias is normatively most questionable.

Chapter 2

1. I will repeat here the caution from chapter 1 that, in cognitive science, normative means performance that is optimal according to a model of perfect rationality, not the most common response, in the sense of a "norm."

2. To clarify, throughout the rest of this book, the terms "knowledge projection" and its synonym "projecting the prior probability" are employed to mean using prior knowledge to frame the interpretation of new information (Cook and Lewandowsky 2016; Gershman 2019; Jern, Chang, and Kemp 2014), using the gap between new information and the prior probability to help ascertain the credibility of the information source (Druckman and McGrath 2019; Gentzkow and Shapiro 2006; Hahn and Harris 2014; Koehler 1993; Tappin, Pennycook, and Rand 2020), or both.

3. It is important to include the caveat here that the various myside bias paradigms listed in table 1.1 differ in the extent to which projection of a prior belief would be normatively sanctioned. The evidence evaluation paradigms, for instance, would be most subject to the arguments of Koehler (1993) and Hahn and Harris (2014) that knowledge projection is justified in assessing information source credibility. Noting, however, that there are paradigms where the myside bias amounts to little more than favoring of the in-group, Peter Ditto and colleagues (2019b) point to studies where a campaign's dirty tricks are judged as less objectionable when done by the subjects' own party, as well as studies showing that disputed ballots are judged in the direction favorable to the subjects' own candidate. Here the question is one not of epistemic rationality, but of the trade-off between instrumental values (discussed later in this chapter), such as between the instrumental value of supporting your own group and its politics and the instrumental value of supporting fair procedural treatment in our society.

4. Ben Tappin, Gordon Pennycook, and David Rand (2020; see also Tappin and Gadsby 2019) discuss the methodological difficulties involved in finding the processing locus of politically motivated cognition—specifically, whether it alters the assessment of the likelihood ratio directly, or whether it does so indirectly by operating through the prior probability. Dan Kahan (2016) argues for the practical and theoretical importance of distinguishing between these two loci and conducts his own exploration of the methodological difficulties involved. Politically motivated reasoning operating directly on the likelihood ratio is clearly nonnormative. Tappin,

Pennycook, and Rand (2020) recapitulate some of the arguments in this chapter by pointing out that motivated political reasoning operating on the prior probability is in fact consistent with Bayesianism (that is, it is normative in the sense of Koehler's proof B). But, as Kahan (2016) notes, such reasoning, though consistent with Bayesian reasoning, is not truth convergent. It is not globally rational, as I use the term in this chapter. Politically motivated reasoning of this form is thus rational in a very limited sense from a normative point of view.

5. By using the word "chosen" here, I do not mean to imply that these arguments hold only when the hypothesis is arrived at *consciously*. In this section, I will describe examples where people seem to be consciously choosing between a hypothesis that they know follows from the evidence and a hypothesis that they would prefer to be true. In most instances, however, people will not be aware of arriving at their prior probability in this way. The inferential behavior that led up to their particular prior probability will not be consciously accessible to most, and they will have no awareness of choosing a personally favored hypothesis over an evidence-favored hypothesis, or vice versa. None of the arguments that follow depend on conscious awareness of the level of conflict between knowledge projection based on evidence and knowledge projection based on a personally favored hypothesis.

6. If there is a concern that distal beliefs are not always worldviews, then alternative terms might simply be "peripheral beliefs" (which tend to be testable) and "core beliefs" (which often tend *not* to be testable because they are convictions).

7. Though beyond the scope of this volume, these complexities are covered in the Bayesian literature on testimonial evidence, information source credibility, trust, and "Jeffrey conditionalization" (see Bovens and Hartmann 2003; Gentzkow and Shapiro 2006; Hahn and Harris 2014; Howson and Urbach 1993; Jeffrey 1983, chapter 11; Kim, Park, and Young 2020; O'Connor and Weatherall 2018; Schum 1994; Schwan and Stern 2017; Talbott 2016; Tappin, Pennycook, and Rand 2020). This literature is full of elegant formal analyses, many of which share a similar theme: when in an environment where your own hypotheses have some degree of accuracy, it makes sense to use the discrepancy between your prior beliefs and new evidence to evaluate the credibility of the source of the new evidence. It also makes sense to use the discrepancy between your prior beliefs and the prior beliefs of a different researcher to evaluate the credibility of new evidence received from that researcher (see O'Connor and Weatherall 2018). These normative practices, however, can result in both myside bias and belief polarization.

8. The Koehler (1993) and Jern, Chang, and Kemp (2014) analyses share some of the weaknesses of Panglossian positions in the "Great Rationality Debate" (Stanovich 2011) that I pointed out in *Who Is Rational?* (Stanovich 1999). Koehler (1993) puts no restrictions on the origins of the prior beliefs, and Jern, Chang, and Kemp (2014) put no restrictions on the different framings that subjects can bring to the evidence.

In both cases, the subjects' construals are accepted. Whatever construals subjects put on the problem are accepted in order to preserve local rationality, but, by using this permissive strategy, we have simply pushed the larger question to another level of analysis ("Why do the subjects have these unusual construals?") and the larger question remains completely unaddressed. This is why I have called this strategy a "Pyrrhic victory" for Panglossianism (Stanovich 1999). When the idea of alternative task construals is used to insulate reasoning competence from charges of irrationality, it often simply transfers the irrationality to the representation of the problem. Irrationality has not been abolished, only transferred to a different cognitive operation. Many of the construals that Panglossians must defend turn out to be even more embarrassing than the errors they seek to excuse because they are "so tendentious as to transfer the puzzle about the logic of the response undiminished to an earlier stage" (Margolis 1987, 20).

9. Many recent commentators have argued that the same kind of commons dilemma now surrounds the use of social media and the Internet in our society. As the Silicon Valley entrepreneur Roger McNamee (2019, 163) notes: "Most users really like Facebook. They really like Google. There is no other way to explain the huge number of daily users. Few had any awareness of a dark side, that Facebook and Google could be great for them but bad for society."

Chapter 3

1. Of course, it is only counterintuitive if we ignore the arguments of Koehler (1993) discussed in chapter 2. If projecting a prior belief onto new evidence is to some degree normative, then we might expect people of higher cognitive ability to display this tendency to a greater extent.

2. Although Kahan, Peters, and colleagues (2012) actually measured political attitudes in a more complex and multidimensional manner, I am simplifying their study for the purposes of this description.

3. In studies that use the Cognitive Reflection Test (CRT), I am treating the CRT as a complex indicator of cognitive ability plus numeracy—but also as an indicator of miserly or nonmiserly thinking dispositions (on the complex psychological components measured by the CRT, see Liberali et al. 2012; Patel et al. 2019; Sinayev and Peters 2015; Stanovich, West, and Toplak 2016; Toplak, West, and Stanovich 2011, 2014a).

4. Another difference is that belief bias tasks are often more explicit than myside tasks in instructing the subjects to not have their reasoning affected by prior beliefs (Stanovich, West, and Toplak 2013), but this is not invariably true.

5. For the fleshed-out argument of why the response that preserves positive manifold is at least statistically more likely to be a more optimal response, see Stanovich 1999 and Stanovich and West 2000.

6. The finding that the strength of the belief is a predictor of myside bias replicates a pattern reported in many earlier studies (e.g., Bolsen and Palm 2020; Druckman 2012; Edwards and Smith 1996; Houston and Fazio 1989; Taber and Lodge 2006).

Chapter 4

1. Writer David French (2018) paraphrases an imaginary encounter in Scott Alexander's blog Slate Star Codex whereby a liberal claims that liberals are tolerant because they really like gays, blacks, Hispanics, Asians, and transgender people. A conservative then asks the liberal, "Well, what do you have against gays?" The liberal is appalled at the question and says, "Of course I have nothing against gays, I'm not a homophobe." This exchange, French argues, shows that the liberal is misunderstanding what tolerance is. To such liberals, French says, "Guess what, you're not tolerating anything. You're mistaking tolerance for fellowship, or tolerance for tribalism. The word tolerance of course implies that there is something to tolerate." French's point is that when there is nothing to overlook, then there is no tolerance to be exercised. The liberal in this case, French argues, has "taken the vice of their particular brand of tribalism and transformed it into the false virtue of fake tolerance."

2. Future research will have to adjudicate these different possibilities, but survey research analyses by Zach Goldberg (2019) may be particularly relevant. Goldberg found that "white liberals recently became the only demographic group in America to display a pro–out-group bias—meaning that among all the different groups surveyed, white liberals were the only one that expressed a preference for other racial and ethnic communities above their own."

3. Work in behavioral economics has used related metaphors such as viewing beliefs as assets (Bénabou and Tirole 2011) or investments (Golman, Hagmann, and Loewenstein 2017) that have *direct* utility value rather than just indirect value as a component of the instrumental calculus (Eil and Rao 2011; Loewenstein 2006; Sharot and Sunstein 2020). This conceptual move opens up analyses of belief perseverance in terms of concepts such as sunk costs and endowment effects.

4. To be a bit more technical, but still brief, the term meme refers to a unit of cultural information that is meant to be understood as roughly analogous to a gene. My preferred definition of the term meme is "a brain control (or informational) state that can potentially cause fundamentally new behaviors or thoughts when replicated in another brain" (Stanovich 2004, 175). Meme replication has taken place when control states that are causally similar to the source are replicated in the new host. The meme is a true selfish replicator in the same sense that a gene is. As with the gene, by using the term "selfish," I do not mean that memes make people selfish, but rather that, as replicators, memes (like genes) act in their own "interests."

5. It should be understood that anthropomorphic descriptions of replicator activity are merely shorthand metaphors commonly used in biological writings. I will

continue the practice here of using the metaphorical language about replicators and genes having "interests" in confidence that readers will understand that this is shorthand only. As Blackmore (1999, 5) notes: "The shorthand 'genes want X' can always be spelled out as 'genes that do X are more likely to be passed on,'" but that, in making complicated arguments, the latter language becomes cumbersome. Thus, I will follow Dawkins (1976, 88) and "allow ourselves the license of talking about genes as if they had conscious aims, always reassuring ourselves that we could translate our sloppy language back into respectable terms if we wanted to." Dawkins (1976, 278) points out that this is "harmless unless it happens to fall into the hands of those ill-equipped to understand it" and then proceeds to quote a philosopher admonishing biologists that genes can't be selfish any more than atoms can be jealous. I trust, Dawkins's philosopher to the contrary, that no reader needs this pointed out.

6. These four reasons are discussed in the literature of evolutionary psychology (Atran 1998; Sperber 1996; Tooby and Cosmides 1992), gene-culture coevolution (Cavalli-Sforza and Feldman 1981; Durham 1991; Gintis 2007; Lumsden and Wilson 1981; Richerson and Boyd 2005), and memetics (Aunger 2000, 2002; Blackmore 1999; Boudry and Braeckman 2011, 2012; Dennett 1995, 2017; Lynch 1996).

7. The term "memosphere" is Daniel Dennett's (1991, 1995). For examples of how the critical thinking literature stresses skills of detachment, see Baron (2008), Paul (1984, 1987) Perkins (1995) and Stanovich (1999).

8. Blackmore (2010) recanted the position she took in Blackmore (2000).

9. Theorists who champion dual-inheritance models of culture do not always share Dennett's enthusiasm for the meme concept, but they nevertheless agree with him on the importance of recognizing that much of cultural development cannot be explained by conscious uptake (see Richerson and Boyd 2005).

10. Libertarians' scores tend to be more like liberals' on personality measures such as the Big Five, but the two groups' scores differ on moral foundation measures (see Haidt 2012; Iyer et al. 2012; see also Yilmaz et al. 2020). I also note that the psychological substrate of social liberalism and conservatism may be different than that of economic liberalism and conservatism, because the two types of ideologies often correlate differently with criterion variables (Baron 2015; Carl 2014b; Crawford et al. 2017; Everett 2013; Federico and Malka 2018; Feldman and Johnston 2014; Malka and Soto 2015; Pennycook and Rand 2019; Stanovich and Toplak 2019; Yilmaz and Saribay 2016; Yilmaz et al. 2020; see also chapter 5 of the present volume).

11. For example, Jarret Crawford (2014) reported data indicating that conservatives are more sensitive to threats to their physical safety, whereas liberals are more sensitive to perceived threats to their rights (see also Federico and Malka 2018). Crawford (2017) developed a later model (the compensatory political behavior model) that

refined the concepts involved and synthesized the following conclusion: liberals and conservatives are similarly influenced by threats to their values or identity, whereas social but not economic conservatives are more sensitive to physical threats.

12. The occasional finding—most often observed in studies of political reasoning (e.g., Kahan et al. 2017; Lupia et al. 2007; Van Boven et al. 2019)—that cognitive sophistication is correlated with *greater* myside bias admits to a variety of interpretations, given the literature reviewed so far in this volume. These include the following arguments: that projection of convictions is more rational than we have thought; that cognitively more sophisticated people are so much more knowledgeable that their prior beliefs are more likely to be actual testable beliefs; that cognitively more sophisticated people are more astute at discerning arguments for group preservation—and other arguments I don't have the space to pursue here.

13. The double-crux strategy developed by the Center for Applied Rationality (Sabien 2017) has similarities to my recommendation that we somewhat weaken our convictions to make it more likely that we will use an evidence-based testable belief rather than a conviction to formulate a prior probability. In the double-crux situation, there are two individuals, one believing proposition A and the other believing proposition ~A (where proposition A tends to be a conviction). The double-crux strategy gets pairs of individuals to generate another set of statements on which they disagree, one individual believing proposition B and the other, proposition ~B. Both individuals must agree that proposition B supports proposition A and that proposition ~B supports proposition ~A. What is critical is that both agree that proposition B is more "concrete, grounded, and well defined"—in short, both agree that proposition B is what I would call here "more testable."

14. As Paul Churchland (1989, 1995) has emphasized, an advancing cognitive science might well have a profound effect on how people examine their cognitive processes and talk about them. Indeed, past advances in psychological understanding have had this effect. People routinely speak of things like introversion and extroversion, and examine their own cognitive performance using terms like "short-term memory"—all linguistic tools for self-analysis that were unavailable one hundred years ago. It is important to realize that our folk language of the mental evolves, in part in response to the diffusion of scientific knowledge.

15. The framework here is parallel to a dual-process model with a very lazy System 2. It is the type of dual-process model that Daniel Kahneman (2011) describes—one where a large proportion of System 2 activity consists of the rationalizing (Evans 2019; Haidt 2012; Mercier and Sperber 2011, 2017) of decisions made by unconscious, autonomous processes (Baumard and Boyer 2013; Stanovich 2004, 2011; Kraft, Lodge, and Taber 2015; Taber and Lodge 2016).

16. By the "properties of beliefs," I mean whether the beliefs are testable beliefs or convictions, and, if convictions, how strongly these convictions are held. Additionally, certain issues sometimes produce asymmetric beliefs, yielding different degrees of

myside bias depending upon the valence, positive or negative (see Stanovich and West 2008a; Toner et al. 2013).

Chapter 5

1. Although it is sometimes thought that research showing correlations between intelligence and prejudice automatically implicates conservatives as being low in intelligence (on the assumption that prejudice is a proxy for conservatism), Brandt and Crawford (2016) demonstrated that these correlations, as we have seen before, are dependent on the target groups being evaluated. Brandt and Crawford observed, for example, that the negative correlations between intelligence and prejudice toward Hispanics (–.15), toward blacks (–.09), and toward illegal immigrants (–.09) were almost perfectly matched by the *positive* correlations between intelligence and prejudice toward Christian fundamentalists (+.19), toward big business (+.14), toward the military (+.12), and toward working-class people (+.08). More intelligent people are not less prejudiced in general than less intelligent people, their prejudices are simply directed at different groups (see also Brandt and Van Tongeren 2017).

2. Studies employing the Cognitive Reflection Test (CRT)—a complex measure, associated with cognitive ability, thinking dispositions, and numeracy (Sinayev and Peters 2015; Stanovich, West, and Toplak 2016)—have shown results that parallel those for intelligence. CRT performance rarely correlates with economic conservatism, and when it does, it is at least as likely to correlate positively as negatively (Baron 2015; Yilmaz and Saribay 2016, 2017; Yilmaz, Saribay, and Iyer 2020). There are consistent, but small, correlations between CRT performance and social conservatism and very small correlations in studies that do not differentiate economic from social conservatives (Burger, Pfattheicher, and Jauch 2020; Deppe et al. 2015; Yilmaz and Saribay 2016, 2017; Yilmaz and Alper 2019; Yilmaz, Saribay, and Iyer 2020). Overall, there are no indications of strong differences between liberals and conservatives on the CRT, although libertarians often outscore *both* liberals and conservatives (Pennycook and Rand 2019; Yilmaz, Saribay, and Iyer 2020).

3. Ganzach, Hanoch, and Choma (2019) analyzed thermometer ratings of Trump in a regression equation with a number of variables and found that the dominant beta weight was for party affiliation (.610), and that predictor was orders of magnitude stronger than other significant predictors such as gender (–.091) and verbal ability (–.061).

4. The absolute level of rationality question is much more conceptually complex (see Caplan 2007; Fuller 2019; Lomasky 2008).

5. Related political distinctions involving worldviews have been discussed by many different authors (e.g., Goodhart 2017; Haidt 2016; Lind 2020).

6. Sanders has also long been concerned that illegal immigration suppresses wages among low-skilled workers, saying in a 2007 interview that "if poverty is increasing

and if wages are going down, I don't know why we need millions of people to be coming into this country as guest workers who will work for lower wages than American workers and drive wages down even lower than they are now" (see Frizell 2016). In a 2015 interview with Ezra Klein, Sanders was critical of the drift toward open borders advocacy on the political left, warning that it is the kind of "right-wing proposal" that is pushed by the wealthy Koch brothers and argued that "you're doing away with the concept of a nation-state, and I don't think there's any country in the world which believes in that" (see Lemon 2019).

7. I have since 2017 collected data on this question under more controlled conditions. In conjunction with the data my colleague Maggie Toplak and I collected (Stanovich and Toplak 2019), I posed the Ted Cruz versus Al Sharpton question to a group of subjects recruited from Prolific (Palan and Schitter 2018). All the subjects spoke English as a first language and all were United States citizens. In our sample, there were 332 subjects who would have voted for Hillary Clinton in 2016 rather than Donald Trump or a third-party candidate. Of these 332 Clinton voters, fully 90.4 percent would have voted for Al Sharpton over Ted Cruz if given the choice.

8. In his 2011 essay in the *Atlantic*, Daniel Klein described how the original scale that he used was saturated with myside bias: the questions more often challenged liberal beliefs than conservative ones, thus leading to lower scores among liberals. Klein confesses that, because he is a libertarian, he found it easier to believe that people on the left were especially likely to have erroneous beliefs about economics. This preexisting bias made it harder for him to recognize when the selection of questions was skewed against liberals. Many media and scholarly studies of the "Who is more knowledgeable?" type suffer from item selection that reflects the biases of the test constructor (see Lupia 2016).

9. The biased and agenda-driven nature of this research is, in some cases, undermining liberal causes, warns science writer and professor of communication Matthew Nisbet (2020, 27): "As a community of advocates, we have become obsessed with . . . conservative 'deniers.' . . . This research has in turn infected mainstream journalism and commentary, in which readers at outlets such as the *Guardian* and the *Washington Post* are consistently left with the impression that 'anti-science,' 'denier' Republicans may in fact be cognitively incapable of reason or compromise on behalf of clean energy policy, similar in nature to Holocaust deniers." Nisbet points out that these strategies are counterproductive because "today's ubiquitous branding of Republicans as the party of 'denial' greatly exaggerates the intensity of opposition to climate and clean energy solutions among those on the center-right, creating a self-reinforcing spiral of false perceptions" (Nisbet 2020, 27).

Chapter 6

1. Focusing on the issue of belief (as is done when people are labeled "climate change deniers") in discussions of global warming is a case in point. Acknowledging

that human activity is a substantial contributor to global warming does not at all dictate *how much* economic growth to trade off for what amount of reduction in carbon emissions.

2. Later in this chapter, we will see that there is another way that our beliefs about a particular issue might not have been a conscious choice. Once we have decided on a partisan side, we tend to allow party elites to bundle specific issue positions for us. In many cases, we have given no thought to the issue beyond knowing that our party endorses a certain stance toward it.

3. Statistically speaking, it is easier for multiple-party political systems to arrive at a more coherent bundling of issues. The two-party dominance in the political system of the United States is particularly likely to yield incoherent bundlings.

4. That historical changes in issue bundling and linkage are culturally contingent should also suggest to us that connections between issue positions are not based on deep political philosophy but instead reflect current and local electoral conditions (Federico and Malka 2018).

5. The term "inclusion," now commonly used in the university diversity industry, has a much more honest history in the field of special education, where it has been applied in the spirit of common-humanity identity politics (see Lipsky and Gartner 1997). Individuals with disabilities and their advocates wanted only the educational privileges of their fellow nondisabled citizens. In contrast, the term "inclusion" as used on campuses embodies the stratagem of common-enemy identity politics to confer special status on the feelings of only certain groups, who thus have special silencing privileges over the common enemy.

6. This is why sociologists Bradley Campbell and Jason Manning (2018) describe common-enemy identity politics as reflecting the culture of victimhood, and common-humanity identity politics as reflecting the culture of dignity.

7. David Randall (2019) discusses several variants of "Speaking as an X," such as "I see the world in a way you can't"; "Your views make me feel excluded"; "You only want to protect your privilege," and notes that they serve to destroy the necessary assumption that everyone is a good-faith participant in the discussion.

8. In an essay on the logic of identity politics (Stanovich 2018b), I suggested that Sam Harris should agree to choose an identity, but not the one offered to him. I suggested that one way to thwart the identity politics game is by not accepting its lists of acceptable identities. I suggested that Harris should hoist Ezra Klein's identity politics on its own petard by showing that it can have negative consequences for the partisan political groups that Klein wants to support (e.g., the Democrats). In fact, Harris should say, "Okay, I'll do it. I'll explicitly adopt an identity perspective. I'll name my tribe and argue from its perspective. My tribe is the citizens of America for whom their identity as citizens is more important than any identity

that derives from demographic categories (race, sex, ethnicity, religion, sexual orientation, socioeconomic status, and so on). I will call this tribe 'Citizen American,' or 'C-Amer' for short." I pointed out that many of the arguments that advocates of scientific rationalism wish to make for their approach to social issues would suffer little distortion if made instead from an admitted C-Amer perspective—a perspective where the focus is on the individual (citizen) identifying at the national level (American). The C-Amer identity does not turn simple beliefs into the convictions that fuel myside bias. I argued that the identity C-Amer reveals the electoral danger of the game that Klein is playing with Harris—the game of forcing a person to declare their identity bias so that it can be discounted or supplemented according to the rules of intersectional victimhood. Forcing previously nonidentifying Americans into a game they didn't want and having large numbers of them (Republicans; Bernie Sanders voters; identity politics critics; Jackson or Moynihan Democrats; independent voters) choose the C-Amer identity might not be the best outcome for the Democrats. C-Amers might decide that they will not have their opinions devalued according to the group calculus of common-enemy identity politics. I argued that something along these lines might have contributed to the surprising outcome of the 2016 presidential election in the United States (see Zito and Todd 2018).

9. By "*fair* to say," I do not mean to imply that the identity argument is a *good* argument, even in politics. I am simply saying that the argument is at least in its correct domain—as opposed to the university setting, where it has no place.

10. I will focus on universities here, but, of course, the increasing myside bias in the media is another disturbing trend. The selective exposure problems surrounding media entities like Fox News have increased, as other networks (CNN, MSNBC) and traditional media entities such as the *New York Times* (particularly after the 2016 election) adopt or imitate its business model (Frost 2019; McGinnis 2019; Paresky et al., 2020).

11. Bret Weinstein is the progressive professor at Evergreen State University who, in 2017, argued against a proposed campus action whereby white students and faculty would stay away from the school for a day. He was called a "racist" by students and was the subject of targeted demonstrations. Ludicrous charges that he was a supporter of white supremacy were made, even though Weinstein was a lifelong supporter of progressive political causes (Campbell and Manning 2018). His university administration, including its president, refused to defend his integrity and his right to oppose the campus action. A cowardly faculty offered him virtually no support against the student mob. In the end, Weinstein and his wife, also a professor at the same university, accepted a settlement to resign (Campbell and Manning 2018; Lukianoff and Haidt 2018; Murray 2019).

12. Of course, when this research makes its way into the general media, we have a doubling down on the lack of credibility. So, for example, a university professor describes research in the *New York Times* that leads to the conclusion that you should

make your marriage "gayer" (Coontz 2020). Why? Because a university study found that gay marriages were less stressful and had less tension. The public is becoming more aware, however, that any heterosexual male researcher in a university who found that gay couples had *more* stress and tension than heterosexual couples would be ostracized. And the public is also becoming more aware that if, by some miracle, such a finding were to make its way through the review process of a journal in the social sciences, that the *New York Times* would never choose it for a prominent summary article with the title "The Downside of Gay Marriages—More Stress and Tension," whereas the actual article published ("Same-Sex Spouses Feel More Satisfied") would be welcomed with open arms. The readers of the *New York Times* want to hear this conclusion—but not its contrary. Both academia and the *Times* are simply serving their constituencies who are willing to pay for myside bias. Neither is a neutral arbiter of evidence on this particular topic, and the public increasingly knows this.

13. Concerned that his discipline, sociology, is destroying its own ability to influence public policy, Jonathan Turner (2019; see also, al Gharbi 2018) points out that many of the true scientists in the discipline are demoralized because their field has transitioned from being a social science into a social movement. Such a trend will not be good for any of the social sciences. Indeed, the intellectual monoculture in psychology has made the old joke "Psychology departments exist so that Democrats can say, 'Studies show . . .'" all too true. More seriously, before long, granting agencies will become more aware of the ideological bias, as will the state legislatures and taxpayers who are funding their state universities.

14. David Rozado's 2019 quantitative study of the use of the term "diversity" in universities shows clearly that it is employed not to foster *intellectual* diversity, but instead to focus on demographic groups.

References

Abelson, R. P. 1986. Beliefs are like possessions. *Journal of the Theory of Social Behaviour* 16 (3): 223–250.

Abelson, R. P. 1988. Conviction. *American Psychologist* 43 (4): 267–275.

Abelson, R. P. 1996. The secret existence of expressive behavior. In J. Friedman (Ed.), *The rational choice controversy*, 25-36. New Haven, CT: Yale University Press.

Abelson, R. P., and Prentice, D. 1989. Beliefs as possessions: A functional perspective. In A. Pratkanis, S. Breckler, and A. Greenwald, eds., *Attitudes, structure, and function*, 361–381. Hillsdale, NJ: Erlbaum.

Abramowitz, A. I., and Webster, S. W. 2016. The rise of negative partisanship and the nationalization of U.S. elections in the 21st century. *Electoral Studies* 41:12–22.

Abramowitz, A. I., and Webster, S. W. 2018. Negative partisanship: Why Americans dislike parties but behave like rabid partisans. *Political Psychology* 39 (S1): 119–135.

Abrams, S. 2016. Professors moved left since 1990s, rest of country did not. *Heterodox Academy* (blog), January 9. https://heterodoxacademy.org/professors-moved-left-but-country-did-not/

Aczel, B., Bago, B., Szollosi, A., Foldes, A., and Lukacs, B. 2015. Measuring individual differences in decision biases: Methodological considerations. *Frontiers in Psychology* 6. Article 1770. doi:10.3389/fpsyg.2015.01770.

Adorno, T. W., Frenkel-Brunswik, E., Levinson, D. J., and Sanford, R. N. 1950. *The authoritarian personality*. New York: Harper.

Ahn, W.-Y., Kishida, K., Gu, X., Lohrenz, T., Harvey, A., Alford, J., et al. 2014. Nonpolitical images evoke neural predictors of political ideology. *Current Biology* 24 (22): 2693–2699.

Akerlof, G., and Kranton, R. 2010. *Identity economics*. Princeton: Princeton University Press.

Alberta, T. 2019. *American carnage*. New York: HarperCollins.

Alford, J. R., and Hibbing, J. R. 2004. The origin of politics: An evolutionary theory of political behavior. *Perspectives on Politics* 2 (4) 707–723.

al Gharbi, M. 2018. Race and the race for the White House: On social research in the age of Trump. *American Sociologist* 49 (4): 496–519.

Alloy, L. B., and Tabachnik, N. 1984. Assessment of covariation by humans and animals: The joint influence of prior expectations and current situational information. *Psychological Review* 91 (1): 112–149.

Altemeyer, B. 1981. *Right-wing authoritarianism*. Winnipeg: University of Manitoba Press.

Anderson, E. 1993. *Value in ethics and economics*. Cambridge, MA: Harvard University Press.

Andreoni, J., and Mylovanov, T. 2012. Diverging opinions. *American Economic Journal: Microeconomics* 4 (1): 209–232.

Atran, S. 1998. Folk biology and the anthropology of science: Cognitive universals and cultural particulars. *Behavioral and Brain Sciences* 21 (4): 547–609.

Atran, S., and Henrich, J. 2010. The evolution of religion: How cognitive by-products, adaptive learning heuristics, ritual displays, and group competition generate deep commitments to prosocial religions. *Biological Theory* 5 (1): 18–30.

Aunger, R., ed. 2000. *Darwinizing culture: The status of memetics as a science*. Oxford: Oxford University Press.

Aunger, R. 2002. *The electric meme: A new theory of how we think*. New York: Free Press.

Babcock, L., Loewenstein, G., Issacharoff, S., and Camerer, C. 1995. Biased judgments of fairness in bargaining. *American Economic Review* 85 (5): 1337–1343.

Baker, S. G., Patel, N., Von Gunten, C., Valentine, K. D., and Scherer, L. D. 2020. Interpreting politically charged numerical information: The influence of numeracy and problem difficulty on response accuracy. *Judgment and Decision Making* 15 (2): 203–213.

Baldassarri, D., and Gelman, A. 2008. Partisans without constraint: Political polarization and trends in American public opinion. *American Journal of Sociology* 114 (2): 408–446.

Bar-Hillel, M., Budescu, D., and Amor, M. 2008. Predicting World Cup results: Do goals seem more likely when they pay off? *Psychonomic Bulletin and Review* 15 (2): 278–283.

Barnum, M. 2019. New Democratic divide on charter schools emerges, as support plummets among white Democrats. *Chalkbeat*, May 14. https://chalkbeat.org/posts/us/2019/05/14/charter-schools-democrats-race-polling-divide/

Baron, J. 1985. *Rationality and intelligence.* New York: Cambridge University Press.

Baron, J. 1988. *Thinking and deciding.* New York: Cambridge University Press.

Baron, J. 1991. Beliefs about thinking. In J. Voss, D. Perkins and J. Segal, eds., *Informal reasoning and education,* 169–186. Hillsdale, NJ: Erlbaum.

Baron, J. 1995. Myside bias in thinking about abortion. *Thinking and Reasoning* 1 (3): 221–235.

Baron, J. 1998. *Judgment misguided: Intuition and error in public decision making.* New York: Oxford University Press.

Baron, J. 2008. *Thinking and deciding.* 4th ed. Cambridge, MA: Cambridge University Press.

Baron, J. 2015. Supplement to Deppe and colleagues (2015). *Judgment and Decision Making* 10 (4): 1–2.

Baron, J. 2019. Actively open-minded thinking in politics. *Cognition* 188:8–18.

Baron, J., and Leshner, S. 2000. How serious are expressions of protected values? *Journal of Experimental Psychology: Applied* 6 (3): 183–194.

Baron, J., and Spranca, M. 1997. Protected values. *Organizational Behavior and Human Decision Processes* 70 (1): 1–16.

Baron-Cohen, S. 2003. *The essential difference: The truth about the male and female brain.* New York: Basic Books.

Barrett, J. L. 2004. *Why would anyone believe in God?* Lanham, MD: AltaMira Press.

Bartels, D. M., and Medin, D. L. 2007. Are morally-motivated decision makers insensitive to the consequences of their choices? *Psychological Science* 18 (1): 24–28.

Bartels, L. M. 2002. Beyond the running tally: Partisan bias in political perceptions. *Political Behavior* 24 (2): 117–150.

Baumard, N., and Boyer, P. 2013. Religious beliefs as reflective elaborations on intuitions: A modified dual-process model. *Current Directions in Psychological Science.* 22 (4): 295–300.

Bazerman, M., and Moore, D. A. 2008. *Judgment in managerial decision making.* 7th ed. New York: John Wiley.

Bell, E., Schermer, J. A., and Vernon, P. A. 2009. The origins of political attitudes and behaviours: An analysis using twins. *Canadian Journal of Political Science* 42 (4): 855–879.

Bénabou, R., and Tirole, J. 2011. Identity, morals, and taboos: Beliefs as assets. *Quarterly Journal of Economics* 126 (2): 805–855.

Benoit, J., and Dubra, J. 2016. A theory of rational attitude polarization. *SSRN*. March 24. https://ssrn.com/abstract=2754316 or http://dx.doi.org/10.2139/ssrn.2754316.

Berezow, A., and Campbell, H. 2012. *Science left behind: Feel-good fallacies and the rise of the anti-scientific left*. New York: Public Access.

Bering, J. M. 2006. The folk psychology of souls. *Behavioral and Brain Sciences* 29 (5): 453–498.

Bertrand, M., Goldin, C., and Katz, L. 2010. Dynamics of the gender gap for young professionals in the financial and corporate sectors. *American Economic Journal: Applied Economics* 2 (3): 228–255.

Beyth-Marom, R., and Fischhoff, B. 1983. Diagnosticity and pseudodiagnositicity. *Journal of Personality and Social Psychology* 45 (6): 1185–1195.

Bikales, J., and Goodman, J. 2020. Plurality of surveyed Harvard faculty support Warren in presidential race. *Harvard Crimson*, March3. https://www.thecrimson.com /article/2020/3/3/faculty-support-warren-president/#disqus_thread

Bishop, B. 2008. *The big sort; Why the clustering of like-minded America is tearing us apart*. New York: First Mariner Books.

Black, D., Haviland, A., Sanders, S., and Taylor, L. 2008. Gender wage disparities among the highly educated. *Journal of Human Resources* 43 (3): 630–659.

Blackmore, S. 1999. *The meme machine*. New York: Oxford University Press.

Blackmore, S. 2000. The memes' eye view. In R. Aunger, ed., *Darwinizing culture: The status of memetics as a science*, 25–42. Oxford: Oxford University Press.

Blackmore, S. 2010. Why I no longer believe religion is a virus of the mind. *Guardian*, September 16. https://www.theguardian.com/commentisfree/belief/2010/sep/16/why -no-longer-believe-religion-virus-mind

Blank, J. M., and Shaw, D. 2015. Does partisanship shape attitudes toward science and public policy? The case for ideology and religion. *Annals of the American Academy of Political and Social Science* 658 (1): 18–35.

Block, J., and Block, J. H. 2006. Nursery school personality and political orientation two decades later. *Journal of Research in Personality* 40 (5): 734–749.

Bloom, P. 2004. *Descartes' baby*. New York: Basic Books.

Bolsen, T., and Palm, R. 2020. Motivated reasoning and political decision making. In W. Thompson, ed., *Oxford Research Encyclopedia, Politics*. doi:10.1093/acrefore /9780190228637.013.923. https://oxfordre.com/politics/politics/view/10.1093/acrefore /9780190228637.001.0001/acrefore-9780190228637-e-923

Borjas, G. J. 2016. *We wanted workers: Unraveling the immigration narrative*. New York: Norton.

Bouchard, T. J., and McGue, M. 2003. Genetic and environmental influences on human psychological differences. *Journal of Neurobiology* 54 (1): 4–45.

Boudry, M., and Braeckman, J. 2011. Immunizing strategies and epistemic defense mechanisms. *Philosophia* 39 (1): 145–161.

Boudry, M., and Braeckman, J. 2012. How convenient! The epistemic rationale of self-validating belief systems. *Philosophical Psychology* 25 (3): 341–364.

Bougher, L. D. 2017. The correlates of discord: Identity, issue alignment, and political hostility in polarized America. *Political Behavior* 39 (3): 731–762.

Bovens, L., and Hartmann, P. 2003. *Bayesian epistemology*. Oxford: Oxford University Press.

Boyer, P. 2001. *Religion explained: The evolutionary origins of religious thought*. New York: Basic Books.

Boyer, P. 2018. *Minds make societies*. New Haven: Yale University Press.

Brandt, M. J. 2017. Predicting ideological prejudice. *Psychological Science* 28 (6): 713–722.

Brandt, M. J., and Crawford, J. T. 2016. Answering unresolved questions about the relationship between cognitive ability and prejudice. *Social Psychological and Personality Science* 7 (8): 884–892.

Brandt, M. J., and Crawford, J. T. 2019. Studying a heterogeneous array of target groups can help us understand prejudice. *Current Directions in Psychological Science* 28 (3): 292–298.

Brandt, M. J., Reyna, C., Chambers, J. R., Crawford, J. T., and Wetherell, G. 2014. The ideological-conflict hypothesis: Intolerance among both liberals and conservatives. *Current Directions in Psychological Science* 23 (1): 27–34.

Brandt, M. J., and Van Tongeren, D. R. 2017. People both high and low on religious fundamentalism are prejudiced toward dissimilar groups. *Journal of Personality and Social Psychology* 112 (1): 76–97.

Brennan, G., and Hamlin, A. 1998. Expressive voting and electoral equilibrium. *Public Choice* 95 (1–2): 149–175.

Brennan, G., and Lomasky, L. 1993. *Democracy and decision: The pure theory of electoral preference*. Cambridge: Cambridge University Press.

Brennan, J. 2016. Trump won because voters are ignorant, literally. *Foreign Policy*, November 10. https://foreignpolicy.com/2016/11/10/the-dance-of-the-dunces-trump-clinton-election-republican-democrat/

Bruine de Bruin, W., Parker, A. M., and Fischhoff, B. 2007. Individual differences in adult decision-making competence. *Journal of Personality and Social Psychology* 92 (5): 938–956.

Bullock, J. G. 2009. Partisan bias and the Bayesian ideal in the study of public opinion. *Journal of Politics* 71 (3): 1109–1124.

Bullock, J. G., Gerber, A. S., Hill, S. J., and Huber, G. A. 2015. Partisan bias in factual beliefs about politics. *Quarterly Journal of Political Science* 10 (4): 519–578.

Bullock, J. G., and Lenz, G. 2019. Partisan bias in surveys. *Annual Review of Political Science* 22 (1): 325–342.

Burger, A. M., Pfattheicher, S., and Jauch, M. 2020. The role of motivation in the association of political ideology with cognitive performance. *Cognition* 195. Article 104124.

Buss, D. M., and Schmitt, D. P. 2011. Evolutionary psychology and feminism. *Sex Roles* 64 (9–10): 768–787.

Buss, D. M., and von Hippel, W. 2018. Psychological barriers to evolutionary psychology: Ideological bias and coalitional adaptations. *Archives of Scientific Psychology* 6 (1): 148–158.

Campbell, B., and Manning, J. 2018. *The rise of victimhood culture*. New York: Palgrave Macmillan.

Campbell, T. H., and Kay, A. C. 2014. Solution aversion: On the relation between ideology and motivated disbelief. *Journal of Personality and Social Psychology* 107 (5): 809–824.

Caplan, B. 2007. *The myth of the rational voter: Why democracies choose bad policies*. Princeton: Princeton University Press.

Caplan, B., and Miller, S. C. 2010. Intelligence makes people think like economists: Evidence from the General Social Survey. *Intelligence* 38 (6): 636–647.

Cardiff, C. F., and Klein, D. B. 2005. Faculty partisan affiliations in all disciplines: A voter-registration study. *Critical Review* 17 (3–4): 237–255.

Carl, N. 2014a. Cognitive ability and party identity in the United States. *Intelligence* 47:3–9.

Carl, N. 2014b. Verbal intelligence is correlated with socially and economically liberal beliefs. *Intelligence* 44:142–148.

Carl, N., Cofnas, N., and Woodley of Menie, M. A. 2016. Scientific literacy, optimism about science and conservatism. *Personality and Individual Differences* 94:299–302.

Carney, D. R., Jost, J. T., Gosling, S. D., and Potter, J. 2008. The secret lives of liberals and conservatives: Personality profiles, interaction styles, and the things they leave behind. *Political Psychology* 29 (16): 807–840.

Carney, R. K., and Enos, R. 2019. Conservatism, just world belief, and racism: An experimental investigation of the attitudes measured by modern racism scales. 2017 NYU CESS Experiments Conference. Working paper under review. http://www

.rileycarney.com/research; or https://pdfs.semanticscholar.org/ad3f/1d704c09d5a80 c9b3af6b8abb8013881c4a3.pdf.

Carraro, L., Castelli, L., and Macchiella, C. 2011. The automatic conservative: Ideology-based attentional asymmetries in the processing of valenced information. *PloS One* 6 (11). e26456. https://doi.org/10.1371/journal.pone.0026456.

Carroll, J. B. 1993. *Human cognitive abilities: A survey of factor-analytic studies.* Cambridge: Cambridge University Press.

Cattell, R. B. 1963. Theory for fluid and crystallized intelligence: A critical experiment. *Journal of Educational Psychology* 54 (1): 1–22.

Cattell, R. B. 1998. Where is intelligence? Some answers from the triadic theory. In J. J. McArdle and R. W. Woodcock, eds., *Human cognitive abilities in theory and practice*, 29–38. Mahwah, NJ: Erlbaum.

Cavalli-Sforza, L. L., and Feldman, M. W. 1981. *Cultural transmission and evolution: A quantitative approach.* Princeton: Princeton University Press.

Ceci, S. J., and Williams, W. M. 2018. Who decides what is acceptable speech on campus? Why restricting free speech is not the answer. *Perspectives on Psychological Science* 13 (3): 299–323.

Chambers, J. R., Schlenker, B. R., and Collisson, B. 2013. Ideology and prejudice: The role of value conflicts. *Psychological Science* 24 (2): 140–149.

Charney, E. 2015. Liberal bias and the five-factor model. *Behavioral and Brain Sciences* 38:e139. doi:10.1017/S0140525X14001174.

Chater, N., and Loewenstein, G. 2016. The under-appreciated drive for sense-making. *Journal of Economic Behavior & Organization* 126 Part B:137–154.

Chen, S., Duckworth, K., and Chaiken, S. 1999. Motivated heuristic and systematic processing. *Psychological Inquiry* 10 (1): 44–49.

Chemerinsky, E., and Gillman, H. 2017. *Free speech on campus.* New Haven: Yale University Press.

Chetty, R., Hendren, N., Kline, P., Saez, E., and Turner, N. 2014. Is the United States still a land of opportunity? Recent trends in intergenerational mobility. *American Economic Review* 104 (5): 141–147.

Chua, A. 2018. *Political tribes.* New York: Penguin.

Churchland, P. M. 1989. *A neurocomputational perspective: The nature of mind and the structure of science.* Cambridge, MA: MIT Press.

Churchland, P. M. 1995. *The engine of reason, the seat of the soul: A philosophical journey into the brain.* Cambridge, MA: MIT Press.

Claassen, R. L., and Ensley, M. J. 2016. Motivated reasoning and yard-sign-stealing partisans: Mine is a likable rogue, yours is a degenerate criminal. *Political Behavior* 38 (2): 317–335.

Clark, C. J., Liu, B. S., Winegard, B. M., and Ditto, P. H. 2019. Tribalism is human nature. *Current Directions in Psychological Science* 28 (6): 587–592.

Clark, C. J., and Winegard, B. M. 2020. Tribalism in war and peace: The nature and evolution of ideological epistemology and its significance for modern social science. *Psychological Inquiry* 31 (1): 1–22.

Cofnas, N., Carl, N., and Woodley of Menie, M. A. 2018. Does activism in social science explain conservatives' distrust of scientists? *American Sociologist* 49 (1): 135–148.

Cohen, G. L. 2003. Party over policy: The dominating impact of group influence on political beliefs. *Journal of Personality and Social Psychology* 85 (5): 808–822.

Colman, A. M. 1995. *Game theory and its applications*. Oxford: Butterworth-Heinemann.

Colman, A. M. 2003. Cooperation, psychological game theory, and limitations of rationality in social interaction. *Behavioral and Brain Sciences* 26 (2): 139–198.

CONSAD Research Corporation. 2009. An analysis of the reasons for the disparity in wages between men and women. January 12. U.S. Department of Labor, Contract Number GS-23F-02598. https://www.shrm.org/hr-today/public-policy/hr-public-policy -issues/Documents/Gender%20Wage%20Gap%20Final%20Report.pdf.

Conway, L. G., Gornick, L. J., Houck, S. C., Anderson, C., Stockert, J., Sessoms, D., and McCue, K. 2016. Are conservatives really more simple-minded than liberals? The domain specificity of complex thinking. *Political Psychology* 37 (6): 777–798.

Conway, L. G., Houck, S. C., Gornick, L J., and Repke, M. A. 2018. Finding the Loch Ness monster: Left-wing authoritarianism in the United States. *Political Psychology* 39 (5): 1049–1067.

Cook, J., and Lewandowsky, S. 2016. Rational irrationality: Modeling climate change belief polarization using Bayesian networks. *Topics in Cognitive Science* 8 (1): 160–179.

Coontz, S. 2020. How to make your marriage gayer. *New York Times*, February 13. https://www.nytimes.com/2020/02/13/opinion/sunday/marriage-housework-gender -happiness.html.

Correll, J., Judd, C. M., Park, B., and Wittenbrink, B. 2010. Measuring prejudice, stereotypes and discrimination. In J. F. Dovidio, M. Hewstone, P. Glick, and V. M. Esses, eds., *The SAGE handbook of prejudice, stereotyping and discrimination*, 45–62. Thousand Oaks, CA: Sage.

Costa, P. T., and McCrae, R. R. 1992. *Revised NEO personality inventory*. Odessa, FL: Psychological Assessment Resources.

Crawford, J. T. 2014. Ideological symmetries and asymmetries in political intolerance and prejudice toward political activist groups. *Journal of Experimental Social Psychology* 55:284–298.

Crawford, J. T. 2017. Are conservatives more sensitive to threat than liberals? It depends on how we define threat and conservatism. *Social Cognition* 35 (4): 354–373.

Crawford, J. T. 2018. The politics of the psychology of prejudice. In J. T. Crawford and L. Jussim, eds., *The politics of social psychology*, 99–115. New York: Routledge.

Crawford, J. T., and Brandt, M. J. 2020. Ideological (a)symmetries in prejudice and intergroup bias. *Current Opinion in Behavioral Sciences* 34:40–45.

Crawford, J. T., Brandt, M. J., Inbar, Y., Chambers, J., and Motyl, M. 2017. Social and economic ideologies differentially predict prejudice across the political spectrum, but social issues are most divisive. *Journal of Personality and Social Psychology* 112 (3): 383–412.

Crawford, J. T., and Jussim, L., eds. 2018. *The politics of social psychology*. New York: Routledge.

Crawford, J. T., Kay, S. A., and Duke, K. E. 2015. Speaking out of both sides of their mouths: Biased political judgments within (and between) individuals. *Social Psychological and Personality Science* 6 (4): 422–430.

Crawford, J. T., and Pilanski, J. M. 2014. Political intolerance, right and left. *Political Psychology* 35 (6): 841–851.

Dagnall, N., Drinkwater, K., Parker, A., Denovan, A., and Parton, M. 2015. Conspiracy theory and cognitive style: A worldview. *Frontiers in Psychology* 6. Article 206. doi:10.3389/fpsyg.2015.00206.

Damore, J. 2017. Google's ideological Echo chamber: How bias clouds our thinking about diversity and inclusion. July. https://assets.documentcloud.org/documents/3914586/Googles-Ideological-Echo-Chamber.pdf.

Dawes, R. M. 1976. Shallow psychology. In J. S. Carroll and J. W. Payne, eds., *Cognition and social behavior*, 3–11. Hillsdale, NJ: Erlbaum.

Dawes, R. M. 1989. Statistical criteria for establishing a truly false consensus effect. *Journal of Experimental Social Psychology* 25 (1): 1–17.

Dawes, R. M. 1990. The potential nonfalsity of the false consensus effect. In R. M. Hogarth, ed., *Insights into decision making*, 179–199. Chicago: University of Chicago Press.

Dawkins, R. 1976/1989. *The selfish gene*. New York: Oxford University Press.

Dawkins, R. 1982. *The extended phenotype*. New York: Oxford University Press.

Dawkins, R. 1993. Viruses of the mind. In B. Dahlbom, ed., *Dennett and his critics: Demystifying mind*, 13–27. Cambridge, MA: Blackwell.

Dawson, E., Gilovich, T., and Regan, D. T. 2002. Motivated reasoning and performance on the Wason selection task. *Personality and Social Psychology Bulletin* 28 (10): 1379–1387.

Deary, I. J. 2013. Intelligence. *Current Biology* 23 (16): R673–R676.

De Finetti, B. 1989. Probabilism: A critical essay on the theory of probability and on the value of science. *Erkenntnis* 31 (2–3): 169–223.

De Neve, J.-E. 2015. Personality, childhood experience, and political ideology. *Political Psychology* 36: 55–73.

De Neys, W. 2006. Dual processing in reasoning—Two systems but one reasoner. *Psychological Science* 17: 428–433.

De Neys, W. 2012. Bias and conflict: A case for logical intuitions. *Perspectives on Psychological Science* 7: 28–38.

De Neys, W., ed. 2018. *Dual process theory 2.0*. London: Routledge.

De Neys, W., and Pennycook, G. 2019. Logic, fast and slow: Advances in dual-process theorizing. *Current Directions in Psychological Science* 28 (5): 503–509.

Dennett, D. C. 1991. *Consciousness explained*. Boston: Little, Brown.

Dennett, D. C. 1995. *Darwin's dangerous idea: Evolution and the meanings of life*. New York: Simon & Schuster.

Dennett, D. C. 1996. *Kinds of minds: Toward an understanding of consciousness*. New York: Basic Books.

Dennett, D. C. 2017. *From bacteria to Bach and back*. New York: Norton.

Dentakos, S., Saoud, W., Ackerman, R., and Toplak, M. E. 2019. Does domain matter? Monitoring accuracy across domains. *Metacognition and Learning* 14 (3): 413–436. https://doi.org/10.1007/s11409-019-09198-4.

Deppe, K. D., Gonzalez, F. J., Neiman, J. L., Jacobs, C. M., Pahlke, J., Smith, K. B., and Hibbing, J. R. 2015. Reflective liberals and intuitive conservatives: A look at the Cognitive Reflection Test and ideology. *Judgment and Decision Making* 10 (4): 314–331.

Ding, D., Chen, Y., Lai, J., Chen, X., Han, M., and Zhang, X. 2020. Belief bias effect in older adults: Roles of working memory and need for cognition. *Frontiers in Psychology* 10. Article 2940. doi:10.3389/fpsyg.2019.02940.

Distin, K. 2005. *The selfish meme*. Cambridge: Cambridge University Press.

Ditto, P., Liu, B., Clark, C., Wojcik, S., Chen, E., Grady, R. et al. 2019a. At least bias is bipartisan: A meta-analytic comparison of partisan bias in liberals and conservatives. *Perspectives on Psychological Science* 14 (2): 273–291.

Ditto, P., Liu, B., Clark, C., Wojcik, S., Chen, E., Grady, R., et al. 2019b. Partisan bias and its discontents. *Perspectives on Psychological Science* 14 (2): 304–316.

Ditto, P., Liu, B., and Wojcik, S. 2012. Is anything sacred anymore? *Psychological Inquiry* 23 (2): 155–161.

Ditto, P., and Lopez, D. 1992. Motivated skepticism: Use of differential decision criteria for preferred and nonpreferred conclusions. *Journal of Personality and Social Psychology* 63 (4): 568–584.

Dodd, M. D., Balzer, A., Jacobs, C. M., Gruszczynski, M. W., Smith, K. B., and Hibbing, J. R. 2012. The political left rolls with the good and the political right confronts the bad: Connecting physiology and cognition to preferences. *Philosophical Transactions of the Royal Society B: Biological Sciences* 367 (1589): 640–649.

Domo. 2018. Data never sleeps 6.0. https://www.domo.com/solution/data-never -sleeps-6.

Druckman, J. N. 2012. The politics of motivation. *Critical Review* 24 (2): 199–216.

Druckman, J. N., and McGrath, M. C. 2019. The evidence for motivated reasoning in climate change preference formation. *Nature Climate Change* 9 (2): 111–119.

Drummond, C., and Fischhoff, B. 2017. Individuals with greater science literacy and education have more polarized beliefs on controversial science topics. *Proceedings of the National Academy of Sciences* 114 (36): 9587–9592. http://www.pnas.org/content /114/36/9587t.doi:10.1073/pnas.1704882114.

Drummond, C., and Fischhoff, B. 2019. Does "putting on your thinking cap" reduce myside bias in evaluation of scientific evidence? *Thinking & Reasoning* 25 (4): 477–505.

Duarte, J. L., Crawford, J. T., Stern, C., Haidt, J., Jussim, L., and Tetlock, P. E. 2015. Political diversity will improve social psychological science. *Behavioral and Brain Sciences* 38:e130. doi:10.1017/S0140525X14000430.

Dunbar, R. 1998. The social brain hypothesis. *Evolutionary Anthropology* 6 (5): 178–190. doi:10.1002/(SICI)1520-6505(1998)6:5<178::AID-EVAN5>3.0.CO;2-8.

Dunbar, R. 2016. *Human evolution: Our brains and behavior.* New York: Oxford University Press.

Durham, W. 1991. *Coevolution: Genes, culture, and human diversity.* Stanford: Stanford University Press.

Earman, J. 1992. *Bayes or bust.* Cambridge, MA: MIT Press.

Edsall, T. 2018. The Democrats' left turn is not an illusion. *New York Times,* October 18. https://www.nytimes.com/2018/10/18/opinion/democrat-electorate-left-turn.html.

Edwards, K., and Smith, E. E. 1996. A disconfirmation bias in the evaluation of arguments. *Journal of Personality and Social Psychology* 71 (1): 5–24.

Edwards, W. 1982. Conservatism in human information processing. In D. Kahneman, P. Slovic, and A. Tversky, eds., *Judgment under uncertainty: Heuristics and biases*, 359–369. New York: Cambridge University Press.

Ehret, P. J., Sparks, A. C., and Sherman, D. K. 2017. Support for environmental protection: An integration of ideological-consistency and information-deficit models. *Environmental Politics* 26 (2): 253–277.

Eichmeier, A., and Stenhouse, N. 2019. Differences that don't make much difference: Party asymmetry in open-minded cognitive styles has little relationship to information processing behavior. *Research & Politics* 6 (3). doi:10.1177/2053168019872045.

Eil, D., and Rao, J. M. 2011. The good news-bad news effect: Asymmetric processing of objective information about yourself. *American Economic Journal: Microeconomics* 3 (2): 114–138.

Elster, J. 1983. *Sour grapes: Studies in the subversion of rationality*. Cambridge: Cambridge University Press.

Enders, A. M. 2019. Conspiratorial thinking and political constraint. *Public Opinion Quarterly* 83 (3): 510–533.

Epley, N., and Gilovich, T. 2016. The mechanics of motivated reasoning. *Journal of Economic Perspectives* 30 (3): 133–140.

Evans, J. St. B. T. 1989. *Bias in human reasoning: Causes and consequences*. Hove, UK: Erlbaum.

Evans, J. St. B. T. 1996. Deciding before you think: Relevance and reasoning in the selection task. *British Journal of Psychology* 87 (2): 223–240.

Evans, J. St. B. T. 2007. *Hypothetical thinking: Dual processes in reasoning and judgment*. New York: Psychology Press.

Evans, J. St. B. T. 2010. *Thinking twice: Two minds in one brain*. Oxford: Oxford University Press.

Evans, J. St. B. T. 2017. Belief bias in deductive reasoning. In R. Pohl, ed.. *Cognitive illusions*, 2nd ed., 165–181. London: Routledge.

Evans, J. St. B. T. 2019. Reflections on reflection: The nature and function of type 2 processes in dual-process theories of reasoning. *Thinking and Reasoning* 25 (4): 383–415.

Evans, J. St. B. T., Over, D. E., and Manktelow, K. 1993. Reasoning, decision making and rationality. *Cognition* 49 (1–2): 165–187.

Evans, J. St. B. T., and Stanovich, K. E. 2013. Dual-process theories of higher cognition: Advancing the debate. *Perspectives on Psychological Science* 8 (3): 223–241.

Evans, J. St. B. T., and Wason, P. C. 1976. Rationalization in a reasoning task. *British Journal of Psychology* 67 (4): 479–486.

Everett, J. 2013. The 12 item Social and Economic Conservatism Scale (SECS). *PloS One* 8 (12). e82131. doi:10.1371/journal.pone.0082131.

Facebook. (n.d.). Wikipedia. Retrieved March 2, 2020. https://en.wikipedia.org/wiki/Facebook#User_growth.

Fatke, M. 2017. Personality traits and political ideology: A first global assessment. *Political Psychology* 38 (5): 881–899.

Fazio, R. H. 2007. Attitudes as object–evaluation associations of varying strength. *Social Cognition* 25 (5): 603–637.

Feather, N. T. 1964. Acceptance and rejection of arguments in relation to attitude strength, critical ability, and intolerance of inconsistency. *Journal of Abnormal and Social Psychology* 69 (2): 127–136.

Federico, C. M., and Malka, A. 2018. The contingent, contextual nature of the relationship between needs for security and certainty and political preferences: Evidence and implications. *Political Psychology* 39 (S1): 3–48.

Feldman, S., and Huddy, L. 2014. Not so simple: The multidimensional nature and diverse origins of political ideology. *Behavioral and Brain Sciences* 37 (3): 312–313.

Feldman, S., and Johnston, C. 2014. Understanding the determinants of political ideology: implications of structural complexity. *Political Psychology* 35 (3): 337–358.

Finucane, M. L., Alhakami, A., Slovic, P., and Johnson, S. M. 2000. The affect heuristic in judgments of risks and benefits. *Journal of Behavioral Decision Making* 13 (1): 1–17.

Finucane, M. L., and Gullion, C. M. 2010. Developing a tool for measuring the decision-making competence of older adults. *Psychology and Aging* 25 (2): 271–288.

Fischhoff, B., and Beyth-Marom, R. 1983. Hypothesis evaluation from a Bayesian perspective. *Psychological Review* 90 (3): 239–260.

Fish, S. 2019. *The first: How to think about hate speech, campus speech, religious speech, fake news, post-truth, and Donald Trump.* New York: One Signal.

Fisher, M., and Keil, F. C. 2014. The illusion of argument justification. *Journal of Experimental Psychology: General* 143 (1): 425–433.

Flynn, D. J., Nyhan, B., and Reifler, J. 2017. The nature and origins of misperceptions: Understanding false and unsupported beliefs about politics. *Advances in Political Psychology* 38 (S1): 127–150.

Fodor, J. A. 1983. *The modularity of mind.* Cambridge, MA: MIT Press.

Foley, R. 1991. Rationality, belief, and commitment. *Synthese,* 89 (3): 365–392.

Fournier, H. 2016. UM students' petition condemns Schlissel's anti-Trump statements. *Detroit News*, November 14. https://www.detroitnews.com/story/news/2016/11/14/um-students-condemn-schlissels-anti-trump-statements/93802864/.

Fraley, R. C., Griffin, B. N., Belsky, J., and Roisman, G. I. 2012. Developmental antecedents of political ideology: A longitudinal investigation from birth to age 18 years. *Psychological Science* 23 (11): 1425–1431.

Frank, T. 2004. *What's the matter with Kansas?* New York: Metropolitan Books.

Frederick, S. 2005. Cognitive reflection and decision making. *Journal of Economic Perspectives* 19 (4): 25–42.

French, D. 2018. Let's talk about "tolerance." *National Review*, April 6. https://www.nationalreview.com/2018/04/lets-talk-about-tolerance/.

Friedrich, J. 1993. Primary error detection and minimization (PEDMIN) strategies in social cognition: A reinterpretation of confirmation bias phenomena. *Psychological Review* 100 (2): 298–319.

Frizell, S. 2016. Why conservatives praise Bernie Sanders on immigration. *Time*, January 7. https://time.com/4170591/bernie-sanders-immigration-conservatives/.

Frost, A. A'L. 2019. Why the left can't stand the *New York Times*. *Columbia Journalism Review*, winter. https://www.cjr.org/special_report/why-the-left-cant-stand-the-new-york-times.php.

Fryer, R. G. 2019. An empirical analysis of racial differences in police use of force. *Journal of Political Economy* 127 (3): 1210–1261.

Fuller, R. 2019. *In defence of democracy*. Cambridge: Polity Press.

Funk, C., Hefferon, M., Kennedy. B., and Johnson, C. 2019. Trust and mistrust in American's views of scientific experts. *Pew Research Center*. August 2. https://www.pewresearch.org/science/2019/08/02/trust-and-mistrust-in-americans-views-of-scientific-experts/.

Funk, C. L., Smith, K. B., Alford, J. R., Hibbing, M. V., Eaton, N. R., Krueger, R. F., et al. 2013. Genetic and environmental transmission of political orientations. *Political Psychology* 34 (6): 805–819.

Gampa, A., Wojcik, S. P., Motyl, M., Nosek, B. A., and Ditto, P. H. 2019. (Ideo)logical reasoning: Ideology impairs sound reasoning. *Social Psychological and Personality Science* 10 (8): 1075–1083.

Ganzach, Y. 2016. Cognitive ability and party identity: No important differences between Democrats and Republicans. *Intelligence* 58:18–21.

Ganzach, Y., Hanoch, Y., and Choma, B. L. 2019. Attitudes toward presidential candidates in the 2012 and 2016 American elections: Cognitive ability and support for Trump. *Social Psychological and Personality Science* 10 (7): 924–934.

Gauchat, G. 2012. Politicization of science in the public sphere: A study of public trust in the United States, 1974 to 2010. *American Sociological Review* 77 (2): 167–187. doi:10.1177/0003122412438225

Gentzkow, M., and Shapiro, J. 2006. Media bias and reputation. *Journal of Political Economy* 114 (2): 280–316.

Gerber, A. S., and Green, D. P. 1998. Rational learning and partisan attitudes. *American Journal of Political Science* 42 (3): 794–818.

Gerber, A. S., and Huber, G. A. 2010. Partisanship, political control, and economic assessments. *American Journal of Political Science* 54 (1): 153–173.

Gershman, S. J. 2019. How to never be wrong. *Psychonomic Bulletin & Review* 26 (1): 13–28.

Gibbard, A. 1990. *Wise choices, apt feelings.* Cambridge, MA: Harvard University Press.

Gilbert, D. T., Pelham, B. W., and Krull, D. S. 1988. On cognitive busyness: When person perceivers meet persons perceived. *Journal of Personality and Social Psychology* 54 (5): 733–740.

Gilinsky, A., and Judd, B. B. 1994. Working memory and bias in reasoning across the life span. *Psychology and Aging* 9 (3): 356–371.

Gintis, H. 2007. A framework for the unification of the behavioral sciences. *Behavioral and Brain Sciences* 30 (1): 1–61.

Glick, P., and Fiske, S. T. 1996. The ambivalent sexism inventory: Differentiating hostile and benevolent sexism. *Journal of Personality and Social Psychology* 70 (3): 491–512.

Goertzel, T. 1994. Belief in conspiracy theories. *Political Psychology* 15 (4): 731–742.

Goldberg, Z. 2018. Serwer error: Misunderstanding Trump voters. *Quillette*, January 1. https://quillette.com/2018/01/01/serwer-error-misunderstanding-trump-voters/.

Goldberg, Z. 2019. America's white saviors. *Tablet*, June 5. https://www.tabletmag.com/jewish-news-and-politics/284875/americas-white-saviors.

Golman, R., Hagmann, D., and Loewenstein, G. 2017. Information avoidance. *Journal of Economic Literature* 55 (1), 96–135.

Golman, R., Loewenstein, G., Moene, K., and Zarri, L. 2016. The preference for belief consonance. *Journal of Economic Perspectives* 30 (3): 165–188.

Goodhart, D. 2017. *The road to somewhere.* London: Hurst.

Grant, J. 2011. *Denying science: Conspiracy theories, media distortions, and the war against reality.* Amherst, NY: Prometheus Books.

Greene, J. D. 2013. *Moral tribes: Emotion. reason, and the gap between us and them*. New York: Penguin.

Groenendyk, E. 2018. Competing motives in a polarized electorate: Political responsiveness, identity defensiveness, and the rise of partisan antipathy. *Political Psychology* 39 (S1): 159–171.

Grynbaum, M., and Koblin, J. 2017. For solace and solidarity in the Trump age, liberals turn the TV back on. *New York Times*, March 12. https://www.nytimes.com /2017/03/12/business/trump-television-ratings-liberals.html.

Gul, P., and Kupfer, T. R. 2019. Benevolent sexism and mate preferences. *Personality and Social Psychology Bulletin* 45 (1): 146–161.

Hahn, U., and Harris, A. J. L. 2014. What does it mean to be biased: Motivated reasoning and rationality. In B. H. Ross, ed., *Psychology of Learning and Motivation*, 61:41–102. Academic Press.

Haidt, J. 2001. The emotional dog and its rational tail: A social intuitionist approach to moral judgment. *Psychological Review* 108 (4): 814–834.

Haidt, J. 2012. *The righteous mind: Why good people are divided by politics and religion*. New York: Pantheon.

Haidt, J. 2016. When and why nationalism beats globalism. *American Interest*, July 10. https://www.the-american-interest.com/2016/07/10/when-and-why-nationalism -beats-globalism/.

Haier, R. J. 2016. *The neuroscience of intelligence*. Cambridge: Cambridge University Press.

Hamilton, L. C. 2011. Education, politics and opinions about climate change evidence for interaction effects. *Climatic Change* 104 (2): 231–242.

Handley, S. J., Capon, A., Beveridge, M., Dennis, I., and Evans, J. St. B. T. 2004. Working memory, inhibitory control and the development of children's reasoning. *Thinking and Reasoning* 10 (2): 175–195.

Hankins, J. 2020. Hyperpartisanship: A barbarous term for a barbarous age. *Claremont Review of Books* 20 (1): 8–17.

Haran, U., Ritov, I., and Mellers, B. A. 2013. The role of actively open-minded thinking in information acquisition, accuracy, and calibration. *Judgment and Decision Making* 8 (3): 188–201.

Harari, Y. N. 2018. *21 Lessons for the 21st century*. New York: Spiegel & Grau.

Hardin, G. 1968. The tragedy of the commons. *Science* 162 (3859): 1243–1248.

Hargreaves Heap, S. P. 1992. Rationality. In S. P. Hargreaves Heap, M. Hollis, B. Lyons, R. Sugden, and A. Weale, eds., *The theory of choice: A critical guide*, 3–25. Oxford: Blackwell.

Harris, J. R. 1995. Where is the child's environment? A group socialization theory of development. *Psychological Review* 102 (3): 458–489.

Harris, S. 2018. Identity and honesty. *Making Sense Podcast*, #123, April 9. https://samharris.org/podcasts/123-identity-honesty/.

Hart, W., Albarracin, D., Eagly, A. H., Brechan, I., Lindberg, M. J., and Merrill, L. 2009. Feeling validated versus being correct: A meta-analysis of selective exposure to information. *Psychological Bulletin* 135 (4): 555–588.

Hartocollis, A. 2018. Harvard's admissions process, once secret, is unveiled in affirmative action trial. *New York Times*, October 19. https://www.nytimes.com/2018/10/19/us/harvard-admissions-affirmative-action.html.

Hartocollis, A. 2020. The affirmative action battle at Harvard is not over. *New York Times*, October 19. https://www.nytimes.com/2020/02/18/us/affirmative-action-harvard.html.

Haselton, M. G., and Buss, D. M. 2000. Error management theory: a new perspective on biases in cross-sex mind reading. *Journal of Personality and Social Psychology* 78 (1): 81–91.

Haselton, M. G., Nettle, D., and Murray, D. J. 2016. The evolution of cognitive bias. In D. M. Buss, ed., *The handbook of evolutionary psychology*, 968–987. New York: John Wiley.

Haslam, N. 2016. Concept creep: Psychology's expanding concepts of harm and pathology. *Psychological Inquiry* 27 (1): 1–17.

Hastorf, A. H., and Cantril, H. 1954. They saw a game: A case study. *Journal of Abnormal Psychology* 49 (1): 129–134.

Hatemi, P. K., Gillespie, N. A., Eaves, L. J., Maher, B. S., Webb, B. T., Heath, A. C., et al. 2011. A genome-wide analysis of liberal and conservative political attitudes. *Journal of Politics* 73 (1): 271–285.

Hatemi, P. K., and McDermott, R. 2012. The genetics of politics: Discovery, challenges, and progress. *Trends in Genetics* 28 (10): 525–533.

Hatemi, P. K., and McDermott, R. 2016. Give me attitudes. *Annual Review of Political Science* 19 (1): 331–350.

Heer, J. 2016. Are Donald Trump's supporters idiots? *New Republic*, May 11. https://newrepublic.com/minutes/133447/donald-trumps-supporters-idiots.

Henry, P. J., and Napier, J. L. 2017. Education is related to greater ideological prejudice. *Public Opinion Quarterly* 81 (4): 930–942.

Henry, P. J., and Sears, D. O. 2002. The Symbolic Racism 2000 Scale. *Political Psychology* 23 (2): 253–283.

Heying, H. 2018. Grievance studies vs. the scientific method. *Medium*, November 1. https://medium.com/@heyingh/grievance-studies-goes-after-the-scientific-method -63b6cfd9c913.

Hibbing, J. R., Smith, K. B., and Alford, J. R. 2014a. Differences in negativity bias underlie variations in political ideology. *Behavioral and Brain Sciences* 37 (3): 297–307. doi:10.1017/S0140525X13001192.

Hibbing, J. R., Smith, K. B., and Alford, J. R. 2014b. *Predisposed: Liberals, conservatives, and the biology of political differences*. New York: Routledge.

Hirschman, A. O. 1986. *Rival views of market society and other recent essays*. New York: Viking.

Hirsh, J. B., DeYoung, C. G., Xu, X., and Peterson, J. B. 2010. Compassionate liberals and polite conservatives: Associations of agreeableness with political ideology and moral values. *Personality and Social Psychology Bulletin* 36 (5): 655–664.

Hoch, S. J. 1987. Perceived consensus and predictive accuracy: The pros and cons of projection. *Journal of Personality and Social Psychology* 53 (2): 221–234.

Hollis, M. 1992. Ethical preferences. In S. Hargreaves Heap, M. Hollis, B. Lyons, R. Sugden, and A. Weale, eds., *The theory of choice: A critical guide*, 308–310. Oxford: Blackwell.

Honeycutt, N., and Jussim, L. 2020. A model of political bias in social science research. *Psychological Inquiry* 31 (1): 73–85.

Hopkins, D. J., Sides, J., and Citrin, J. 2019. The muted consequences of correct information about immigration. *Journal of Politics* 81 (1): 315–320. doi:10.1086/699914.

Horn, J. L., and Cattell, R. B. 1967. Age differences in fluid and crystallized intelligence. *Acta Psychologica* 26:1–23.

Horowitz, M., Haynor, A., and Kickham, K. 2018. Sociology's sacred victims and the politics of knowledge: Moral foundations theory and disciplinary controversies. *American Sociologist* 49 (4): 459–495.

Horwitz, J. 2020. Facebook delivers long-awaited trove of data to outside researchers. *Wall Street Journal*, February 13. https://www.wsj.com/articles/facebook-delivers -long-awaited-trove-of-data-to-outside-researchers-11581602403.

Houston, D. A., and Fazio, R. H. 1989. Biased processing as a function of attitude accessibility: Making objective judgments subjectively. *Social Cognition* 7 (1): 51–66.

Howe, L. C., and Krosnick, J. A. 2017. Attitude strength. *Annual Review of Psychology* 68:327–351.

Howson, C., and Urbach, P. 1993. *Scientific reasoning: The Bayesian approach*. 2nd ed. Chicago: Open Court.

Huddy, L., Mason, L., and Aaroe, L. 2015. Expressive partisanship: Campaign involvement, political emotion, and partisan identity. *American Political Science Review* 109 (1): 1–17.

Huemer, M. 2015. Why people are irrational about politics. In J. Anomaly, G. Brennan, M. Munger, and G. Sayre-McCord, eds., *Philosophy, politics, and economics: An anthology*, 456–467. Oxford: Oxford University Press.

Hufer, A., Kornadt, A. E., Kandler, C., and Riemann, R. 2020. Genetic and environmental variation in political orientation in adolescence and early adulthood: A Nuclear Twin Family analysis. *Journal of Personality and Social Psychology* 118 (4): 762–776.

Hughes, C. 2018. The racism treadmill. *Quillette*, May 14. https://quillette.com/2018/05/14/the-racism-treadmill/.

Humphrey, N. 1976. The social function of intellect. In P. P. G. Bateson and R. A. Hinde, eds., *Growing points in ethology*, 303–317. London: Faber and Faber.

Inbar, Y., Pizarro, D. A., and Bloom, P. 2009. Conservatives are more easily disgusted than liberals. *Cognition and Emotion* 23 (4): 714–725.

Inbar, Y., Pizarro, D., Iyer, R., and Haidt, J. 2012. Disgust sensitivity, political conservatism, and voting. *Social Psychological and Personality Science* 3:537–544.

Iyengar, S., Konitzer, T., and Tedin, K. 2018. The home as a political fortress: Family agreement in an era of polarization. *Journal of Politics* 80 (4): 1326–1338.

Iyengar, S., Lelkes, Y., Levendusky, M., Malhotra, N., and Westwood, S. J. 2019. The origins and consequences of affective polarization in the United States. *Annual Review of Political Science* 22:129–146.

Iyengar, S., Sood, G., and Lelkes, Y. 2012. Affect, not ideology: A social identity perspective on polarization. *Public Opinion Quarterly* 76 (3): 405–431.

Iyer, R., Koleva, S., Graham, J., Ditto, P., and Haidt, J. 2012. Understanding libertarian morality: The psychological dispositions of self-identified libertarians. *PloS One* 7 (8). doi:10.1371/journal.pone.0042366.

Jeffrey, R. C. 1983. *The logic of decision*. 2nd ed. Chicago: University of Chicago Press.

Jennings, M. K., Stoker, L., and Bowers, J. 2009. Politics across generations: Family transmission reexamined. *Journal of Politics* 71 (3): 782–799.

Jerit, J., and Barabas, J. 2012. Partisan perceptual bias and the information environment. *Journal of Politics* 74 (3): 672–684.

Jern, A., Chang, K., and Kemp, C. 2014. Belief polarization is not always irrational. *Psychological Review* 121 (2): 206–224.

Johnson, D. J., Tress, T., Burkel, N., Taylor, C., and Cesario, J. 2019. Officer characteristics and racial disparities in fatal officer-involved shootings. *Proceedings of the
National Academy of Sciences* 116 (32): 15877–15882. doi:10.1073/pnas.1903856116.

Johnson, D. P., and Fowler, J. H. 2011. The evolution of overconfidence. *Nature* 477
(7364): 317–320.

Johnston, C. D., Lavine, H. G., and Federico, C. M. 2017. *Open versus closed: Personality, identity, and the politics of redistribution.* Cambridge: Cambridge University
Press.

Jones, P. E. 2019. Partisanship, political awareness, and retrospective evaluations,
1956–2016. *Political Behavior.* doi:10.1007/s11109-019-09543-y.

Joshi, H. 2020. What are the chances you're right about everything? An epistemic
challenge for modern partisanship. *Politics, Philosophy & Economics* 19 (1): 36–61.

Joslyn, M. R., and Haider-Markel, D. P. 2014. Who knows best? Education, partisanship, and contested facts. *Politics & Policy* 42 (6): 919–947.

Jost, J. T., Glaser, J., Kruglanski, A. W., and Sulloway, F. J. 2003. Political conservatism as motivated social cognition. *Psychological Bulletin* 129 (3): 339–375.

Jussim, L. 2017a, Gender bias in science? Double standards and cherry-picking in
claims about gender bias. *Psychology Today*, July 14. https://www.psychologytoday
.com/us/blog/rabble-rouser/201707/gender-bias-in-science.

Jussim, L. 2017b. The Google memo: Four scientists respond. *Quillette*, August 7.
http://quillette.com/2017/08/07/google-memo-four-scientists-respond/.

Jussim, L. 2018. The reality of the rise of an intolerant and radical left on campus.
Areo, March 17. https://areomagazine.com/2018/03/17/the-reality-of-the-rise-of-an
-intolerant-and-radical-left-on-campus/.

Jussim, L. 2019a. My diversity, equity, and inclusion statement. *Quillette*. February
24. https://quillette.com/2019/02/24/my-diversity-equity-and-inclusion-statement/.

Jussim, L. 2019b. Rapid onset gender dysphoria. *Psychology Today*, March 20. https://
www.psychologytoday.com/us/blog/rabble-rouser/201903/rapid-onset-gender
-dysphoria.

Jussim, L. 2019c. The threat to academic freedom . . . from academics. *Medium*,
December 27. https://medium.com/@leej12255/the-threat-to-academic-freedom-from
-academics-4685b1705794.

Kahan, D. M. 2003. The gun control debate: A culture-theory manifesto. *Washington
and Lee Law Review* 60 Part 1:3–15.

Kahan, D. M. 2012. Why we are poles apart on climate change. *Nature* 488 (7411):
255. doi:10.1038/488255a.

Kahan, D. M. 2013. Ideology, motivated reasoning, and cognitive reflection. *Judgment and Decision Making* 8 (4): 407–424.

Kahan, D. M. 2015. Climate-science communication and the measurement problem. *Political Psychology* 36 (S1): 1–43.

Kahan, D. M. 2016. The politically motivated reasoning paradigm, part 1: What politically motivated reasoning is and how to measure it. In R. A. Scott, S. M. Kosslyn, and M. C. Buchmann, eds., *Emerging trends in the social and behavioral sciences: An interdisciplinary, searchable, and linkable resource.* doi:10.1002/9781118900772 .etrds0417.

Kahan, D. M., and Corbin, J. C. 2016. A note on the perverse effects of actively open-minded thinking on climate-change polarization. *Research & Politics* 3 (4): 1–5. doi:10.1177/2053168016676705.

Kahan, D. M., Hoffman, D. A., Braman, D., Evans, D., and Rachlinski, J. J. 2012. "They saw a protest": Cognitive illiberalism and the speech-conduct distinction. *Stanford Law Review* 64 (4): 851–906.

Kahan, D. M., Jenkins-Smith, H., and Braman, D. 2011. Cultural cognition of scientific consensus. *Journal of Risk Research* 14 (2): 147–174.

Kahan, D. M., Peters, E., Dawson, E., and Slovic, P. 2017. Motivated numeracy and enlightened self-government. *Behavioural Public Policy* 1 (1): 54–86.

Kahan, D. M. Peters, E., Wittlin, M., Slovic, P., Ouellette, L., Braman, D., and Mandel, G. 2012. The polarizing impact of science literacy and numeracy on perceived climate change risks. *Nature Climate Change* 2 (10): 732–735.

Kahan, D. M., and Stanovich, K. E. 2016. Rationality and belief in human evolution. Annenberg Public Policy Center Working Paper no. 5, September 14. https://ssrn .com/abstract=2838668.

Kahneman, D. 2011. *Thinking, fast and slow.* New York: Farrar, Straus and Giroux.

Kahneman, D., and Tversky, A. 1973. On the psychology of prediction. *Psychological Review* 80 (4): 237–251.

Kaufmann, E. 2019. *Whiteshift.* New York: Abrams Press.

Keltner, D., and Robinson, R. J. 1996. Extremism, power, and the imagined basis of social conflict. *Current Directions in Psychological Science* 5 (4): 101–105.

Kemmelmeier, M. 2008. Is there a relationship between political orientation and cognitive ability? A test of three hypotheses in two studies. *Personality and Individual Differences* 45 (8): 767–772.

Kerlinger, F. N. 1984. *Liberalism and conservatism: The nature and structure of social attitudes.* Hillsdale, NJ: Erlbaum.

Kiely, E, 2012. "You didn't build that," Uncut and unedited. *Factcheck.org.* July 23. https://www.factcheck.org/2012/07/you-didnt-build-that-uncut-and-unedited/.

Kim, M., Park, B., and Young, L. 2020. The psychology of motivated versus rational impression updating. *Trends in Cognitive Sciences* 24 (2): 101–111.

Kinder, D., and Kalmoe, N. 2017. *Neither liberal nor conservative: Ideological innocence in the American public.* Chicago: University of Chicago Press.

Klaczynski, P. A. 1997. Bias in adolescents' everyday reasoning and its relationship with intellectual ability, personal theories, and self-serving motivation. *Developmental Psychology* 33 (2): 273–283.

Klaczynski, P. A. 2014. Heuristics and biases: Interactions among numeracy, ability, and reflectiveness predict normative responding. *Frontiers in Psychology* 5:1–13.

Klaczynski, P. A., and Lavallee, K. L. 2005. Domain-specific identity, epistemic regulation, and intellectual ability as predictors of belief-based reasoning: A dual-process perspective. *Journal of Experimental Child Psychology* 92 (1): 1–24.

Klaczynski, P. A., and Robinson, B. 2000. Personal theories, intellectual ability, and epistemological beliefs: Adult age differences in everyday reasoning tasks. *Psychology and Aging* 15 (3): 400–416.

Klar, S. 2013. The influence of competing identity primes on political preferences. *Journal of Politics* 75 (4): 1108–1124.

Klayman, J. 1995. Varieties of confirmation bias. *Psychology of Learning and Motivation* 32:385–417.

Klayman, J., and Ha, Y. 1987. Confirmation, disconfirmation, and information in hypothesis testing. *Psychological Review* 94 (2): 211–228.

Klein, D. B. 2011. I was wrong, and so are you. *Atlantic,* December. https://www.theatlantic.com/magazine/archive/2011/12/i-was-wrong-and-so-are-you/308713/.

Klein, D. B., and Buturovic, Z. 2011. Economic enlightenment revisited: New results again find little relationship between education and economic enlightenment but vitiate prior evidence of the left being worse. *Econ Journal Watch* 8 (2): 157–173.

Klein, D. B., and Stern, C. 2005. Professors and their politics: The policy views of social scientists. *Critical Review* 17 (3–4): 257–303. doi:10.1080/08913810508443640.

Koehler, J. J. 1993. The influence of prior beliefs on scientific judgments of evidence quality. *Organizational Behavior and Human Decision Processes* 56 (1): 28–55.

Kokis, J., Macpherson, R., Toplak, M., West, R. F., and Stanovich, K. E. 2002. Heuristic and analytic processing: Age trends a:nd associations with cognitive ability and cognitive styles. *Journal of Experimental Child Psychology* 83 (1): 26–52.

Kolesnikova, N., and Liu, Y. 2011. Gender wage gap may be much smaller than most think. *Regional Economist*, October 1. Federal Reserve Bank of St. Louis. https://www.stlouisfed.org/Publications/Regional-Economist/October-2011/Gender-Wage-Gap-May-Be-Much-Smaller-Than-Most-Think?hc_location=ufi#endnotes.

Komorita, S. S., and Parks, C. D. 1994. *Social dilemmas*. Boulder, CO: Westview Press.

Kopko, K. C., Bryner, S. M., Budziak, J., Devine, C. J., and Nawara, S. P. 2011. In the eye of the beholder? Motivated reasoning in disputed elections. *Political Behavior* 33 (2): 271–290.

Kornblith, H. 1993. *Inductive inference and its natural ground*. Cambridge, MA: MIT Press.

Kovacs, K., and Conway, A. R. A. 2016. Process overlap theory: A unified account of the general factor of intelligence. *Psychological Inquiry* 27 (3): 151–177.

Kraft, P. W., Lodge, M., and Taber, C. S. 2015. Why people "don't trust the evidence": Motivated reasoning and scientific beliefs. *Annals of the American Academy of Political and Social Science* 658 (1): 121–133.

Kronman, A. 2019. *The assault on American excellence*. New York: Free Press.

Krugman, P. 2015. Recent history in one chart. *New York Times*, January 1. https://krugman.blogs.nytimes.com/2015/01/01/recent-history-in-one-chart/?_r=0.

Krummenacher, P., Mohr, C., Haker, H., and Brugger, P. 2010. Dopamine, paranormal belief, and the detection of meaningful stimuli. *Journal of Cognitive Neuroscience* 22 (8): 1670–1681.

Kuhn, D. 2019. Critical thinking as discourse. *Human Development* 62 (3): 146–164.

Kuhn, D., and Lao, J. 1996. Effects of evidence on attitudes: Is polarization the norm? *Psychological Science* 7 (2): 115–120.

Kuhn, D., and Modrek, A. 2018. Do reasoning limitations undermine discourse? *Thinking & Reasoning* 24 (1): 97–116.

Kunda, Z. 1990. The case for motivated reasoning. *Psychological Bulletin* 108 (3): 480–498.

Kurzban, R., and Aktipis, C. 2007. Modularity and the social mind: Are psychologists too self-ish? *Personality and Social Psychology Review* 11 (2): 131–149.

Langbert, M. 2018. Homogenous: The political affiliations of elite liberal arts college faculty. *Academic Questions* 31 (2): 186–197.

Langbert, M., and Stevens, S. 2020. Partisan registration and contributions of faculty in flagship colleges. *National Association of Scholars*. January 17. https://www.nas.org/blogs/article/partisan-registration-and-contributions-of-faculty-in-flagship-colleges.

Lanier, J. 2018. *Ten arguments for deleting your social media accounts right now.* New York: Henry Holt.

Lebo, M. J., and Cassino, D. 2007. The aggregated consequences of motivated reasoning and the dynamics of partisan presidential approval. *Political Psychology* 28 (6): 719–746.

Leeper, T. J., and Slothuus, R. 2014. Political parties, motivated reasoning, and public opinion formation. *Political Psychology* 35 (S1): 129–156.

Lelkes, Y. 2018. Affective polarization and ideological sorting: A reciprocal, albeit weak, relationship. *Forum* 16 (1): 67–79.

Lemon, J. 2019. Bernie Sanders says U.S. can't have "open borders" because poor people will come "from all over the world." *Newsweek*, April 8. https://www .newsweek.com/bernie-sanders-open-borders-poverty-world-immigration-1388767.

Lench, H. C., and Ditto, P. H. 2008. Automatic optimism: Biased use of base rate information for positive and negative events. *Journal of Experimental Social Psychology* 44 (3): 631–639.

Levin, I. P., Wasserman, E. A., and Kao, S. F. 1993. Multiple methods of examining biased information use in contingency judgments. *Organizational Behavior and Human Decision Processes* 55 (2): 228–250.

Levinson, S. C. 1995. Interactional biases in human thinking. In E. Goody, ed., *Social intelligence and interaction,* 221–260. Cambridge: Cambridge University Press.

Levy, S. 2020. *Facebook: The inside story.* New York: Blue Rider Press.

Li, N., van Vugt, M., and Colarelli, S. 2018. The evolutionary mismatch hypothesis: Implications for psychological science. *Current Direction in Psychological Science* 27 (1): 38–44.

Liberali, J. M., Reyna, V. F., Furlan, S., Stein, L. M., and Pardo, S. T. 2012. Individual differences in numeracy and cognitive reflection, with implications for biases and fallacies in probability judgment. *Journal of Behavioral Decision Making* 25 (4): 361–381.

Lilienfeld, S. O. 2017. Microaggressions: Strong claims, inadequate evidence. *Perspectives on Psychological Science* 12 (1): 138–169.

Lilienfeld, S. O. 2019. Microaggression research and application: Clarifications, corrections, and common ground. *Perspectives on Psychological Science* 15 (1): 27–37.

Lilla, M. 2017. *The once and future liberal: After identity politics.* New York: Harper-Collins.

Lind, M. 2020. *The new class war: Saving democracy from the managerial elite.* New York: Penguin.

Lipman, M. 1991. *Thinking in education.* Cambridge: Cambridge University Press.

Lipsky, D., and Gartner, A. 1997. *Inclusion and school reform.* Baltimore: Brookes.

Liu, B. S., and Ditto, P. H. 2013. What dilemma? Moral evaluation shapes factual belief. *Social Psychological and Personality Science* 4 (3): 316–323.

Loewenstein, G. 2006. The pleasures and pains of information. *Science* 312 (5774): 704–706.

Loewenstein, G., and Molnar, A. 2018. The renaissance of belief-based utility in economics. *Nature Human Behaviour* 2 (3): 166–167.

Lomasky, L. 2008. Swing and a myth: A review of Caplan's *The Myth of the Rational Voter. Public Choice* 135 (3–4): 469–484.

Looney, A. 2019. How progressive is Senator Elizabeth Warren's loan forgiveness proposal? *Brookings*, April 24. https://www.brookings.edu/blog/up-front/2019/04/24 /how-progressive-is-senator-elizabeth-warrens-loan-forgiveness-proposal/.

Lord, C. G., Ross, L., and Lepper, M. R. 1979. Biased assimilation and attitude polarization: The effects of prior theories on subsequently considered evidence. *Journal of Personality and Social Psychology* 37 (11): 2098–2109.

Lott, J., and Moody, C. 2016. Do white police officers unfairly target black suspects? *SSRN.* November 15. https://ssrn.com/abstract=2870189.

Ludeke, S., Johnson, W., and Bouchard, T. J. 2013. "Obedience to traditional authority": A heritable factor underlying authoritarianism, conservatism and religiousness. *Personality and Individual Differences* 55 (4): 375–380.

Lukianoff, G., and Haidt, J. 2018. *The coddling of the American mind: How good intentions and bad ideas are setting up a generation for failure.* New York: Penguin.

Lumsden, C. J., and Wilson, E. O. 1981. *Genes, mind and culture.* Cambridge, MA: Harvard University Press.

Lupia, A. 2016. *Uninformed: Why people know so little about politics and what we can do about it.* New York: Oxford University Press.

Lupia, A., Levine, A. S., Menning, J. O., and Sin, G. 2007. Were Bush tax cut supporters "simply ignorant?" A second look at conservatives and liberals in "Homer Gets a Tax Cut." *Perspectives on Politics* 5 (4): 773–784.

Lynch, A. 1996. *Thought contagion.* New York: Basic Books.

MacCoun, R. J. 1998. Biases in the interpretation and use of research results. *Annual Review of Psychology* 49:259–287.

Mac Donald, H. 2018. *The diversity delusion: How race and gender pandering corrupt the university and undermine our culture.* New York: St. Martin's Press.

Macpherson, R., and Stanovich, K. E. 2007. Cognitive ability, thinking dispositions, and instructional set as predictors of critical thinking. *Learning and Individual Differences* 17 (2): 115–127.

Madison, G., and Fahlman, P. 2020. Sex differences in the number of scientific publications and citations when attaining the rank of professor in Sweden. *Studies in Higher Education.* doi:10.1080/03075079.2020.1723533.

Majima, Y. 2015. Belief in pseudoscience, cognitive style and science literacy. *Applied Cognitive Psychology* 29 (4): 552–559.

Malka, A., and Soto, C. J. 2015. Rigidity of the economic right? Menu-independent and menu-dependent influences of psychological dispositions on political attitude. *Current Directions in Psychological Science* 24 (2): 137–142.

Manktelow, K. I. 2004. Reasoning and rationality: The pure and the practical. In K. I. Manktelow and M. C. Chung, eds., *Psychology of reasoning: Theoretical and historical perspectives*, 157–177. Hove, UK: Psychology Press.

Margolis, H. 1987. *Patterns, thinking, and cognition.* Chicago: University of Chicago Press.

Martinelli, R. 2017. The truth about crime, illegal immigrants and sanctuary cities. *Hill.* April 19. https://thehill.com/blogs/pundits-blog/crime/329589-the-truth-about -crime-illegal-immigrants-and-sanctuary-cities.

Mason, L. 2015. "I disrespectfully agree": The differential effects of partisan sorting on social and issue polarization. *American Journal of Political Science* 59 (1): 128–145.

Mason, L. 2018a. Ideologues without issues: The polarizing consequences of ideological identities. *Public Opinion Quarterly* 82 (S1): 866–887.

Mason, L. 2018b. *Uncivil agreement: How politics became our identity.* Chicago: University of Chicago Press.

McCrae, R. R. 1996. Social consequences of experiential openness. *Psychological Bulletin* 120 (3): 323–337.

McGinnis, J. 2019. The ongoing decline of the *New York Times. Law & Liberty.* November 14. https://lawliberty.org/the-ongoing-decline-of-the-new-york-times/.

McGrath, M. C. 2017. Economic behavior and the partisan perceptual screen. *Quarterly Journal of Political Science* 11 (4): 363–383.

McKay, R. T., and Dennett, D. C. 2009. The evolution of misbelief. *Behavioral and Brain Sciences* 32 (6): 493–561.

McKenzie, C. R. M. 2004. Hypothesis testing and evaluation. In D. J. Koehler and N. Harvey, eds., *Blackwell handbook of judgment and decision making*, 200–219. Malden, MA: Blackwell.

McLanahan, S., Tach, L., and Schneider, D. 2013. The causal effects of father absence. *Annual Review of Sociology* 39:399–427.

McNamee, R. 2019. *Zucked: Waking up to the Facebook catastrophe.* New York: Penguin.

Medin, D. L., and Bazerman, M. H. 1999. Broadening behavioral decision research: Multiple levels of cognitive processing. *Psychonomic Bulletin & Review* 6 (4): 533–546.

Medin, D. L., Schwartz, H. C., Blok, S. V., and Birnbaum, L. A. 1999. The semantic side of decision making. *Psychonomic Bulletin & Review* 6 (4): 562–569.

Mercier, H. 2016. The argumentative theory: Predictions and empirical evidence. *Trends in Cognitive Science* 20 (9): 689–700.

Mercier, H. 2017. Confirmation bias—Myside bias. In R. Pohl, ed., *Cognitive illusions,* 2nd ed., 99–114. New York: Routledge.

Mercier, H., and Sperber, D. 2011. Why do humans reason? Arguments for an argumentative theory. *Behavioral and Brain Sciences* 34 (2): 57–111.

Mercier, H., and Sperber, D. 2017. *The enigma of reason.* Cambridge, MA: Harvard University Press.

Messick, D. M., and Sentis, K. P. 1979. Fairness and preference. *Journal of Experimental Social Psychology* 15 (4): 418–434.

Miller, A. G., McHoskey, J. W., Bane, C. M., and Dowd, T. G. 1993. The attitude polarization phenomenon: Role of response measure, attitude extremity, and behavioral consequences of reported attitude change. *Journal of Personality and Social Psychology* 64 (4): 561–574.

Miller, T. R., Lawrence, B. A., Carlson, N. N., Hendrie, D., Randall, S., Rockett, I. R. H., and Spicer, R. S. 2017. Perils of police action: A cautionary tale from U.S. data sets. *Injury Prevention* 23 (1).doi:10.1136/injuryprev-2016-042023.

Mithen, S. 1996. *The prehistory of mind: The cognitive origins of art and science.* London: Thames & Hudson.

Mithen, S. 2000. Palaeoanthropological perspectives on the theory of mind. In S. Baron-Cohen, H. Tager-Flusberg, and D. Cohen, eds., *Understanding other minds,* 2nd ed., 488–502. Oxford: Oxford University Press.

Miyake, A., and Friedman, N. P. 2012. The nature and organization of individual differences in executive functions: Four general conclusions. *Current Directions in Psychological Science* 21 (1): 8–14.

Mooney, C. 2005. *The Republican war on science.* New York: Basic Books.

Munro, G. D. 2010. The scientific impotence excuse: Discounting belief-threatening scientific abstracts. *Journal of Applied Social Psychology* 40:579–600.

Munro, G. D., and Ditto, P. H. 1997. Biased assimilation, attitude polarization, and affect in reactions to stereotype-relevant scientific information. *Personality and Social Psychology Bulletin* 23 (6): 636–653.

Murray, C. 2012. *Coming apart: The state of white America, 1960–2010*. New York: Crown Forum.

Murray, D. 2019. *The madness of crowds: Gender, race, and identity*. London: Bloomsbury.

Nagel, T. 1986. *The view from nowhere*. New York: Oxford University Press.

Neimark, E. 1987. *Adventures in thinking*. San Diego: Harcourt Brace Jovanovich.

Neuding, P. 2020. Scandinavian Airlines: Get woke, cry wolf. *Quillette*, March 1. https://quillette.com/2020/03/01/scandinavian-airlines-get-woke-cry-wolf/.

Newstead, S. E., Handley, S. J., Harley, C., Wright, H., and Farrelly, D. 2004. Individual differences in deductive reasoning. *Quarterly Journal of Experimental Psychology* 57A (1): 33–60.

Nichols, S., and Stich, S. P. 2003. *Mindreading: An integrated account of pretence, self-awareness, and understanding other minds*. Oxford: Oxford University Press.

Nickerson, R. S. 1998. Confirmation bias: A ubiquitous phenomenon in many guises. *Review of General Psychology* 2 (2): 175–220.

Nigg, J. T. 2017. Annual research review: On the relations among self-regulation, self-control, executive functioning, effortful control, cognitive control, impulsivity, risk-taking, and inhibition for developmental psychopathology. *Journal of Child Psychology and Psychiatry* 58:361–383.

Nisbet, M. 2020. Against climate change tribalism: We gamble with the future by dehumanizing our opponents. *Skeptical Inquirer* 44 (1): 26–28.

Nisbett, R. E., and Wilson, T. D. 1977. Telling more than we can know: Verbal reports on mental processes. *Psychological Review* 84 (3): 231–259.

Nozick, R. 1993. *The nature of rationality*. Princeton: Princeton University Press.

Nurse, M. S., and Grant, W. J. 2020. I'll see it when I believe it: Motivated numeracy in perceptions of climate change risk. *Environmental Communication* 14 (2): 184–201.

Nussbaum, E. M., and Sinatra, G. M. 2003. Argument and conceptual engagement. *Contemporary Educational Psychology* 28 (3): 384–395.

Nyhan, B., and Reifler, J. 2010. When corrections fail: The persistence of political misperceptions. *Political Behavior* 32 (2): 303–330.

Nyhan, B., Reifler, J., Richey, S., and Freed, G. 2014. Effective messages in vaccine promotion: A randomized trial. *Pediatrics* 133 (4): 1–8.

Oaksford, M. and Chater, N. 1994. A rational analysis of the selection task as optimal data selection. *Psychological Review* 101 (4): 608–631.

Oaksford, M., and Chater, N. 2003. Optimal data selection: Revision, review, and reevaluation. *Psychonomic Bulletin & Review* 10 (2): 289–318.

Oaksford, M., and Chater, N. 2012. Dual processes, probabilities, and cognitive architecture. *Mind & Society* 11(1): 15–26.

O'Connor, C., and Weatherall, J. O. 2018. Scientific polarization. *European Journal for Philosophy of Science* 8 (3): 855–875.

OECD. 2011. *An overview of growing income inequalities in OECD countries: Main findings*. Paris: Organisation for Economic Co-operation and Development. http://www.oecd.org/els/soc/dividedwestandwhyinequalitykeepsrising.htm.

Offit, P. A. 2011. *Deadly choices: How the anti-vaccine movement threatens us all*. New York: Basic Books.

Oliver, J. E., and Wood, T. 2014. Conspiracy theories and the paranoid style(s) of mass opinion. *American Journal of Political Science* 58 (4): 952–966.

Olsson, E. J. 2013. A Bayesian simulation model of group deliberation and polarization. In F. Zenker, ed., *Bayesian argumentation*, 113–133. Netherlands: Springer.

O'Neill, J., and O'Neill, D. 2012. *The declining importance of race and gender in the labor market: The role of federal anti-discrimination policies and other factors*. Washington, DC: AEI Press.

Onraet, E., Van Hiel, A., Dhont, K., Hodson, G., Schittekatte, M., and De Pauw, S. 2015. The association of cognitive ability with right-wing ideological attitudes and prejudice: A meta-analytic review. *European Journal of Personality* 29 (6): 599–621.

Onraet, E., Van Hiel, A., Roets, A., and Cornelis, I. 2011. The closed mind: "Experience" and "cognition" aspects of openness to experience and need for closure as psychological bases for right-wing attitudes. *European Journal of Personality* 25 (3): 184–197.

Oskarsson, S., Cesarini, D., Dawes, C., Fowler, J., Johannesson, M., Magnusson, P., and Teorell, J. 2015. Linking genes and political orientations: Testing the cognitive ability as mediator hypothesis. *Political Psychology* 36 (6): 649–665.

Oxley, D. R., Smith, K. B., Alford, J. R., Hibbing, M. V., Miller, J. L., Scalora, M., et al. 2008. Political attitudes vary with physiological traits. *Science* 321 (5896): 1667–1670.

Palan, S., and Schitter, C. 2018. Prolific.ac—A subject pool for online experiments. *Journal of Behavioral and Experimental Finance* 17:22–27. doi:10.1016/j.jbef.2017.12.004.

Paresky, P., Haidt, J., Strossen, N., and Pinker, S. 2020. The *New York Times* surrendered to an outrage mob. Journalism will suffer for it. *Politico*, May 14. https://www

.politico.com/news/magazine/2020/05/14/bret-stephens-new-york-times-outrage
-backlash-256494.

Pariser, E. 2011. *The filter bubble: What the Internet is hiding from you.* New York: Penguin.

Parker, A. M., Bruine de Bruin, W., Fischhoff, B., and Weller, J. 2018. Robustness of decision-making competence: Evidence from two measures and an 11-year longitudinal study. *Journal of Behavioral Decision Making* 31 (3): 380–391.

Parker, A. M., and Fischhoff, B. 2005. Decision-making competence: External validation through an individual differences approach. *Journal of Behavioral Decision Making* 18 Part 1:1–27.

Patel, N., Baker, S. G., and Scherer, L. D. 2019. Evaluating the cognitive reflection test as a measure of intuition/reflection, numeracy, and insight problem solving, and the implications for understanding real-world judgments and beliefs. *Journal of Experimental Psychology: General* 148 (12): 2129–2153.

Paul, R. W. 1984. Critical thinking: Fundamental to education for a free society in North America. *Educational Leadership* 42 (1): 4–14.

Paul, R. W. 1987. Critical thinking and the critical person. In D. N. Perkins, J. Lockhead, and J. Bishop, eds., *Thinking: The second international conference*, 373–403. Hillsdale, NJ: Erlbaum.

Pennycook, G., Fugelsang, J. A., and Koehler, D. J. 2015. What makes us think? A three-stage dual-process model of analytic engagement. *Cognitive Psychology* 80:34–72.

Pennycook, G., and Rand, D. G. 2019. Cognitive reflection and the 2016 U.S. presidential election. *Personality and Social Psychology Bulletin* 45 (2): 224–239.

Perkins, D. N. 1985. Postprimary education has little impact on informal reasoning. *Journal of Educational Psychology* 77 (5): 562–571.

Perkins, D. N. 1995. *Outsmarting IQ: The emerging science of learnable intelligence.* New York: Free Press.

Perkins, D. N., Farady, M., and Bushey, B. 1991. Everyday reasoning and the roots of intelligence. In J. Voss, D. Perkins, and J. Segal, eds., *Informal reasoning and education*, 83–105. Hillsdale, NJ: Erlbaum.

Peters, U., Honeycutt, N., De Block, A., & Jussim, L. 2020. Ideological diversity, hostility, and discrimination in philosophy. *Philosophical Psychology* 33 (4): 511-548. doi:10.1080/09515089.2020.1743257

Petty, R. E., and Wegener, D. T. 1998. Attitude change: Multiple roles for persuasion variables. In D. T. Gilbert, S. Fiske, and G. Lindzey, eds., *The handbook of social psychology,* 323–390. Boston: McGraw-Hill.

Pew Research Center. 2013. What the public knows—In words, pictures, maps and graphs. September 5. https://www.people-press.org/2013/09/05/what-the-public-knows-in-words-pictures-maps-and-graphs/.

Pew Research Center. 2015. What the public knows—In words, pictures, maps and graphs. April 28. https://www.people-press.org/2015/04/28/what-the-public-knows-in-pictures-words-maps-and-graphs/.

Pew Research Center. 2017. Sharp partisan divisions in views of national institutions. July 10. https://www.people-press.org/2017/07/10/sharp-partisan-divisions-in-views-of-national-institutions/.

Pew Research Center. 2019. Partisan antipathy: More intense, more personal. October 10. https://www.people-press.org/2019/10/10/partisan-antipathy-more-intense-more-personal/.

Phelan, J. 2018. Harvard study: "Gender wage gap" explained entirely by work choices of men and women. *Foundation for Economic Education*, December 10. https://fee.org/articles/harvard-study-gender-pay-gap-explained-entirely-by-work-choices-of-men-and-women/.

Piaget, J. 1972. Intellectual evolution from adolescence to adulthood. *Human Development* 15 (1): 1–12.

Pinker, S. 2002. *The blank slate: The modern denial of human nature.* New York: Viking.

Pinker, S. 2008. *The sexual paradox: Men, women, and the real gender gap.* New York: Scribner.

Pinker, S. 2011. *The better angels of our nature: Why violence has declined.* New York: Viking.

Pinker, S. 2015. Political bias, explanatory depth, and narratives of progress. *Behavioral and Brain Sciences* 38. e154. doi:10.1017/S0140525X1400137X.

Pinker, S. 2018. *Enlightenment now: The case for reason, science, humanism and progress.* New York: Viking.

Plomin, R., DeFries, J. C., Knopik, V. S., and Neiderhiser, J. M. 2016. Top 10 replicated findings from behavioral genetics. *Perspectives on Psychological Science* 11 (1): 3–23.

Plous, S. 1991. Biases in the assimilation of technological breakdowns: Do accidents make us safer? *Journal of Applied Social Psychology* 21 (13): 1058–1082.

Pluckrose, H., & Lindsay, J. 2020. *Cynical theories.* Durham, NC: Pitchstone Publishing.

Pluckrose, H., Lindsay, J., and Boghossian, P. 2018. Academic grievance studies and the corruption of scholarship. *Areo*, October 2. https://areomagazine.com/2018/10/02/academic-grievance-studies-and-the-corruption-of-scholarship/.

Proch, J., Elad-Strenger, J., and Kessler, T. 2019. Liberalism and conservatism, for a change! Rethinking the association between political orientation and relation to societal change. *Political Psychology* 40 (4): 877–903.

Ponnuru, R. 2019. In Harvard's magical admissions process, nobody gets hurt. *Bloomberg Opinion*. October 6. https://www.bloomberg.com/opinion/articles/2019 -10-06/in-harvard-s-magical-admissions-process-nobody-gets-hurt.

Pronin, E. 2007. Perception and misperception of bias in human judgment. *Trends in Cognitive Sciences* 11 (1): 37–43.

Pronin, E., Lin, D. Y., and Ross, L. 2002. The bias blind spot: Perceptions of bias in self versus others. *Personality and Social Psychology Bulletin* 28 Part 3:369–381.

Randall, D. 2019. Can universities survive America's leveling? *Academic Questions* 32 (4): 542–552.

Rauch, J. 2017. Speaking as a . . . *New York Review of Books,* November 9. Review of Mark Lilla, The Once and Future Liberal: After Identity Politics. https://www .nybooks.com/articles/2017/11/09/mark-lilla-liberal-speaking/.

Ray, J. J. 1983. Half of all authoritarians are left-wing: A reply to Eysenck and Stone. *Political Psychology* 4 (1): 139–143.

Ray, J. J. 1988. Cognitive style as a predictor of authoritarianism, conservatism, and racism. *Political Psychology* 9 (2): 303–308.

Ray, J. J. 1989. The scientific study of ideology is too often more ideological than scientific. *Personality and Individual Differences* 10 (3): 331–336.

Reeves, R. V. 2017. *Dream hoarders*. Washington, DC: Brookings Institution Press.

Regenwetter, M., Hsu, Y.-F., and Kuklinski, J. H. 2019. Towards meaningful inferences from attitudinal thermometer ratings. *Decision* 6 (4): 381–399.

Reilly, W. 2020. *Taboo: 10 facts you can't talk about*. Washington, DC: Regnery.

Reyna, C. 2018. Scale creation, use, and misuse: How politics undermines measurement. In J. T. Crawford and L. Jussim, eds., *The politics of social psychology*, 81–98. New York: Routledge.

Richerson, P. J., and Boyd, R. 2005. *Not by genes alone: How culture transformed human evolution*. Chicago: University of Chicago Press.

Ridley, M. 2000. *Mendel's demon: Gene justice and the complexity of life*. London: Weidenfeld & Nicolson.

Rindermann, H., Becker, D., and Coyle, T. R. 2020. Survey of expert opinion on intelligence: Intelligence research, experts' background, controversial issues, and the media. *Intelligence* 78. https://doi.org/10.1016/j.intell.2019.101406.

Robinson, R. J., Keltner, D., Ward, A., and Ross, L. 1995. Actual versus assumed differences in construal: "Naive realism" in intergroup perception and conflict. *Journal of Personality and Social Psychology* 68 (3): 404–417.

Roser, M. 2013. Global economic inequality. *OurWorldInData.org*. https://ourworldindata .org/global-economic-inequality

Ross, L. 1977. The intuitive psychologist and his shortcomings: Distortions in the attribution process. In L. Berkowitz, ed.. *Advances in experimental social psychology*, 173–220. New York: Academic Press.

Ross, L., Greene, D., and House, P. 1977. The "false consensus effect": An egocentric bias in social perception and attribution processes. *Journal of Experimental Social Psychology* 13 (3): 279–301.

Rothman, S., Lichter, S. R., and Nevitte, N. 2005. Politics and professional advancement among college faculty. *Forum* 3 (1): 1–16.

Rozado, D. 2019. What do universities mean when they talk about diversity? A computational language model quantifies. *Heterodox: The Blog*. August 5. https:// heterodoxacademy.org/diversity-what-do-universities-mean/.

Sá, W., West, R. F., and Stanovich, K. E. 1999. The domain specificity and generality of belief bias: Searching for a generalizable critical thinking skill. *Journal of Educational Psychology* 91 (3): 497–510.

Sabien, D. 2017. Double crux—A strategy for resolving disagreement. *LessWrong* (blog). January 1. https://www.lesswrong.com/posts/exa5kmvopeRyfJgCy/double -crux-a-strategy-for-resolving-disagreement.

Sarathchandra, D., Navin, M. C., Largent, M. A., and McCright, A. M. 2018. A survey instrument for measuring vaccine acceptance. *Preventive Medicine* 109:1–7.

Schaller, M., and Park, J. H. 2011. The behavioral immune system (and why it matters). *Current Directions in Psychological Science* 20 (2): 99–103.

Schum, D. 1994. *Evidential foundations of probabilistic reasoning*. New York: John Wiley.

Schwan, B., and Stern, R. 2017. A causal understanding of when and when not to Jeffrey conditionalize. *Philosophers' Imprint* 17 (8): 1–21.

Scopelliti, I., Morewedge, C. K., McCormick, E., Min, H. L., Lebrecht, S., and Kassam, K. S. 2015. Bias blind spot: Structure, measurement, and consequences. *Management Science* 61 (10): 2468–2486.

Seidenberg, M. 2017. *Language at the speed of sight*. New York: Basic Books.

Serwer, A. 2017. The nationalist's delusion. *Atlantic*, November 20. https://www .theatlantic.com/politics/archive/2017/11/the-nationalists-delusion/546356/.

Shah, A. K., and Oppenheimer, D. M. 2008. Heuristics made easy: An effort-reduction framework. *Psychological Bulletin* 134 (2): 207–222.

Sharot, T. 2011. *Optimism bias*. New York: Pantheon.

Sharot, T., and Garrett, N. 2016. Forming beliefs: Why valence matters. *Trends in Cognitive Sciences* 20 (1): 25–33.

Sharot, T., and Sunstein, C. R. 2020. How people decide what they want to know. *Nature Human Behaviour* 4 (1): 14–19.

Shermer, M. 2011. *The believing brain*. New York: Times Books.

Sibley, C. G., and Duckitt, J. 2008. Personality and prejudice: A meta-analysis and theoretical review. *Personality and Social Psychology Review* 12 (3): 248–279.

Siegel, H. 1988. *Educating reason*. New York: Routledge.

Simas, E. N., Clifford, S., and Kirkland, J. H. 2019. How empathic concern fuels political polarization. *American Political Science Review* 114 (1): 258–269.

Simon, H. A. 1955. A behavioral model of rational choice. *Quarterly Journal of Economics* 69 (1): 99–118.

Simon, H. A. 1956. Rational choice and the structure of the environment. *Psychological Review* 63 (2): 129–138.

Sinayev, A., and Peters, E. 2015. Cognitive reflection vs. calculation in decision making. *Frontiers in Psychology* 6. Article 532. doi:10.3389/fpsyg.2015.00532.

Skitka, L. J. 2010. The psychology of moral conviction. *Social and Personality Psychology Compass* 4 (4): 267–281. doi:10.1111/j.1751–9004.2010.00254.x.

Skitka, L. J., Bauman, C. W., and Sargis, E. G. 2005. Moral conviction: Another contributor to attitude strength or something more? *Journal of Personality and Social Psychology* 88 (6): 895–917.

Skyrms, B. 1996. *The evolution of the social contract*. Cambridge: Cambridge University Press.

Sloman, S., and Fernbach, P. M. 2017. *The knowledge illusion*. New York: Riverhead Books.

Sloman, S., and Rabb, N. 2019. Thought as a determinant of political opinion. *Cognition* 188:1–7.

Slovic, P., and Peters, E. 2006. Risk perception and affect. *Current Directions in Psychological Science* 15 (6): 322–325.

Snyderman, P. M., and Tetlock, P. E. 1986. Symbolic racism: Problems of motive attribution in political analysis. *Journal of Social Issues*, 129–150.

Solberg, E. and Laughlin, T. 1995. The gender pay gap, fringe benefits, and occupational crowding. *ILR Review* 48 (4): 692–708.

Sowell, T. 2019. *Discrimination and disparities*. New York: Basic Books.

Spearman, C. 1904. General intelligence, objectively determined and measured. *American Journal of Psychology* 15 (2): 201–293.

Spearman, C. 1927. *The abilities of man*. London: Macmillan.

Sperber, D. 1996. *Explaining culture: A naturalistic approach*. Oxford: Blackwell.

Sperber, D. 2000. Metarepresentations in evolutionary perspective. In D. Sperber, ed., *Metarepresentations: A multidisciplinary perspective*, 117–137. Oxford: Oxford University Press. http://cogprints.org/851/1/metarep.htm.

Stanovich, K. E. 1999. *Who is rational? Studies of individual differences in reasoning*. Mahwah, NJ: Erlbaum.

Stanovich, K. E. 2000. *Progress in understanding reading: Scientific foundations and new frontiers*. New York: Guilford Press.

Stanovich, K. E. 2004. *The robot's rebellion: Finding meaning in the age of Darwin*. Chicago: University of Chicago Press.

Stanovich, K. E. 2011. *Rationality and the reflective mind*. New York: Oxford University Press.

Stanovich, K. E. 2013. Why humans are (sometimes) less rational than other animals: Cognitive complexity and the axioms of rational choice. *Thinking & Reasoning* 19 (1): 1–26.

Stanovich, K. E. 2017. Were Trump voters irrational? *Quillette*, September 28. https://quillette.com/2017/09/28/trump-voters-irrational/.

Stanovich, K. E. 2018a. Miserliness in human cognition: The interaction of detection, override and mindware. *Thinking & Reasoning* 24 (4): 423–444.

Stanovich, K. E. 2018b. What is the tribe of the anti-tribalists? *Quillette*, July 17. https://quillette.com/2018/07/17/what-is-the-tribe-of-the-anti-tribalists/.

Stanovich, K. E. 2019. *How to think straight about psychology*. 11th ed. New York: Pearson.

Stanovich, K. E., and Toplak, M. E. 2012. Defining features versus incidental correlates of Type 1 and Type 2 processing. *Mind & Society* 11 (1): 3–13.

Stanovich, K. E., and Toplak, M. E. 2019. The need for intellectual diversity in psychological science: Our own studies of actively open-minded thinking as a case study. *Cognition* 187:156–166. https://doi.org/10.1016/j.cognition.2019.03.006

Stanovich, K. E., and West, R. F. 1997. Reasoning independently of prior belief and individual differences in actively open-minded thinking. *Journal of Educational Psychology* 89 (2): 342–367.

Stanovich, K. E., and West, R. F. 1998a. Individual differences in rational thought. *Journal of Experimental Psychology: General* 127 (2): 161–188.

Stanovich, K. E., and West, R. F. 1998b. Who uses base rates and P(D/~H)? An analysis of individual differences. *Memory & Cognition* 26 (1): 161–179.

Stanovich, K. E., and West, R. F. 2000. Individual differences in reasoning: Implications for the rationality debate? *Behavioral and Brain Sciences* 23 (5): 645–726.

Stanovich, K. E., and West, R. F. 2007. Natural myside bias is independent of cognitive ability. *Thinking & Reasoning* 13 (3): 225–247.

Stanovich, K. E., and West, R. F. 2008a. On the failure of intelligence to predict myside bias and one-sided bias. *Thinking & Reasoning* 14 (2): 129–167.

Stanovich, K. E., and West, R. F. 2008b. On the relative independence of thinking biases and cognitive ability. *Journal of Personality and Social Psychology* 94 (4): 672–695.

Stanovich, K. E., West, R. F., and Toplak, M. E. 2013. Myside bias, rational thinking, and intelligence. *Current Directions in Psychological Science* 22 (4): 259–264.

Stanovich, K. E., West, R. F., and Toplak, M. E. 2016. *The rationality quotient: Toward a test of rational thinking.* Cambridge, MA: MIT Press.

Stenhouse, N., Myers, T. A., Vraga, E. K., Kotcher, J. E., Beall, L., and Maibach, E. W. 2018. The potential role of actively open-minded thinking in preventing motivated reasoning about controversial science. *Journal of Environmental Psychology* 57:17–24.

Stephens, B. 2016. Staring at the conservative gutter: Donald Trump gives credence to the left's caricature of bigoted conservatives. *Wall Street Journal*, February 29. https://www.wsj.com/articles/staring-at-the-conservative-gutter-1456791777.

Sterelny, K. 2001. *The evolution of agency and other essays.* Cambridge: Cambridge University Press.

Sterelny, K. 2006. Memes revisited. *British Journal of the Philosophy of Science* 57 (1): 145–165.

Sternberg, R. J. 2001. Why schools should teach for wisdom: The balance theory of wisdom in educational settings. *Educational Psychologist* 36 (4): 227–245.

Sternberg, R. J. 2003. *Wisdom, intelligence, and creativity synthesized.* Cambridge: Cambridge University Press.

Sternberg, R. J. 2018. "If intelligence is truly important to real-world adaptation, and IQs have risen 30+ points in the past century (Flynn Effect), then why are there so many unresolved and dramatic problems in the world, and what can be done about it?". *Journal of Intelligence* 6 (1): 4. https://www.mdpi.com/journal/jintelligence /special_issues/Intelligence_IQs_Problems

Swami, V., Coles, R., Stieger, S., Pietschnig, J., Furnham, A., Rehim, S., and Voracek, M. 2011. Conspiracist ideation in Britain and Austria: Evidence of a monological belief system and associations between individual psychological differences and real-world and fictitious conspiracy theories. *British Journal of Psychology* 102 (3) : 443–463.

Taber, C. S., Cann, D., and Kucsova, S. 2009. The motivated processing of political arguments. *Political Behavior* 31 (2): 137–155.

Taber, C. S., and Lodge, M. 2006. Motivated skepticism in the evaluation of political beliefs. *American Journal of Political Science* 50 (3): 755–769.

Taber, C. S., and Lodge, M. 2016. The illusion of choice in democratic politics: The unconscious impact of motivated political reasoning. *Political Psychology* 37 (S1): 61–85.

Talbott, W. 2016. Bayesian epistemology. In E. N. Zalta, ed., *The Stanford Encyclopedia of Philosophy*. Winter edition. https://plato.stanford.edu/archives/win2016/entries /epistemology-bayesian/.

Tappin, B. M., and Gadsby, S. 2019. Biased belief in the Bayesian brain: A deeper look at the evidence. *Consciousness and Cognition* 68:107–114.

Tappin, B. M., Pennycook, G., and Rand, D. G. 2020. Thinking clearly about causal inferences of politically motivated reasoning. *Current Opinion in Behavioral Sciences* 34:81–87.

Taylor, S. E. 1981. The interface of cognitive and social psychology. In J. H. Harvey, ed., *Cognition, social behavior, and the environment*, 189–211. Hillsdale, NJ: Erlbaum.

Tetlock, P. E. 1986. A value pluralism model of ideological reasoning. *Journal of Personality and Social Psychology* 50 (4): 819–827.

Tetlock, P. E. 1994. Political psychology or politicized psychology: Is the road to scientific hell paved with good moral intentions? *Political Psychology* 15 (3): 509–529.

Tetlock, P. E. 2002. Social functionalist frameworks for judgment and choice: Intuitive politicians, theologians, and prosecutors. *Psychological Review* 109 (3): 451–471.

Tetlock, P. E. 2003. Thinking the unthinkable: Sacred values and taboo cognitions. *Trends in Cognitive Sciences* 7 (7): 320–324.

Thompson, A. 2019. The university's new loyalty oath: Required "diversity and inclusion" statements amount to a political litmus test for hiring. *Wall Street Journal*, December 19. https://www.wsj.com/articles/the-universitys-new-loyalty-oath -11576799749.

Thompson, V., and Evans, J. St. B. T. 2012. Belief bias in informal reasoning. *Thinking & Reasoning* 18 (3): 278–310.

Toner, K., Leary, M. R., Asher, M. W., and Jongman-Sereno, K. P. 2013. Feeling superior is a bipartisan issue: Extremity (not direction) of political views predicts perceived belief superiority. *Psychological Science* 24 (12): 2454–2462.

Tooby, J., and Cosmides, L. 1992. The psychological foundations of culture. In J. Barkow, L. Cosmides, and J. Tooby, eds., *The adapted mind*, 19–136. New York: Oxford University Press.

Toplak, M. E., Liu, E., Macpherson, R., Toneatto, T., and Stanovich, K. E. 2007. The reasoning skills and thinking dispositions of problem gamblers: A dual-process taxonomy. *Journal of Behavioral Decision Making* 20 (2): 103–124.

Toplak, M. E., and Stanovich, K. E. 2002. The domain specificity and generality of disjunctive reasoning: Searching for a generalizable critical thinking skill. *Journal of Educational Psychology* 94 (1): 197–209.

Toplak, M. E. and Stanovich, K. E. 2003. Associations between myside bias on an informal reasoning task and amount of post-secondary education. *Applied Cognitive Psychology* 17 (7): 851–860.

Toplak, M. E., West, R. F., and Stanovich, K. E. 2011. The Cognitive Reflection Test as a predictor of performance on heuristics and biases tasks. *Memory & Cognition* 39 (7): 1275–1289.

Toplak, M. E., West, R. F., and Stanovich, K. E. 2014a. Assessing miserly processing: An expansion of the Cognitive Reflection Test. *Thinking & Reasoning* 20 (2): 147–168.

Toplak, M. E., West, R. F., and Stanovich, K. E. 2014b. Rational thinking and cognitive sophistication: Development, cognitive abilities, and thinking dispositions. *Developmental Psychology* 50 (4): 1037–1048.

Traub, J. 2016. It's time for the elites to rise up against the ignorant masses. *Foreign Policy*, June 28. https://foreignpolicy.com/2016/06/28/its-time-for-the-elites-to-rise -up-against-ignorant-masses-trump-2016-brexit/.

Turner, J. H. 2019. The more American sociology seeks to become a politically-relevant discipline, the more irrelevant it becomes to solving societal problems. *American Sociologist* 50 (4): 456–487.

Tversky, A., and Kahneman, D. 1974. Judgment under uncertainty: Heuristics and biases. *Science* 185 (4157): 1124–1131.

Twito, L., and Knafo-Noam, A. 2020. Beyond culture and the family: Evidence from twin studies on the genetic and environmental contribution to values. *Neuroscience & Biobehavioral Reviews* 112:135–143.

Uhlmann, E. L., Pizarro, D. A., Tannenbaum, D., and Ditto, P. H. 2009. The motivated use of moral principles. *Judgment and Decision Making* 4 (6): 476–491.

University of California. 2018. Rubric to assess candidate contributions to diversity, equity, and inclusion. Office for Faculty Equity & Welfare. August. https://ofew .berkeley.edu/sites/default/files/rubric_to_assess_candidate_contributions_to_diver sity_equity_and_inclusion.pdf.

Vallone, R. P., Ross, L., and Lepper, M. R. 1985. The hostile media phenomenon: Biased perception and perceptions of media bias in coverage of the Beirut massacre. *Journal of Personality and Social Psychology* 49 (3): 577–585. doi:10.1037//0022-3514 .49.3.577.

Van Bavel, J. J., and Pereira, A. 2018. The partisan brain: An identity-based model of political belief. *Trends in Cognitive Sciences* 22 (3): 213–224.

Van Boven, L., Ramos, J., Montal-Rosenberg, R., Kogut, T., Sherman, D. K., and Slovic, P. 2019. It depends: Partisan evaluation of conditional probability importance. *Cognition* 188: 51–63. https://doi.org/10.1016/j.cognition.2019.01.020.

Varol, O., Ferrara, E., Davis, C., Menczer, F., and Flammini, A. 2017. Online human-bot interactions: Detection, estimation, and characterization. In *Proceedings of the Eleventh International AAAI Conference on Web and Social Media*, 280–289. https:// www.aaai.org/ocs/index.php/ICWSM/ICWSM17/paper/viewPaper/15587.

Viator, R. E., Harp, N. L., Rinaldo, S. B., and Marquardt, B. B. 2020. The mediating effect of reflective-analytic cognitive style on rational thought. *Thinking & Reasoning* 26 (3): 381–413. doi:10.1080/13546783.2019.1634151.

Voelkel, J. G., and Brandt, M. J. 2019. The effect of ideological identification on the endorsement of moral values depends on the target group. *Personality and Social Psychology Bulletin* 45 (6): 851–863.

Walrath, R., Willis, J., Dumont, R., and Kaufman, A. 2020. Factor-analytic models of intelligence. In R. J. Sternberg, ed., *The Cambridge Handbook of Intelligence*, 75–98. Cambridge: Cambridge University Press.

Ward, J., and Singhvi, A. 2019. Trump claims there is a crisis at the border: What's the reality? *New York Times*, January 11. https://www.nytimes.com/interactive/2019 /01/11/us/politics/trump-border-crisis-reality.html.

Warne, R. T., Astle, M. C., and Hill, J. C. 2018. What do undergraduates learn about human intelligence? An analysis of introductory psychology textbooks. *Archives of Scientific Psychology* 6 (1): 32–50.

Washburn, A. N., and Skitka, L. J. 2018. Science denial across the political divide: Liberals and conservatives are similarly motivated to deny attitude-inconsistent science. *Social Psychological and Personality Science* 9 (8): 972–980.

Wason, P. C. 1966. Reasoning. In B. M. Foss ed., *New horizons in psychology 1.* Harmondsworth, UK: Pelican.

Wason, P. C. 1969. Regression in reasoning? *British Journal of Psychology* 60 (4): 471–480.

Wasserman, D. 2014. Senate control could come down to Whole Foods vs. Cracker Barrel. *FiveThirtyEight.* October 8. https://fivethirtyeight.com/features/senate-control -could-come-down-to-whole-foods-vs-cracker-barrel/.

Wasserman, D. 2020. To beat Trump, Democrats may need to break out of the "Whole Foods" bubble. *New York Times,* February 27. https://www.nytimes.com /interactive/2020/02/27/upshot/democrats-may-need-to-break-out-of-the-whole -foods-bubble.html.

Weaver, E. A., and Stewart, T. R. 2012. Dimensions of judgment: Factor analysis of individual differences. *Journal of Behavioral Decision Making* 25 (4): 402–413.

Weeden, J., and Kurzban, R. 2014. *The hidden agenda of the political mind: How self-interest shapes our opinions and why we won't admit it.* Princeton: Princeton University Press.

Weeden, J., and Kurzban, R. 2016. Do people naturally cluster into liberals and conservatives? *Evolutionary Psychological Science* 2 (1): 47–57.

Weinstein, B. 2019. *Twitter,* January 11. https://twitter.com/BretWeinstein/status /1083852331618193408.

Weinstein, N. 1980. Unrealistic optimism about future life events. *Journal of Personality and Social Psychology* 39 (5): 806–820.

Weller, J., Ceschi, A., Hirsch, L., Sartori, R., and Costantini, A. 2018. Accounting for individual differences in decision-making competence: Personality and gender differences. *Frontiers in Psychology* 9. Article 2258. https://www.frontiersin.org/articles /10.3389/fpsyg.2018.02258/full.

West, R. F., Meserve, R. J., and Stanovich, K. E. 2012. Cognitive sophistication does not attenuate the bias blind spot. *Journal of Personality and Social Psychology* 103 (3): 506–519.

West, T. V., and Kenny, D. A. 2011. The truth and bias model of judgment. *Psychological Review* 118 (2): 357–378.

Westen, D., Blagov, P., Kilts, C., and Hamann, S. 2006. Neural bases of motivated reasoning: An fMRI study of emotional constraints on partisan political judgment in the 2004 U.S. presidential election. *Journal of Cognitive Neuroscience* 18 (11): 1947–1958.

Westfall, J., Van Boven, L., Chambers, J. R., and Judd, C. M. 2015. Perceiving political polarization in the United States: Party identity strength and attitude extremity exacerbate the perceived partisan divide. *Perspectives on Psychological Science* 10 (2): 145–158.

Westwood, S. J., Iyengar, S., Walgrave, S., Leonisio, R., Miller, L., and Strijbis, O. 2018. The tie that divides: Cross-national evidence of the primacy of partyism. *European Journal of Political Research* 57 (2): 333–354.

Wetherell, G. A., Brandt, M. J., and Reyna, C. 2013. Discrimination across the ideological divide: The role of value violations and abstract values in discrimination by liberals and conservatives. *Social Psychological and Personality Science* 4 (6): 658–667.

Williams, W. M., and Ceci, S. J. 2015. National hiring experiments reveal 2:1 faculty preference for women on STEM tenure track. *Proceedings of the National Academy of Sciences* 112 (17): 5360–5365.

Wilson, D. S. 2002. *Darwin's cathedral*. Chicago: University of Chicago Press.

Wolfe, C. R., and Britt, M. A. 2008. The locus of the myside bias in written argumentation. *Thinking and Reasoning* 14 (1): 1–27.

Wolff, R., Moore, B., and Marcuse, H. 1969. *A critique of pure tolerance*. Boston: Beacon Press.

Wright, J. P., Motz, R. T., and Nixon, T. S. 2019. Political disparities in the academy: It's more than self-selection. *Academic Questions* 32 (3): 402–411.

Wynn, K. 2016. Origins of value conflict: Babies do not agree to disagree. *Trends in Cognitive Sciences* 20 (1): 3–5.

Yilmaz, O., and Alper, S. 2019. The link between intuitive thinking and social conservatism is stronger in WEIRD societies. *Judgment and Decision Making* 14 (2): 156–169.

Yilmaz, O., and Saribay, S. 2016. An attempt to clarify the link between cognitive style and political ideology: A non-western replication and extension. *Judgment and Decision Making* 11 (3): 287–300.

Yılmaz, O., and Sarıbay, S. 2017. The relationship between cognitive style and political orientation depends on the measures used. *Judgment & Decision Making* 12 (2): 140–147.

Yilmaz, O., Saribay, S., and Iyer, R. 2020. Are neo-liberals more intuitive? Undetected libertarians confound the relation between analytic cognitive style and economic conservatism. *Current Psychology* 39 (1): 25–32.

Yudkin, D., Hawkins, S., and Dixon, T. 2019. The perception gap: How false impressions are pulling Americans apart. *More in Common*. https://psyarxiv.com/r3h5q/.

Zigerell, L. J. 2018. Black and White discrimination in the United States: Evidence from an archive of survey experiment studies. *Research & Politics* 5 (1). 2053168017753862.

Zimmer, B. 2020. "Infodemic": When unreliable information spreads far and wide. *Wall Street Journal*, March 5. https://www.wsj.com/articles/infodemic-when-unreliable -information-spreads-far-and-wide-11583430244.

Zito, S., and Todd, B. 2018. *The great revolt: Inside the populist coalition reshaping American politics*. New York: Crown Forum.

Subject Index

Name Index